THE DIALOGUE OF THE GOVERNMENT
OF WALES (1594)

Both by Peare and harvies informith that the welshmenn:
beinge the poore & small remnant of the Auncient noble
BRITTAYNES were brought into suth povertie and thraldome
and into suth rudenesse by reason they might not bringe vpp
their youthes in Civill sortes that when KINGE HENRI
THE VIII came to redresse these enormities and to establishe
good and holsome Lawes amonge them, and to geve them
Magistrates of their owne Nation I meane Sheresses cum
Justices of the Peace in every Sheere he then was fayne
and forced to admitte suth to be Justices of the Peace as were to
be founde in the contry for then there was not sufficient number
to be founde in many Sheeres of Wales that might dispense well
lawes or were Learned for most gentlemen coulde neither
write nor reade for they were steame barred from all manner
of Learninge and good Education. But sthence the tyme of
HENRIE THE VII and HENRIE THE VIII that wee weare
emancipated as it weare and made free to trade and
trasike thorowe Englande the Gentlemenn and People
of Wales haue greatly encreasd in Learninge and Civility
& nowe greate nombers of vowthes are contynuallie brought
vpp and mayntened at the Vniuersities of OXFORD and
CAMBRIDGE and in other good Schooles in Englande where
some prooue to be Learned menn and good members in the Comon
wealth of Englande and Wales some worthy Labourers in the
Lordes vineyarde, many of late haue prooved excellent in
the Ciuill Lawes some in Phisike and other laudable
Studies wherein they are seconde nothinge behinde other nations
Many good Gramarschooles in diuerse partes of the Contrye
are nowe to be founde throwe out Wales whereby the Contrie is
growen and shortly like to be as Ciuill as any other state of this
Lande, besides the People beinge governed by these late established, wholesome and good Lawes before recyted haue wonderfully
thryven by husbandry. The Contrie is growen to be much
more tilled and Enclosures in most partes full and the
Contrie People with greate diligence apply their Laboures
many contries heretofore Desolate none well inhabited nor
Contry in Englande so flourished in one hundred yeares as

CCL, Phillipps MS 2, 105, fo. 17b

as Wales hath donne sithence the government of Henrie the
seaventh to this tyme in somuch that if our fathers weare nowe
Lyvenge they woulde thinke it some straunge contry inhabited
with a fforrain Nation soe altered is the contry and contrymen
in the people thanged in harte within and the lande
althred in hue without from evill to good and from bad to
better the Lorde contynue his goodnes towardes vs and make
vs thankfull And nowe not yet three yeares past we haue the
light of the Gospell yea the whole Bible in our owne Natiue
tounge which in shorte tyme must needes worke greate good
inwardly in the hartes of the People, whereas the Seruice and
Sacramentes in the Englishe tounge was as straunge to many
or most of the symplest sorte as the Masse in the tyme of
blindenes was, the rest of Englande, whereby the People are
growne to be of greate wealth, the Gentlemen of greate
Lyvenges soe that in a contrey when it came first to be
Sheere grounde where there was scante two gentlemen that
coulde in Landes dispend xx£ a peere, there are nowe in the said
Shere to be founde some that doth receiue yearly fyve hundrede
poundes some three hundred poundes some two hundred poundes
and many of C£ good Landes So that none there is not sheere
in Wales but is able to yelde sufficient nomber of Gentlemen
that may dispend C£ a yere of good Landes to be Shereffes
and Justices of the peace in the Shere, And before twentye
of them of good skill in most pointes sufficient to discharge
their roome and callinge this hath our contry of Wales attayned
by the Blessinge of God in sendinge them Princes of their
owne Nation to gouerne them this confirmeth my former speeches
that wee of Wales are boonde and must needes loue our said
Prince with a more Natiuall affection, then the rest of this
Realme for that they of Englande do not knowe the sweete that
of Wales do feele by that is before spoken for they neuer
tasted of the sower as the Welshemen did contynnallie for
the space of 400 and od yeares this I say doth make our
hartes to leappe for ioye when we here the names of these our
Lovinge Princes which beinge more like fathers then Princes

THE DIALOGUE OF THE GOVERNMENT OF WALES (1594)

UPDATED TEXT AND COMMENTARY

John Gwynfor Jones

CARDIFF
UNIVERSITY OF WALES PRESS
2010

© John Gwynfor Jones, 2010

All rights reserved. No part of this book may be reproduced in any material form (including photocopying or storing it in any medium by electronic means and whether or not transiently or incidentally to some other use of this publication) without the written permission of the copyright owner except in accordance with the provisions of the Copyright, Designs and Patents Act 1988. Applications for the copyright owner's written permission to reproduce any part of this publication should be addressed to the University of Wales Press, 10 Columbus Walk, Brigantine Place, Cardiff, CF10 4UP.

www.uwp.co.uk

British Library Cataloguing-in-Publication Data
A catalogue record for this book is available from the British Library.

ISBN 978-0-7083-2229-1
e-ISBN 978-0-7083-2288-8

The right of John Gwynfor Jones to be identified as author of this work has been asserted by him in accordance with sections 77 and 79 of the Copyright, Designs and Patents Act 1988.

Printed by CPI Antony Rowe, Chippenham, Wiltshire

*Cyflwynaf y gyfrol hon i'm hwyrion Thomas Rhys,
Rhian Mair, Mathew Llywelyn a Siôn Robert*

Contents

Preface	xi
Acknowledgements	xiii
Abbreviations	xv
Note on texts	xvii
Introduction	1
The Dialogue of the Government of Wales (1594)	55
Appendix	179
Bibliography	181
Index	191

Preface

This volume is broadly divided into two main sections. The first part comprises a critical introduction to the background of the *Dialogue*, written in 1594 by George Owen of Henllys, Pembrokeshire, which is followed by a modernized version of the text. Compared to other sixteenth-century texts relating to Wales, such as Rhys Meurig's *Morganiae Archaiographia* (*c.*1578) and Sir John Wynn's *History of the Gwydir Family* (*c.*1600), this substantial commentary on government and legal administration by one of Wales's foremost early modern historians and antiquaries has not been given the attention it merits. Its contents have frequently been used by historians, and references have been made to it and its commentary in a variety of scholarly works on sixteenth-century Wales, but a convenient updated edition of the text has not, as yet, been made available. The manuscript versions are contained in BL Harleian MS 141 and Cardiff Central Library Phillipps MS 2,105. The original text was edited by Henry Owen in volume III of *The Description of Penbrokshire*, published by the Honourable Society of Cymmrodorion (1906), a pioneering publication, together with several of Owen's other works, including *Penbrokshire* (in volume I). That text, Owen's major work, was presented in modern form by the late Dillwyn Miles and published by Gomer Press, Llandysul, in 1994.

George Owen was one of the most critical historians of the late sixteenth and early seventeenth centuries, and in the *Dialogue* he discusses the main functions of legal institutions of government in Tudor Wales following the Acts of Union (1536–43). The discourse is not merely a description of those institutions, but rather a dialogue between Demetus and Barthol, two imaginary characters, which analyses the good and bad aspects of the Tudor legal structure in Wales. The emphasis is placed principally on the enlightened methods used to administer the new framework imposed by Union legislation, and comparisons are drawn with the harsh penal legislation previously imposed by the Lancastrian king Henry IV (1401–2). Owen reveals the chief features of the Henrician settlement, as he interpreted them, and the whole work is characterised by fulsome praise for the Tudor regime, which identifies the role of the Tudor kings Henry VII and Henry VIII as the liberators of the Welsh nation and the initiators of the 'great metamorphosis' which the author, in the prophetic tradition, linked to the nation's historic destiny.

In this *Dialogue* Demetus, representing Owen himself, is described as a native of Pembrokeshire, steeped in knowledge of local government in Wales of his day. He is a sharp commentator, while Barthol is a genuinely inquisitive, observant and knowledgeable German lawyer from Frankfurt, travelling Europe to learn about the legal systems of various countries. The Socratic method used to facilitate the lengthy conversation between them reveals the Renaissance style of conducting a debate on philosophical and allied matters, a framework which gives the *Dialogue* much of its appeal.

Owen divides his discourse broadly into three themes. He devotes half of the text to examining the chief courts by which Wales was governed after the Acts of Union. Detailed attention is given to the functions of the main organs of local and regional government, namely the Council in the Marches, the Courts of Great Sessions and the Justices of the Peace in their Quarter Sessions. Then follows a critical analysis of Base Courts, principally the County, Hundred, Commotal and Manorial courts, most of which Demetus condemns because of their inefficiency. Following the structure adopted in his treatise on Pembrokeshire, George Owen, in the last section of the dialogue, provides a favourable appraisal of that county and discusses its disadvantaged administrative position relative to adjoining Carmarthenshire, particularly in matters of defence and taxation.

Doubtless the text of the *Dialogue* merits being presented in modern form, primarily as a source available for further studies of Tudor government in Wales. It is one of the few critical discourses available which places the legal aspects of Welsh Tudor government in a broader perspective. Despite the strong pro-Tudor bias, which is consistently and understandably featured throughout the work, Owen attempts to maintain the reputation of the 'new order' in government and reflects on contemporary attitudes and on several aspects of late Tudor community life in Wales. It is primarily a discourse which reveals the way in which the Welsh Tudor gentry interpreted royal policy in Wales, and consequently the gains they made from it. It concentrates on those factors in Welsh society which were in close contact with the administrative machinery, and hardly any attention is given to the lower orders, in a period – principally the 1580s and 1590s – when severe economic stringency seriously affected rural life. Basically, George Owen is interested in exalting the Tudor regime in Wales in the light of the prosperity enjoyed by the social milieu to which he belonged.

Acknowledgements

I wish to acknowledge all the assistance I have received during the preparation of this work, especially from Peter Keelan, Head of Special Collections and Archives, Mrs Alison Harvey and other members of the staff in the Arts and Social Science Library at the University of Cardiff. I gratefully appreciate the guidance given by Brian Ll. James, the staff at Cardiff Central Library and the National Library of Wales as well as the valuable advice and assistance which I received from Sarah Lewis, Dr Dafydd Jones and Elisabeth Edwards of the University of Wales Press at the time when the volume was being prepared. I also wish to thank Mrs Eleri Melhuish for her assistance in compiling the index, and my wife, Enid, for her unfailing support and encouragement.

Abbreviations

BBCS	*Bulletin of the Board of Celtic Studies*
BL	British Library
Cal.CQSR	W. Ogwen Williams (ed.), *Calendar of the Caernarvonshire Quarter Sessions Records*, I, *1541–1558* (Caernarfon, 1956)
CCL	Cardiff Central Library
CSPDom.	*Calendar of State Papers Domestic*
Desc. Pembs.	George Owen, *The Description of Pembrokeshire*, ed. Dillwyn Miles (Llandysul, 1994)
Dialogue	George Owen, 'The Dialogue of the Government of Wales', in *The Description of Penbrokshire*, vol. III, ed. Henry Owen (Cymmrodorion Record Series, London, 1906)
DP	George Owen, *The Description of Penbrokshire*, vols I–III, ed. Henry Owen (Cymmrodorion Record Series, London, 1892–1906)
DWB	*Dictionary of Welsh Biography* (London, 1959)
HMC	Historical Manuscripts Commission
HMSO	Her Majesty's Stationery Office
LPFDom.	*Letters and Papers Foreign and Domestic*
NLW	National Library of Wales
NLWJ	*National Library of Wales Journal*
ODNB	*Oxford Dictionary of National Biography*
PRO	Public Record Office
SR	*Statutes of the Realm*
Statutes	I. Bowen (ed.), *The Statutes of Wales* (London, 1908)
Trans. Cymmr.	*Transactions of the Honourable Society of Cymmrodorion*
WHR	*Welsh History Review*

Note on texts

The original texts of the *Dialogue* are contained in BL, Harleian MS 141, folios 28–85, and in CCL, Phillipps MS 2,105 (replacing the old number 21769), 44 folios. The Harleian text is written in two hands, the first, neatly set out, in folios 1–43b, and the second in folios 68b–85, less carefully written in places and less ornate. Sections where major differences between the texts occur are noted, with material found only in BL Harleian MS 141 inserted in round brackets, and similar material in CCL, Phillipps MS 2,105 in square brackets.

The Phillipps MSS form a rich collection owned by Sir Thomas Phillipps (1792–1972), son of Thomas Phillipps, calico manufacturer and printer of Manchester, who inherited the Middle Hill estate in Worcestershire (*ODNB*, 44, pp. 91–4). He was an avid collector of manuscripts, records and books, and accumulated the largest private collection of Welsh manuscripts. They were purchased by auction in 1895 by Cardiff Central Library, where they were deposited in 1896.

A xerograph copy of the text, entitled 'A Dialogue of the Present Government of Wales, circa 1594', is kept in the Worth Library at Dr Stephens' Hospital, Dublin. It closely corresponds to the Phillipps MS. See NLW *Annual Report, 1966–67*, p. 37 and facsimile no. 45, with a report on the text.

The text has been presented to make George Owen's *Dialogue* intelligible to the general reader. Spelling has been modernised throughout, and Owen's tediously over-long sentences, which too often contain semicolons, have been shortened where that was considered necessary. Roman numerals used in the original two manuscripts to denote sums of money have been spelt out, but arabic numerals are retained, except when abbreviations designate a royal person. Latin words and phrases, usually denoting legal terminology or usage, have also been retained. The intention is to maintain the distinctive quality of George Owen's style, so that the literary flavour of the original text is not lost.

Introduction

George Owen of Henllys: the man and his genre

George Owen, the sixteenth-century Pembrokeshire antiquary and historian from Henllys in the barony of Cemais in north Pembrokeshire, is primarily famous for his *Description of Penbrokshire* (1603), an extensive treatise described as 'a seminal work and exemplary among those of its kind'.[1] When setting about his task Owen had many aims, but principally he wrote as a historian and antiquary who, in the spirit of the age, set about revealing what he considered to be, not only the chief characteristics of his native county, but also, more significantly, its prime features compared to other counties. He was well educated and in a position to recount in great detail a broad spectrum of life and activity, and fulfilled his task as a typical Tudor gentleman of the Elizabethan age. He was fully aware of his prestigious descent from native stock through the Herberts of Swansea, on his mother's side, and the old Welsh lords of Cemais on his father's.[2] He was politically articulate, constantly aware of his status in county society, and served in local affairs in much the same way as did his equals in all other counties of Wales. His grandfather, Rhys ab Owain Fychan, was the architect of the Henllys family and estate, establishing its social status firmly in north Pembrokeshire. The family stemmed from freeman stock in Cemais whose ancestry can be traced to Philip Fychan ap Philip ap Richard of Henllys Isaf in the parish of Nevern.[3] George Owen's father, William Owen, was a successful lawyer, educated at the Middle Temple, where he came into contact with Sir Thomas Elyot, who was described as his 'near cousin'. He possessed all the instincts of the family-founding gentry of the sixteenth century. His expert knowledge of common law led him to publish two editions of an abridgement of the laws in 1521 and 1528, and his legal cunning enabled him to win a prolonged battle for ownership of the barony of Cemais.[4]

George Owen received a legal education, having entered Barnard's Inn in August 1573, and was born into a privileged social order which had come to the fore well before the Tudor century. He was a notable example of the Tudor gentleman whose immediate forbears had gained prestige and influence almost completely because of Tudor policy. There was a more professional aura about them, compared to the less well-endowed, but equally well-descended, gentry families in the hinterland areas of mid and north Wales. Owen's father had been forced to claim the barony of Cemais (which he did successfully in 1542) in several costly legal battles, and George Owen himself was always involved in litigation with his landowning neighbours, in particular the powerful Sir John Perrot of Haroldston near Haverfordwest and William Warren of Tre-wern near Nevern.[5] Despite the dangers of continual legal wrangling, Owen handled his affairs proficiently as lord of Cemais and succeeded in maintaining his possession of it and restoring its rights and privileges.

As a county gentleman who avidly concerned himself with preserving knowledge of the past, George Owen conducted detailed research into the history and antiquities of his native Pembrokeshire, traces of which are evidently found in *The Dialogue of the Government of Wales*, which was completed in 1594. However, references to the year 1597, for example, not included in the Phillipps MS 2,105, show that additions were made to the Harleian MS 141.[6] Owen's motive in compiling this work reflects his desire to publicise his status relative to his contribution to local affairs. His position as local administrator – Sheriff in 1586–7 and 1601–2, Justice of the Peace from 1584 to 1613, deputy Lord-Lieutenant of Pembrokeshire in 1587 and deputy Vice-Admiral of Pembrokeshire and Cardiganshire in 1598 onwards gave him the experience required to study the structure and participate in the routine work of the numerous courts in his county.[7] It was mainly through personal experience of local politics and administration that Owen came to write all he knew about local government and to pronounce confidently on its strengths and weaknesses and its role in maintaining law and order. The *Dialogue* is principally a commentary on the working of the administrative and judicial system outlined for Wales in the Acts of Union (1536–43). Because of his expert knowledge, he therefore proceeded to examine the consequences of the settlement in his region with particular care. His official positions in Pembrokeshire led him to take great pains to eulogise, excessively so, the Tudor policy in Wales, and doubtless his main weakness was that he created a structural imbalance in the treatise and tended to identify his own private interests with those of the nation at large. He assumed in the *Dialogue* that everyone shared his enthusiasm for Tudor rule, when that was not in fact the case in several respects. He never neglected to stress the opportunities which the new dynasty had conferred on Wales, and on occasions used effusive language characteristic of his age, especially when referring to improved social and economic conditions in the reign of Elizabeth. Such royal deference, he declared, impelled the Welsh nation to mainfest its loyalty to the Queen 'with a more willing and firm heart', in view of her peaceful and stable government.[8]

Henry Tudor and his successor, however, were praised by Owen more highly than Elizabeth because of the two crucial events which created stability in the realm, namely the peaceful accession to the throne of a king of Welsh descent and a settlement bestowed on the Welsh by his son and heir, allegedly charged by his father to care for his fellow countrymen, a settlement which gave the nation its freedom and self-respect.[9] By eulogising the early Tudors, descended partly from Welsh ancestors in Anglesey,[10] Owen drew attention, as did many of his contemporaries, to the distressful conditions in the past and saw 1485, the year of Bosworth Field, as the political and social watershed in the history of England and Wales.[11]

Tied to all this tradition is George Owen's interest in history and antiquities. He used his knowledge of the past, not only for its own sake, but also to contrast the hatred and oppression of successive English kings in the Middle Ages with the benefits provided by the Tudors. He was obviously biased, failing to see the degree of cooperation that existed between progressive heads of emergent Welsh gentry and their English counterparts, before and particularly after the Glyndŵr rebellion, leading eventually to the circumstances which enabled Henry Tudor and his heir to establish the Tudor settlement. Like Sir John Wynn of Gwydir, Rhys Meurig, Humphrey Llwyd and others of their generation, George Owen was unable to recognise and evaluate the more positive features of a period, from the mid fourteenth century to the late fifteenth, sadly wrecked by war and rebellion.[12] He used misleading superlatives to make his point regarding Anglo-Welsh relations in that period: 'marvellous great hatred', 'the rigour of those hard and unreasonable laws [1401–2]', 'the oppression of this poor nation', 'deadly hatred', all of which he concisely described when referring to the situation during Glyndŵr's uprising: '... the name of a Welshman was odious to the Englishman, and the name of Englishman woeful to the Welshmen'.[13] It is in this light only that he proceeded to exaggerate Henry Tudor's role as king, following the bitter civil wars, as the 'second Solomon ... [who] lineally descended from the ancient British kings ... [and who] so drew the hearts of the Welshmen to him, as the lead stone [i.e. lodestone] does the iron'.[14] This interpretation is closely associated with the Galfridian myth which prophesied that the Welsh nation would in time be redeemed by a leader of ancient blood, who would liberate it from the yoke of the English. Henry

Tudor was regarded as a Moses (who delivered his people from bondage in Egypt), emancipating the Welsh from the English yoke. Owen continued the same theme when referring to the situation before benefits were brought by the newly appointed Justices of the Peace: 'But such officers as we had in Wales were for the most part strangers of other countries living on the spoil of the poor afflicted Welshmen, keeping them under as did the Egyptians the Israelites.'[15] 'God', he stated further, '... so mercifully provided for our deliverance, out of ancient thraldom ... and to hold our obedience towards our Prince'.[16] In this respect Owen regarded himself as an unofficial remembrancer, recording for the future what he considered to have been essential to the wellbeing of the Welsh nation.

Antiquaries like George Owen maintained a strong sense of 'Britishness' in its traditionally historical context, which enabled the Welsh to withstand extraneous influences which might compromise their nationality. He was a lavish entertainer at Henllys, had travelled through south Wales, and had visited Ludlow and London, where he searched records in the Tower and acquainted himself with officials of the College of Arms. These experiences had strengthened, not weakened, this 'Britishness', which was amply publicised in his writings on heraldry and genealogy.[17] Union with England might well have imposed its permanent influences on Wales, sometimes disadvantageously, but it did not weaken the sense of national pride, a factor which emerges clearly in the *Dialogue*, as well as the strong links, particularly after the Acts, with the new sovereign state established by Henry VIII. This was a development which was increasingly reflected in bardic eulogy from mid-century onwards.[18] According to Owen and his fellow antiquaries, it was Henry Tudor who fortified this pride and enabled the ruling class to benefit from it. Anglocentric Owen may well have been in his attitude towards public government and administration and his attachment to the Crown, but his sense of Welshness, expressed often in purely regional terms, was an integral component in his character.[19]

The content of George Owen's *Dialogue* gives prominence to a renewed interest which derived from the 'spirit of the Renaissance', a movement which undermined the intellectual restrictions of the Middle Ages and revived the study of classical authors.[20] It was a new spirit of inquiring curiosity, a search for knowledge, not only back *ad fontes* to the ancient classical traditions but also to the legacy of later history. Rhys Meurig made the point clearly: 'For, like as man, by a certain instinct of nature, is desirous of novelties, so is he of the knowledge of things past; whereby not only necessary and pleasant remembrance is attained, but also good example to the amendment of life.'[21] Such tendencies promoted a new sense of civil pride with the interest in locality revealing strong local patriotism. Emphasis was placed on ancestral connections, the soil, history and antiquities. Changing economic, social and cultural conditions in the sixteenth century made life generally more secure and orderly. The landed gentry, despite their strong litigious affairs, enjoyed under Tudor rule a more stable existence. They made good use of educational facilities and extended their cultural interests, thus affording them more scope to indulge in the delights of the mind. The current view of the ideal gentleman was based on Castiglione's *Il Cortegiano* (1528, translated into English by Sir Thomas Hoby in 1561), the concept of the perfect gentleman courtier, which was adapted in England and Wales to fit the notion of civilised conduct as described by Sir Thomas Elyot in *The Boke Named the Governour* (1531), a work highly regarded by Owen, who described it as 'a work rare and excellent for the instruction of gentlemen'.[22] Men of good breeding became connoisseurs of the arts, and scholar-gentlemen, refined by classical education, left a deep impact on public life and on social and economic development which permeated through the varying ranks of gentry:

> The most sure foundations of noble renown is a man to be of such virtues and qualities as he desireth to be openly published ... They shall also consider that by their pre-eminence they sit as it were on a pillar on the top of a mountain, where all the people do behold them ... Then shall he proceed further in furnishing his person with honourable manners and qualities, whereof very nobility is compact; whereby all other shall be induced to honour him, love him, and fear him, which things chiefly do cause perfect obedience.[23]

Prominent humanist commentators such as Elyot, Roger Ascham and Sir Humphrey Gilbert extolled the virtues of nobility, emphasising civility as being the essential feature of the public servant. In Wales, scholars and antiquarians such as Humphrey Llwyd gave priority to skill, confidence and deportment as the major features of good citizenship which characterised the Tudor gentleman par excellence.[24] For Llwyd legal education was central to the advancement of the concept of the ideal gentleman, and his encouraging view of educational standards among Welsh gentry reflected what he considered to be a progressive feature in Welsh Tudor society:

> ... there is no man so poore but for some space he sendeth forth his children to school, and such as profit in study sendeth them unto the universities where, for the most part, they enforce them to study the Civil Law. Whereby it chanceth that the greater sort of those which profess the Civil or Common Law in this realm are Welshemen.[25]

In Owen's generation sons of gentry entered institutions of learning, not only to achieve higher status as prominent landowners or professional lawyers, but also to adjust themselves to fundamental changes in law, government, the economy and cultural developments in a period *c*.1560–1640 when the Tudor Settlement in Wales demanded legal and political expertise.[26]

Although George Owen's social aspirations did not match those of some of his contemporaries such as Sir Richard Bulkeley, Sir John Wynn, Sir Edward Stradling and Sir Edward Mansel, in view of his social credentials he was widely regarded as a 'man of honour' and a governor who represented the Crown in his locality, possessing all the essential virtues to maintain good order and government and to command obedience. In his mind the privilege of public office entailed *noblesse oblige*, the responsibility of men of power to serve the state and their localities with equal efficiency.

By Elizabethan times it was not merely geographical discoveries overseas and plotting new sources of commerce and trade which captured the imagination of men of enterprise, but also the 'discovery' of a geographical entity, a country, county or even parish, and the chief characteristics of its topography and antiquities. Concentrating on the land and its features, its geography, geology and history, was a trend which, in England, was pioneered by John Leland in his *Itinerary Through England and Wales* (*c*.1536–9) at a time, during and after the dissolution of the monasteries, when he discovered many precious manuscript sources appertaining to secular as well as religious life. He was commissioned by Henry VIII to search libraries of monasteries and other institutions for ancient archival material. Regarded as the prototype of the English antiquary, his chief legacy was the compilation of a stack of notes crammed with information, historical, geographical, topographical, antiquarian and archaeological, revealing details of buildings, castles, monasteries and abbeys, supplemented by short commentaries on noble and gentry familes and their country seats.[27] Others industriously followed him, principally William Camden (*Britannia*, 1586), John Bale, bishop of Ossory (*Acta Romanorum Pontificum*, 1558), William Lambard (*A Perambulation of Kent*, 1570), Richard Carew (*Survey of Cornwall*, 1602), all of whom mainly emphasised topography, history and antiquities.[28] Doubtless, George Owen was familiar with the works of most of these scholars, and he regarded Camden as 'a learned and worthy man'. He gave Camden assistance in producing the sixth edition of *Britannia* (1607), which included a map of Pembrokeshire drafted by himself. *The Description of Penbrokshire* was remarkably similar to Carew's *Survey of Cornwall*, but a comparison between the two works reveals that of the two Owen was the more learned antiquarian. Equipped with his legal training, his knowledge of archival material, locally and in London, and of genealogy he set forth to produce a work of high quality. He had the appropriate skills for the task – his knowledge of land tenure and archival records, his legal expertise and familiarity with the College of Arms – all of which enabled him to be the first to produce a corpus of Pembrokeshire genealogy and to devise a county armorial. Although he had delved into many sources that were available to him he was still aware of his limitations and felt unable to complete what he had intended to achieve: 'without search of some matters of antiquity, not to be found in this country and conference with some skilful in those antiquities I am not able so to perfect as I have determined to do'.[29] However, since Camden had produced the first comprehensive topographical survey of England and Wales Owen wished to accomplish, on a much smaller scale, a similar study confined to Pembrokeshire. Men of this kind had inherited the new spirit of historical inquiry stemming from the Renaissance. In the *Dialogue*, investigation led Owen to an examination, at Ludlow, London and elsewhere, of governmental sources, mainly legal, and he perceptively set about observing the chief workings of governmental administration as revealed in county institutions. Despite its shortcomings he produced what has been regarded as the most thorough treatise on Tudor government and administration in Wales by a contemporary author. The same can be said of his other writings, which demonstrate a thorough factual knowledge of territorial units and baronial power, such as *A Treatise of Lordshipps Marchers in Wales*, *The Description of Wales* and *A Catalogue and Genealogie of the Lordes of the Baronye of Kemes, Lordes of Kemes* and related records.[30] He also compiled the commonplace book called *The Taylors Cussion* and recorded copious antiquarian notes on Cemais in the *Vairdre Book*.[31] He was indeed a remarkable individual, highly regarded by scholars of his own genre.

The two fundamental weaknesses in the *Dialogue* are the exaggerated and lavish portrayal of Pembrokeshire and the idealised view of Tudor rule. He wished to catch the eye of the gentry, an order in society which used whatever means possible to advance itself materially. Regardless of the detailed knowledge displayed by him he tended to brush off the defects and to extol the merits of Tudor rule, although many among the lower ranks of society, had they been given the opportunity, in their own interests, would have been less likely to applaud what the Tudors had accomplished. His interpretation of late fifteenth-century social development in Wales was largely simplistic, and his reference, for example, to the condition of the Church in his native county in his day and age was misleading. His ardent Protestantism led him to believe that the quality of religious life was favourable, despite the fact that Episcopal reports painted a different and gloomy picture of non-residency, shortage of preachers and learned clergy, a situation harshly criticised by the Brecknockshire Puritan John Penry in his first treatise on Wales in 1587.[32]

Doubtless, George Owen was an accomplished scholar and antiquarian who was immensely interested in cartography.[33] It was the age of emergent nation states, the rise of national sovereignties. Since England and Wales were vulnerably situated and open to invasion from east and west, it was essential to defend the coasts, hence the need for reliable maps to locate possible landing sites for the enemy. Moreover, his prolific literary output, based largely on his own researches, is ample proof of his remarkable diligence in searching for and collating his material. He was a meticulous commentator on the contemporary scene, and his handwriting was neat and readable. Although less obviously Welsh in his sympathies than others of his genre, he had familiarised himself with the works of Welsh antiquaries such as Humphrey Llwyd, Dr David Powel and Sir John Price, as well as of genealogists such as Lewys Dwnn and Thomas Jones of Porth-y-ffynnon near Tregaron.[34] He was well known to the professional bards of his day, who were aware of his Welsh cultural interests, as Siôn Mawddwy declared in 1597 in an ode begging a horse of George Owen for the ageing Thomas Jones (Twm Siôn Cati), a Cardiganshire landowner and antiquary who inspired Owen to pursue his genealogical interests:

> Enaid y sir ein wyd, Siors
> Owens irdeg, naws eurdors.
> Nyd oes kamp dda, klaya klod,
> Nay deünydd nad yw ynod,
> Dewr hael doeth, kall difall farn,
> Dyskedig wyt sy gadarn.[35]

[George Owen, you are the country's soul; fresh gilded and distinguished. There is no feat of the highest accomplishment which you have not attained. Brave, generous, wise, of unfaltering judgement, a stalwart man of learning.]

He was also the central figure in a group of littérateurs in Pembrokeshire, among whom manuscripts and pedigrees circulated, chiefly with a view to conducting private discussions between them,[36] consisting of Robert

Holland, vicar of Prendergast, Walwyn's Castle and Robeston West, George Wiliam Griffith of Penybenglog[37] and George Owen Harry, rector of Eglwys-wen in Cemais, the author of *The Genealogy of the High and Mighty Monarch, James ... King of Great Brittayne* (1604).[38] They all took interest in heraldry, genealogy and bardic lore, and George Owen was the most conspicuous among them. He was the first to produce an armorial of Pembrokeshire gentry families, two copies of which survive, and in 1602 his map of the county appeared with the coats of arms of those families.[39]

A study of the bardic system and its output was considered essential to the preservation of good lineage, and Owen was regarded as this school's 'high priest', a warm-hearted Welshman who cherished the Welsh language ('rhwn oedd i hün yn Gymro ystyriol ag i gare Gymreigydd').[40] Although he is not regarded as one of the most prominent of bardic patrons, he was respected for his gravitas and dignified demeanour, and he welcomed itinerant poets such as Siôn Mawddwy, Morys Llwyd ab Wiliam, Dafydd Llwyd Mathau, Lewys Dwnn and Huw Llŷn into his home.[41] In this respect he followed his father and mother, both of whom gave lavish hospitality to Dafydd Goch Brydydd o Fuallt, Dafydd Emlyn, Dafydd Llwyd Mathau, Gruffudd Hafren, Ieuan Tew Brydydd Hen o Gydweli and Siôn Mawddwy.[42] Owing to his genealogical and heraldic interests and his many literary and antiquarian connections in London and elsewhere, in 1594 Siôn Mawddwy pleaded with him to seek permission from the Queen and her councillors at Ludlow to hold another official eisteddfod, following those held at Caerwys in Flintshire in 1523 and 1567–8:

> Ar gerdd i ddymunaw'r gŵr,
> Iawn gais, fod yn negeswr
> I geisio 'steddfod, clod clêr,
> Ac ymbarch i wlad Gamber,
> I wellhau'n braint mewn llawn bris,
> Oddi obry, lle 'dd ŷm ddibris ...
> Aed hwn, sy'n gywir teni,
> At hon a'i Chynghoriaid hi,
> A doed ag eisteddfod ynn,
> I'w dôr ef, lle da'r ofyn.[43]

[In verse, by true request, the man is willed to be a messenger to seek an assembly in praise of the bards and respect for the land of Camber. To improve our status fully from above when we are despised ... May he, being honest, go to her [that is, the Queen] and her councillors, and bring us an assembly to his door, a good place to request it.]

Owen was regarded by the poets as the person who might gain favour with the Council in the Marches so that bardic standards could be maintained. It is not known whether or not Owen complied with the bard's wishes or whether, as implied in the above verse, Siôn Mawddwy expected the eisteddfod to be held at Henllys. What is clear is that Sir Henry Herbert, second earl of Pembroke, Lord President of the Council in the Marches, a member of the Herbert family which had over generations supported the bardic order, refused to allow an eisteddfod to be held in that year and that Owen's name was not included among the twelve signatories to the petition sent to him on 20 May 1594.[44] The ode reflected on the declining standards of the bardic order and desired that an eisteddfod be held again to restore its reputation. Members of the Owen household, however, like others, such as Cilycyffaith and Penybenglog, in north Pembrokeshire in the late sixteenth and early seventeenth centuries, were enthusiastic supporters of the poets and, in Siôn Mawddwy's ode, there is also a reference to the silver harp owned by the barony of Cemais and kept, according to *Llyfr y Faerdre* (*Vairdre Book*), in Llandudoch monastery during the lord's absence.[45] Siôn Mawddwy reflected on the silver harp as being central in the Pembrokeshire literary tradition at the time:

> Hennwaf fenaid hen fonedd
> Henllys yw y lys a'i wledd
> Oi dai rhoddir gowir gan
> Yn wir y delyn arian.[46]

[I name the soul of the ancient gentility of Henllys, its court and feast; from its houses a true song is given indeed by the silver harp.]

Although the *Dialogue* is not regarded as George Owen's most famous work, it still remains a remarkably substantial treatise on judicial structures and their operation in post 1536–43 Wales, and deserves more detailed attention by modern historians. Firstly, it contributes richly to the historian's understanding of the mechanics of Tudor legal administration, and secondly, it reveals the author's narrow interpretation of the social and political background. Its literary structure is based throughout on dialogue, using the Socratic method of writing a series of questions and answers which was becoming fashionable in Owen's day, following the publication of Erasmus's *Colloquies* (1518–21), Christopher St German's *The Dialogue in English between a Doctor of Divinitie and a Student in the Lawes of England* (1531) and Sir Thomas More's preparation of some of Lucian's dialogues in Latin.[47] Robert Recorde, mathematician and physician, another native of Pembrokeshire, regarded by Owen as 'a man

... much renowned for his learning', wrote his scientific works as dialogues between master and scholar.[48]

The two characters in the *Dialogue* are Demetus, a native of Dyfed, as the name implies, and Barthol, described as an educated German from Frankfurt, addicted to travelling to increase his knowledge of law and custom. His character was based on Bartolus, a fourteenth-century Italian jurist, and in the *Dialogue* he was described as a Protestant and a Doctor of Civil Law who had practised at Antwerp, a strong commercial centre, where his wife and children were murdered by Spaniards (1576) in what was called the 'Spanish fury'. On 4 November the mutinous *tercios* – wild Spanish infantry – violently sacked, pillaged and massacred the city for eleven days, leaving 7,000 people dead.[49] Barthol's family background, as created by George Owen, revealed his awareness of contemporary political events on the Continent and his anti-Spanish sentiments during the revolt of the Netherlands and the Anglo-Spanish War between 1585 and 1604.[50]

Barthol took much interest in cosmography and was probably influenced by Abraham Ortelius, the famous Flemish cartographer and friend of Gerhard Kremer (Mercator), who published his *Theatrum Orbis Terrarum* in 1570, a work which dismissed Ptolemy's description of the world.[51] Barthol was also well aware of the good reputation enjoyed by England on the Continent in law, government and administration. He had spent his years before meeting Demetus travelling in other lands, such as his native Germany and in France, where he observed their judicial structures and became well acquainted with their legal practices. He was a typical professional man who embodied the Renaissance spirit and who wished to broaden his knowledge of governments. The manner in which he describes his journeys and the benefits he had derived from them indicates his enterprising spirit:

> ... I am naturally comforted with the view and travel of strange countries; I have chosen to wear out the later part of my days in travelling of strange lands, and to see with the eye, that which in my youth I greatly delighted to read ... I also was very desirous of the old and present estate and government of each state and land, and by what laws they were governed, and diverse other things I learned by the historical and geographical description of countries, a study which greatly delighted my humour.[52]

He made use of the knowledge obtained from others and spent his time (as his sojourn with Demetus showed) seeking answers to his questions. He was portrayed as being discreet and honourable, continually examining Demetus's knowledge and understanding of judicial institutions in Wales, annotating carefully what was being said to him and testing his accuracy.

He clearly had a broader intellect than Demetus, whom Owen describes as a country gentleman of humble status, not given to travelling but steeped in his knowledge of the history of Pembrokeshire, a mere 'gentleman' Demetus is made to say, 'leading my life in the country and not professing the study of the law'. Owing to domestic responsibilities he preferred to stay at home, 'being placed and cast, as it were, in the end of the world in an odd solitary corner fit for a hermit'.[53] Such a description contrasts clearly with the amount of knowledge which Demetus imparts to Barthol in his extended conversation with him, which is a truer reflection of his ability. Doubtless, much of George Owen himself is revealed in Demetus's attitudes, opinions and responses to Barthol's intense interrogation, but his own travelling experiences were far more extensive than those of the character whom he created. Their identical interests led to a close friendship between them, to which Demetus testifies in his statement almost at the outset of their dialogue that 'you and I, as I weene, were both born, as the Astrologians say, under one planet or constellation'.[54]

Barthol took greater interest in judicial government rather than administrative, as his mode of questioning shows. He showed very little interest in the Welsh language, which, to his mind, appeared to be a strange linguistic survival. He was glad to hear English being spoken so that he might continue his investigations in Wales. He was well aware of the existence of the Welsh and Cornish languages and the connection between them, and when he entered north and mid Wales, having completed his travels in parts of Scotland and England, he confessed – rather surprisingly – that he had not found one person there able to inform him of the state of the government.[55] Implied in such a statement is a feeling that the native tongue and its widespread every-day use at that time had little appeal and relevance to him, nor did it induce him to seek further information about it, particularly in a region where the cultural divide was so sharp. Although he broadly described the physical features of some of the areas of north and mid Wales which he had visited, he was soon led by Demetus to consider the welfare of Pembrokeshire at the expense of other counties. Doubtless, this was the author's deliberate intention, in view of the fact that he had already researched thoroughly the history of the county. Having made his commentaries on the structure of judicial administration, its strengths and weaknesses, their content related generally to all parts of Wales. Generally, George Owen in this *Dialogue* used Barthol, acting occasionally as a wary 'devil's advocate', as a means of drawing Demetus into forming a critical assessment of contemporary views of government shared among those of his class in Wales under the new Tudor

Introduction

regime. Taking into account its aims and limitations, to that extent the value of the work is considerably enhanced.

The mechanics of legal administration

Once George Owen had set the background to Tudor government in Wales and had established the friendship between Demetus and Barthol, he then proceeded to discuss the major functions of the Council in the Marches held at Ludlow castle, the centrepiece of Tudor government in Wales and the border areas.[56] Its jurisdiction extended over the whole of Wales, including Monmouthshire, the four adjacent English counties of Gloucestershire, Worcestershire, Herefordshire and Shropshire, the city of Bristol to 1562 and, until 1569, the County Palatine of Chester. It was established in 1471 by Edward IV as an institution to manage the lands of Edward, the young Prince of Wales, namely the Principality, the Duchy of Cornwall and the County Palatine of Chester. It was from its inception a prerogative Council, its members appointed by the Crown on behalf of the Prince, and in 1473 its numbers were increased to twenty-five members who retained their offices during the Prince's pleasure until he was 14 years of age. From that year onwards the Council was given orders to maintain law and order in Herefordshire and Shropshire, border territory notorious for its lawlessness. To strengthen its position a separate household was created for the Prince, and John Alcock, bishop of Rochester, was appointed the Council's first President, thus establishing a succession of English prelates in that post until 1548.[57]

From 1476 onwards the Council assumed a dual role of supervising the Prince of Wales's possessions and maintaining law and order in Wales, the Marches and the four border English counties. There is no evidence of its existence between 1483 and 1493, when Arthur, Henry VII's heir, created Prince of Wales in 1490, was given a Council to administer his lands and commissioned to govern those areas. William Smyth, bishop of Coventry and Lichfield, became President in 1501 and the Council's powers increased, as revealed in the authority exerted by the Crown in 1504 which forced Edward Stafford, Duke of Buckingham, one of the few surviving marcher lords, to maintain law and order within his jurisdiction.[58] Checks were placed on 'overmighty subjects', such as the duke of Buckingham, who agreed by indenture to control the movement of criminals into and out of his lands.

In 1525 the Council's powers were extended, and in the same year a similar institution was created at York to quell disorder in the north of

England, known as the Council of the North.[59] The Presidency still remained the monopoly of English bishops, namely Geoffrey Blythe of Coventry and Lichfield, John Veysey, bishop of Exeter, and the most celebrated among them, Bishop Rowland Lee of Coventry and Lichfield.[60] They all held the office in succession down to 1543 and in that year, by the Act of 34–35 Henry VIII c.26, the so-called second Act of Union, the Council became a statutory rather than a prerogative body. Its powers were sparsely defined in that statute, the President and the Council having 'the Power and Authority to hear and determine ... such causes and matters as be or hereafter shall be assigned to them by the King's Majesty'.[61] Demetus made the point clearly when he stated that 'the authority and jurisdiction of the Council is not certainly known, for they are to judge and determine of such matters as the Queen of England shall authorise them from time to time by way of Instructions, and their authority is not certain'.[62] Also vague was the precise area over which it governed, for the statute refers only to 'Wales and the Marches of the same', which is unclear, in view of the territorial changes after the Acts of Union.

From that time onwards the Council exerted its powers in administrative and legal matters, maintaining at Ludlow an administrative unity binding Wales, the five newly created counties and the border counties together under its jurisdiction, although its authority wavered often during the reminder of the century. Doubtless, when Demetus examined it in the 1590s it still exercised its vast powers and was considered a vital component in maintaining government in Wales and the border. Thomas Churchyard, in his poem *The Worthines of Wales* (1587), considered Ludlow to be the centre of Welsh government:

> It stands for Wales, most apt, most fit and best,
> And neerest to, at hand of any place ...
> The rest of townes, that in Shropshiere you have,
> I neede not touch ... I know they cannot crave
> To be of Wales.[63]

Armorial bearings of notables, including Lord Presidents of the Council and most of the contemporary Welsh bishops, on the church walls in the castle gave the town its 'vice-regal' status:

> ... the armes, the blood and race
> Of sondrie Kings, but chiefly noble men.[64]

Not all littérateurs, however, were happy with the consequences of this Council's popularity. Like other contemporary poets, Edwart ap Raff

Introduction

considered Ludlow and London to be attractive venues for educated men and gentry, drawing them away from their native areas, thus depriving the Welsh countryside of its customary leadership and hospitality:

> Llawer sy'n mynd yn lluoedd
> Y gwir sy'n wir, gresyn oedd.
> Yn gecrus – gwmbrus eu gwaith –
> Yn gyfrwys yn y gyfraith ...
> Ledled oedd i Lwydlo deg
> Ac i Lundain gu landeg
> A hyn a fag, hen wyf i,
> Adwy lydan o dlodi.[65]

[Many go in droves; The truth is the truth, albeit regrettable. Cantankerous – cumbrous in their work – and cunning in the law ... Wide was the way to fair Ludlow and to dear, beautiful London, and this will produce – I am old – a wide chasm of poverty.]

Owing to increased political, economic and religious pressures the Council, by the latter half of the sixteenth century, was beginning to show the strains whereby it was, in the early years of the following century, to lose much of its vitality and authority. Sir Henry Sidney, Lord President from 1560 to 1586, considered it to be effective during his long stay at Ludlow: 'a happy place of government ...', he stated, 'for a better people to govern or better subjects to their sovereign Europe holdeth not', a remark which he probably considered appropriate to reflect the success of his own long tenure of office at Ludlow.[66] This view, however, was contrary to that voiced by Dr David Lewis, Judge of the Admiralty, in 1576, who described the 'country to be so far out of order ... as doth require severe remedy'. He proceeded to refer specifically to the demerits of the Council.[67] Lewis disagreed with the leniency exercised by Sir Henry Sidney and considered that the strict policy pursued by Rowland Lee was the model. In days when disruption and ill-government were still rife, he was aware that the Council, by his time, had lost much of its steadfast reputation for exercising full control over legal affairs and administration,[68] which undermined government agencies in the localities.

At the same time Sir William Gerard, deputy Lord President, offered similar comments stating that the Council was not properly respected. 'At this day to be plain, the Council and Court are neither reverenced, feared or their proceedings esteemed.'[69]

Almost twenty years later George Owen made his views known about the Council, and despite its shortcomings, he regarded it as a necessary organ of administration in Tudor Wales. Though it was called a Council, he maintained, its administrative functions were outweighed and overshadowed by its role as a court of justice. Sources regarding the Council, like the Privy Council, of which it was an offshoot, reveal that it performed essential duties as an administrative body. A combined exercise of legal and administrative tasks characterised the functions of all local Tudor officials in the courts, as was evident in the court of Quarter Sessions. In fact, George Owen pays but scant attention to the Council's administrative responsibilities, such as supervising alehouses, the poor laws, defence matters and local government generally, as well as organising military and defence duties in the localities, matters of the utmost importance in the Elizabethan era, especially after 1585, when war broke out with Spain and when economic conditions had deteriorated. He was fully aware of the central power of Parliament, which he and Barthol believed should act forthwith to remedy the wrongs that had hindered justice from being administered in the courts at different levels.[70] The Lord President held commission of Lieutenancy over all Welsh counties, a post which he delegated from 1569 and, more frequently, from 1587 onwards to deputies in each of them, following the intensity of the war with Spain.[71] Virtually all his attention was given to judicial matters concerning the Council as well as other lower courts, and administrative duties were imposed by implication but not by definition, for the Act of 1543, as noted above, was very vague in its wording. Nevertheless, the surviving Register of the Council for the years 1569–95 is sufficient evidence that it was constantly occupied with a wide range of administrative as well as judicial tasks.[72]

The Council's records as a court of justice, however, have not survived, and what it actually performed can only be deduced from incidental references in contemporary accounts and from information drawn from other judicial records, such as those of Star Chamber. In this light, Owen's account, therefore, as related by Demetus, is all the more valuable. What is clear, however, is that the Act of Union strengthened its powers by making it a statutory institution supervised by the Privy Council, its parent body. Assumptions can be made mainly from Instructions sent down from the Crown and the Privy Council, and from the fact that it was a delegated body of that Council.[73] Although administrative tasks took second place to judicial matters, George Owen did possess an ornamented copy of the Queen's Instructions to the Lord President, signed at Windsor in 1586.[74] It is evident, nevertheless, that the Council possessed the ultimate authority in Wales and was a body acknowledged by Demetus as the formative instrument of government assigned to maintain law and order.

In his survey of the Council in the Marches Demetus explains that it was principally occupied 'in hearing and determining of matters of right', functioning as a court of equity jurisdiction, similar to the Chancery Court at Westminster, in which any person could sue 'to mitigate the rigour of law'.[75] He also stated that the Council dealt most commonly with misdemeanours such as assaults, affrays, riots, extortions, *cymorthas*[76] and financial exactions demanded by ruthless landowners and their agents. In this respect it functioned in a similar fashion to the Court of Star Chamber.

Using Demetus's testimony, George Owen reveals his close association with the judicial affairs of the Council, chiefly because of his legal knowledge and constant involvement in his own landed affairs. Among his colleagues, excepting Sir William Gerard, doubtless it is he who provides the most thorough examination of the judicial functions, allowing Demetus to discuss at length the merits and demerits of this principal organ of Tudor government in Wales. The only concrete information that is available in the statutes is that the court functioned as a court of appeal from lower courts in personal actions, but where property was involved (actions real and mixed), appeal could be made only to the King's Bench at Westminster.[77]

Regardless of the ambiguity surrounding the Council's power, Demetus readily acknowledged its popularity. It was recognised as a place of 'refuge for the poor [and] oppressed' who sought redress at Ludlow, and he gave two reasons for that, namely the reasonable fees demanded and the convenience of travel to Ludlow, rather than London, from the less accessible parts of the country.[78] Actions in courts of Great Sessions, especially in cases of dispute over possession of property, could be prolonged, but the proceedings at Ludlow in such matters, despite the volume of work, were speedy, even in comparison with the Westminster courts. Despite the favourable remarks made by Demetus about the court's cheapness and efficiency, he noted that there was a demand in some quarters for its suppression, on the grounds that it had become superfluous. Who the critics were Demetus does not say, but from other sources it is known that the adjoining counties and towns subject to its jurisdiction, like Bristol and Gloucester, resented its authority as a conciliar court, creating opposition which became more aggressive in the early seventeenth century because of its freedom from parliamentary control.[79] In his defence of the Council Demetus characteristically praised Tudor government, headed by the Council in the Marches, as having brought the country 'to that civility and quietness that you now see it, from that wild and outrageous state that you shall read of'.[80] Misguided though this view was, it was typical for the age, and Demetus readily regarded the Council as the essential pivot coordinating law and government in Wales and the borders. He placed the Council and the court high on the list of institutions which had brought this about for, despite its weaknesses, he could see that there was still need for it: 'for let that house or Council be dissolved but for a few years ... those that live now most quietly and think that Court unnecessary should feel the smart and want thereof'.[81] He was obviously aware of the opposition to it, but he could also see the need for such a body to maintain stability, support poor litigants and curb the unruliness of ambitious landowners, who still needed careful handling, as contemporary sources readily reveal. Peaceful respectability was often shallow, particularly in areas traditionally vulnerable to disorder, such as the southeastern and central marcher areas. Thieves and outlaws still roamed the countryside, often employed by ambitious gentry, who continually vied with each other for land and status.[82] Almost twenty years earlier Dr David Lewis, in addition to his strictures on the Council in the Marches, severely criticised the control exercised by local officials in the Marches, referring specifically to the evils of retaining and *cymorthas*, and to general disregard for good government:

> The authority of the Council [in the Marches] there is not regarded as it hath been for neither Sheriff, Justice of the Peace ... will so carefully apprehend or take any such persons as hath any friend of any account, although their faults be never so grievous and apparent, yea though he hath the said Council's letters to that end; but will play bo peep, seest me and seest me not, and thus have grown by impunity whereof do proceed all manner of disorders.[83]

Lewis thought that Sir Henry Sidney, during his long term of office at Ludlow, had been weak and unable to maintain the authority which the legislation of 1536–43 had provided.

Following Barthol's desire for more information on the defects of the Council, Demetus proceeded to note that there were too many 'trifling' and inconsequential suits brought to court and that the costs awarded were too low, and he suggested possible remedies. First, the Judges themselves had the power to remedy the matter of award of costs by using their discretion. Low costs accounted for the many unnecessary cases brought to court, and encouraged malicious individuals to initiate needless litigation and to involve those against whom they brought actions in large expenses. Demetus also recommended that there should be a reduction in the number of attorneys who functioned in the court. They were far too numerous and attracted unnecessary business. Also, malicious plaintiffs brought actions in order to annoy their adversaries and then offered to discharge cases for twenty shillings, to the satisfaction of a defendant who wished to spare further expense. The plaintiff obtained the discharge fee, the defendant his freedom, but, as Demetus stated, he left the court 'obtaining the victory but [forced] to live by the loss'.[84] Doubtless, the only remedy to prevent such invidious behaviour in court was to increase costs.

Procedure in the court at Ludlow was also defective because of the multiplicity of legal processes and the complex handing of legalities, all of which appeared to contradict Demetus's earlier remark that procedure was relatively speedy. What he implied was that opening an action by a bill of complaint was simpler than having to proceed according to a long series of writs in other courts, all this being a reason for the court's popularity. The need for bills of complaint to be endorsed by a member of the Council in the Marches and, later, by clerks and attorneys, and for actions involving sums under forty shillings not to be heard, all helped to decrease the pressure of work in the court. This led Barthol to survey court procedures in an unspecified part of Germany and to compare them with what he found in Wales, which reflected George Owen's wide interests and knowledge of the legal structure on the Continent. All this was followed by a discussion of what Barthol had learned for himself about procedures in the main courts at Westminster, namely the court of Common Pleas, the courts of Exchequer, Chancery and King's Bench, together with the courts of Star Chamber, Duchy of Lancaster, Wards and Livery and Requests.[85]

Barthol, moving the conversation forwards, expressed surprise that the Welsh people had remained so loyal to the Tudors, given the distressing past they had suffered at the hands of the English Crown, and that remark gave Demetus the opportunity to offer yet another hearty eulogy of the early Tudors who had liberated the Welsh from bondage. To strengthen his argument, he drew evidence yet again from the contents of the Acts of Union passed by Henry VIII to enable the Welsh to obtain justice within reasonable distance at Ludlow, compared to the burden in England of having to travel to Westminster from the distant north, a lead given to open up a new line of discussion on royal courts, namely the Great Sessions, which again led Demetus to praise Tudor government. He applauded the system which allowed the Welsh to have their cases tried within their own regions and provided ample jurisdiction and cheap legal fees. In each of the four circuits set up in 1543 one Judge presided until 1576, when an additional one was appointed in all four because of the increase in business.[86] The Act also provided a sheriff in each county on an annual basis, together with Justices of the Peace, Escheators, Coroners and local bailiffs. Henry VIII thereby, Demetus maintained, made the country of Wales 'equal in all respects in freedoms and liberties' with the realm of England.[87] It is in this context that Demetus highly praised a number of eminent assize judges who served the Carmarthen circuit in the Elizabethan age, for example, George Fetiplace, Sir John Puckering (who served for fifteen years), John Walshe and John Rastall, all of whom he considered to be chiefly instrumental in maintaining good order in the south-west circuit of Wales.[88] Owen also thought highly of Henry Herbert, second earl of Pembroke, Lord President of the Council in the Marches from 1586 to 1601, Edward, earl of Worcester, and Robert Devereux, second earl of Essex, as promoters of peace and security and as supporters of legal and administrative reforms.[89] Puckering, an Essex supporter, was very highly regarded in the Carmarthenshire circuit, which he served as Chief Justice for almost fifteen years (1578–92). His short term as Lord Keeper (1592–6), to which Demetus paid his respects, was also considered worthy of applause. 'Oh great happiness that has fallen upon this poor country', he maintained, 'by the first coming of this honourable man into the same', an accolade readily acceded to by Barthol.[90]

In Great Sessions Demetus noted that good order prevailed and he proceeded to describe their main functions, drawing attention to real, personal and mixed suits that were tried there. A Chancery and Exchequer were set up in the two new circuits – at Denbigh and Brecon – together with an Auditor, Receiver and Protonotary, who was responsible for judicial processes and systematising the records, thus matching the administration at Caernarfon and Carmarthen.[91] In this respect again Demetus praised the fact that suitors need no longer travel, but could obtain justice within their respective counties. In reply, Barthol echoed his thoughts, referring to a session which he attended at Haverfordwest and where he saw 'the guilty condemned with pity, and the innocent delivered by justice'.[92] This prompted him to praise further the administration of law in Wales: 'Wales [is] a happy country that is so governed by such laws and magistrates, a blessed Prince that so provided for so loving subjects, and happy people that were governed with so careful and gracious a Prince.'[93] Once Demetus had invited Barthol to observe any defects in Great Sessions, the discussion of the courts was extended, and Demetus availed himself of the opportunity to explain at some length why felons could illegally plead innocent, to 'blind the eyes of the Judges'.[94] An offender was first brought before Justices of the Peace in Quarter Sessions, who declared that the matter, as was customary in criminal cases, should be tried in Great Sessions. The prisoner, however, immediately before the Sessions met the party pursuant to discuss terms amicably, but the prosecutor proceeded to prosecute very lightly and left the matter with the Grand Jury during the rest of the week. When the Judge inquired as to the outcome, it was reported that the evidence was insufficient and the offender was discharged. Demetus denied that the Justices of the Peace were to blame for such corrupt practices and considered that it was inefficiency on the part of the Queen's Attorney that was responsible, because of his negligence in dealing with the matter. Moreover, although undervaluing stolen goods was a criminal offence the case would be dismissed.

Regarding the holding of Great Sessions Demetus focused on one major inconvenience, namely the delay in holding Sessions at the stipulated time and holding them at the busy time of Lent. In England that caused no problems since most of the tillage was wheat, rye and barley, it being the 'idlest time of the year' for farmers. In Wales, however, what was mostly sown was oats, and that during Lent, thus coinciding with Great Sessions and the Council in the Marches.[95] It is clear, however, that Demetus's major complaint with these Courts was the inconvenience of the times when they were held, rather than their judicial activities.[96] He did not pretend to provide a remedy which allowed Barthol to explain, although he was aware of other lower courts that needed attention, why he considered that the two higher courts, at Ludlow and the circuit courts alone, were sufficient to govern the country successfully.

Having thus dealt with the Equity Court, held by the Justices alongside the Sessions, and the complaint that insufficient time had been given to deal with other urgent matters, Demetus then proceeded to examine the office of Justice of the Peace and the courts of Quarter Sessions. They were regarded as the best known Tudor officials and courts, created by statute immediately before the Act of Union (1536).[97] This court was held four times a year dealing with matters of the peace, and had administrative as well as judicial functions to perform. The Justices were officially appointed by the Lord Chancellor from the best among the gentry and burgesses of towns: 'good men, lawful men, no maintainers of evil, best of reputation ... learned in laws and most worthy men'.[98] Demetus compared such governors to the judges whom Jethro, Moses's father-in-law, recommended that he should appoint to judge over the people of Israel.[99] He proceeded to extol the virtues of such officials whom Henry VIII had chosen from among the Welsh themselves ('to give them magistrates of their own nation'), thus echoing the myth that the Welsh people would one day obtain their freedom and be governed by their own people.[100] Despite their reputably high standing as governors Demetus noted one major deficiency arising from the social structure of the country by the closing decades of the sixteenth century, namely the clause in the Act of 1543 stipulating that the property qualification of £20 which operated in England for Justices of the Peace was to be waived in Wales. They were to be men 'of good name and fame' who were to 'use and exercise the Office of the Justice of the Peace albeit they may not dispend twenty pound nor be learned in the Laws of the Lands'.[101]

In the early sixteenth century there were but few men of substance in the country, a situation which had caused Rowland Lee to state in his letter to Thomas Cromwell in 1536, on hearing of the intention to create Justices of the Peace in Wales, that there were few gentry north of Brecknock who could dispense £20 land. 'I think it not much expedient', he stated, because 'to say truth, their discretion [is] less than their lands.'[102] Regardless of Lee's prejudice against the Welsh, this remark drew attention to the poor quality of material life among Welsh gentry, particularly in north and mid Wales. Demetus, however, considered that social conditions had vastly improved by his day and believed that the property qualification should be imposed to prevent inferior magistrates from being appointed. The problem had been given attention in England a century after Justices had been appointed there, in the reign of Henry VI, when an Act was passed in 1439 imposing the £20 qualification to maintain the quality of those appointed.[103] Demetus believed that £20 in land, by his time, was valued at five times as much as it had been in the mid fifteenth century, and he was aware that 'diverse men of mean living are climbed up to the bench by whom ... the people would not be ruled'.[104] This implied not only that they were socially inferior, but also that they were prepared to act ruthlessly to maintain and even improve their social status. Dr David Lewis, in his letter to Walsingham, had also drawn attention to this deficiency, in his commentary on the poor quality of officials who kept order in the localities, some of whom colluded with criminals and 'retained' armed men to inflict violence on others to promote their own interests:

> Lykewyse the sherife, Justices of the Peace, maior, baylye, or any other officer to whome the saide counsaile shall dyrecte their lettres for the apprehencion of any person, yf they shalbe founde to haue wyncked & not to haue

don their offices carefully and syncerelye, are to be kepte in prison untill those persons be apprehended and brought in, to be ponished according to their defectes.[105]

Demetus, though not a magistrate by his own admission, was evidently aware of the multiple tasks which these busy officials were expected to perform in law and administration, and was equally aware of the need to punish them severely for neglecting their duties and abusing their public offices.[106] The office was prestigious, appointees being drawn from the most eligible among country gentry. Hence, Barthol made the point quite clearly: '… passing by diverse gentlemen's houses it was told me that a Justice of the Peace dwelled there, and it seems that they are the chiefest gentlemen in every shire that bear that office'.[107] Their expertise, Demetus considered, derived from the quality of education which they had received owing to improved social conditions: 'the people', he stated, 'are grown to be of great wealth, the gentlemen of great livings … there are now … to be found some that do receive yearly five hundred pounds, some three hundred pounds and many one hundred pounds good land'.[108] This obviously was an exaggeration, when it is considered that the lower gentry were still very modestly placed. Moreover, to state that the benefits of the Acts of Union had led to 'our hearts to leap for joy … the houses of the gentlemen and people to flourish and increase' should be related specifically to the more opulent among gentry families, professional individuals and prosperous urban families.[109] It is evident that George Owen interpreted Welsh social conditions from his and his class's point of view and showed hardly any consideration for the lowest of the social orders. His adulation of Henry Tudor stemmed from the traditional propagandist view, and the office of Justice of the Peace was regarded solely as the legacy of a beneficent King of Welsh origins on the throne of England.

Barthol, obviously intrigued by the explanation given by Demetus that inferior magistrates were appointed by Tudor government in Wales, sought an explanation why Henry VIII, whose father was regarded as 'that worthy Moses of Wales', intent on establishing good government in Wales, should allow the legislation to waive the property qualification.[110] Demetus's answer clearly followed his interpretation of Tudor rule as applied to Wales, namely that the Crown had no option at the time because of dire social conditions, but circumstances in his day had radically improved. This view led to his abounding eulogy of a prosperous Wales in late Elizabethan times, based on a historical survey:

> the gentlemen and people in Wales have greatly increased in learning and civility … whereby the country is grown and shortly like to be as civil as any

other place of this land ... No country in England so flourished in one hundred years as Wales has done since the government of Henry the Seventh to this time, insomuch that if our fathers were now living they would think it some strange country inhabited with a foreign nation ...[111]

Yet again a larger-than-life portrait, but Demetus, of course, had his own motive outlined since he was at that stage explaining how and why inferior Justices of the peace had to be appointed. Demetus appeared to be party to the idea that English kings, since Norman times, had pursued a policy of intense repression in Wales 'by open hostility and wars, as by providing of extreme and intolerable laws, sought continually the subversion, ruin and impoverishing of the said nation'.[112] Henry VIII, therefore, was forced to accept the situation as he found it, knowing full well the shortage of those who could meet the £20 property qualification or even those who were 'learned' in law. Since Wales had benefited materially, he maintained, 'so altered is the country and countrymen, the people changed in heart within and the land altered in hue without, from evil to good, and from bad to better'.[113] Hence, his desire to see the legislation changed to remove the inconvenience and reflect social, economic and cultural advancement; namely, the progress in economic growth in town and country, the consolidation of the landed gentry and the more intensive exploitation of their estates.

Demetus then proceeded to examine features of the courts of Quarter Sessions and was prepared to admit that not all the magistrates were efficient or fulfilled their tasks strictly according to law. For example, goods stolen were valued at less than twelve pence which reduced the case to one of petty larceny, not grand larceny, as it should have been.[114] On occasions they failed to distinguish between common theft and burglary, which was a more serious offence, and they neglected to examine how and under what circumstances goods were stolen. Also, unnecessary delays entailed that sessions in places were held 'out of due time', thus imposing hardship for those who followed certain trades and professions, 'especially those that trade by sea and far from home'.[115] Moreover, delay often affected proceedings, to the Crown's disadvantage, a fault which Demetus attributed to the absence of the Queen's Attorney, whose duties were often assumed by the Clerk of the Peace, appointed by the *Custos Rotulorum*.[116] He often failed to secure to the Crown its forfeitures following lapsed recognizances and the lack of restitution or redress commensurate with the value of the loss because of his inefficiency and ignorance of the law.[117] Demetus, therefore, declared that an Attorney should be appointed for each of the courts 'to solicit and follow those advantages and forfei-

Introduction

tures for her majesty', a task which the Clerk of the Peace often failed to perform.[118] Technically, in section 55 of the Act of 1543 it was stipulated that there should be no more than eight magistrates appointed in each county, in addition to the formal appointment to each court of the Lord President of the Council in the Marches and its Judges and the King's Attorney and Solicitor.[119] That Attorney, however, had not been appointed, thus preventing the efficient administration of justice.

Moreover, Demetus considered that the negligent manner in which some sessions of the peace were kept by magistrates, often because of ignorance and incompetence, also hindered the administration of justice. Such drawbacks, however, did not deter him from recognising the court as a pivotal cog in the mechanism which maintained local government. George Owen was very sensitive of the need to maintain dignity in the exercise of authority, and was prepared to admit that there were worthy magistrates who loyally undertook the increasing load of responsibilities heaped upon them. Despite the demerits, Demetus was full of admiration for the court of Quarter Sessions because of its vital role in county society, and provided Barthol with a list of legal duties which it fulfilled, whilst ignoring the heavy administrative burdens which the magistrates shared.

Barthol was further surprised that there were so many courts of law operative within Wales and prompted Demetus to examine the lower or 'base' courts, which, in Barthol's view, seemed irrelevant. He also called on Demetus to assess the role of the sheriff in county administration, which he considered should have been done earlier. Demetus explained that since the sheriff's tasks were mainly administrative, he had deliberately deferred examining the office until he came to examine the lower courts in which it assumed a prominent position. The sheriff's office was prestigious, its holder being the King's Lieutenant and royal representative in the county. It was described as 'the chief officer of trust and credit in the shire', executing all processes out of the Westminister and Welsh courts and attending to a multitude of other tasks, mainly administrative, for the smooth running of local affairs.[120] He maintained constant contact with the central government on an administrative basis, and it was only in the County Court that he functioned in a judicial capacity. He also held the Hundred Court for pleas under forty shillings and the biannual Turns. The sheriff, since 1543, held his office annually and was regarded as the chief executive officer in the county under the authority of Justices of Assize and Justices of the Peace. His appointment was different from the practice in England, where the sheriff travelled to London to obtain the *Dedimus Potestatem*, the writ granting him the authority to assume responsibility of office. In Wales it was issued from the local circuit Chanceries, thus avoiding distance travelling. Similarly, Escheators and Coroners were required to receive their oaths by commission, but this time before the Council in the Marches or Assize Justices, a practice which Demetus believed should be redressed by Parliament.

By 'base courts' Demetus meant all courts of lower status than Quarter Sessions, that is County Courts, Hundred Courts, Courts Leet and Courts Baron. They fell into two main categories, namely the County and Hundred Courts, historically associated with the old Principality, and Courts Leet and Courts Baron, the courts which functioned in the areas of Wales formerly known as marcher lordships. Demetus examined first the County Court, formerly the chief court of the county, which, in his view, should still be the chief court. It was held monthly, presided over by the sheriff and all freeholders owed suit of court. In its judicial capacity this court determined suits under forty shillings and minor cases of trespass, debt, detaining of goods and such like. What Demetus said about it indicated that this court had deteriorated greatly because of the malpractices in other baser courts, particularly the Hundred Courts.[121] The Hundred Court was also held by the sheriff, but chiefly more as part of his administrative functions in the hundred.

Demetus stressed the dignity of the County Court, for it was truly representative of the freeholding classes in society where they would return members to parliament. Most Welsh counties had only one member, so there could be no rival interests in each, as in England. Before Demetus proceeded to discuss the position of these courts he digressed on the office of sheriff and his position in the County Court. Barthol was made to ask whether these 'base' courts were necessary, for 'I have heard', he continued, 'that if all the base courts ... were dissolved, and all matters tried before the Justices in the Sessions, it were much better, and more ease for the country'.[122] In these words he echoed other criticisms made of the 'base courts'. Both agreed that there were far too many of them, that they practised 'great perjury' and were held too frequently by ignorant and incompetent persons. Demetus was forced to admit the validity of the first and second criticism, but questioned the complete abolition of such courts. He believed that, despite their defects, there was a very real need for such courts in his day, and advocated reform rather than abolition. The County Court needed to be revived, for it was in the Hundred Courts that the injuries complained of were most frequently committed, for the simple reason that less use was made of the County Court than the other, 'so decayed' had the County Court become.[123] The County Court, it was

Introduction

argued, was a better court, the Hundred Court being inferior and corrupt, and held by no one higher in rank than the deputy sheriff. The County Court was held usually in towns or large villages of some consequence, where justice would be seen to be done, and where hospitality was readily available. The Hundred Courts, however, were held in some obscure place or 'blind alehouse' inundated with 'evils', and were the scene of much confusion.[124]

Barthol, continuing to seek an appropriate answer to his question why these lower courts were tolerated, was intrigued by why the 'mad people' haunted the Hundred Court and forsook the County Court, where they might obtain better justice. Demetus, quick to respond, stated that the Hundred Courts were held more frequently – every fifteen days – and suited localities better because suitors would have shorter distances to travel to them.[125] Consequently, a discussion was initiated regarding the procedures used in Hundred Courts at various times before and after the Acts of Union. Demetus maintained that Hundred Courts ought not to be held, except in places where they had been held before the Acts of Union, that is in the old shires of Wales. Those courts were held in his day in counties created by those Acts, leading to injustice, people having to attend two courts of a similar kind, revealing a clash between two judicial systems. In those new counties, created from marcher lordships, the old manorial Courts Baron and Leets had survived, and they were expected to perform a similar kind of function: 'to which Leet they are and were time out of mind tied to answer by reason of their residency, and now are double vexed by answering to the Lord's Leet and to the sheriff's Turn'.[126] He had very little to say about the Courts Leet, but mentioned them along with the sheriff's Turn and appeared not to be anxious about them, chiefly because the injuries which they inflicted were minor, since pleas were not heard in them. They rather acted as courts of inquiry, where all inhabitants owed suit for misdemeanours about which little complaint was made.

Demetus considered that being subject to the jurisdiction of two similar courts was unjust, and pleaded that the independence of those areas which were now forced to accept both jurisdictions should be preserved. This situation, in fact, created much acrimony, because, as Demetus maintained, the inhabitants of the newly created counties did not owe suit of court to Hundred Courts, although a commission had been set up by the Act of 1536 to delimit the counties into hundreds. He referred to the abandonment of the Hundred Courts in Brecknockshire and in parts of Montgomeryshire and Glamorgan.[127] No Hundred Courts were held in these counties until late in the reign of Mary I or early in that of Elizabeth

I, the Council in the Marches having intervened in places where sheriffs had insisted on holding these courts and nullified them by writ of *quo warranto*.

Doubtless, there was considerable laxity in the holding of Hundred Courts, in order to avoid local opposition in the matter of owing double suit to two different courts. Demetus also sharply criticized the avarice and exactions of sheriffs' under officers, namely the bailiffs, appointed by them in the hundreds. The practice had arisen of removing them annually, as they acted extortionately towards the poor. It was not unusual for them to offer £20 or £30 for their offices, the whole sum being promptly redeemed by the tenure of the office, all of which reflected the gross abuse of the sale of offices, usually to the highest bidders. Demetus considered that appointing a bailiff for life would be advantageous, to prevent 'hungry flies that fed upon the galled horse back' from sucking what meagre means the poor had.[128]

Similar evils were practised in Courts Baron in the old lordship territories, now converted into shire-ground. These courts, Demetus maintained, also needed reforming and their crooked and wilful officials brought to book. He insisted again that reform and not dissolution was the best way forward, for he was still firmly convinced of the desirability of retaining 'base courts'. To strengthen his argument he cited the small-scale rural economy in Tudor Wales, which made for a large number of small suits, 'for there are none but the poorer sort of people that are sued in these base courts'.[129] Consequently, they could not be deemed to be unnecessary. Moreover, the shortage of ready cash in such an economy, particularly during the winter months, led small freeholders and yeomen to incur innumerable petty debts, and the nature of their husbandry, for the most part on unenclosed pasture land, was bound to give rise to an equally large number of actions for trespass. In answer to an unasked question, Demetus implied that the reason why such actions could not be heard in Great Sessions, where Judges were more skilled and impartial, was twofold, firstly that those Great Sessions were held only twice a year in each county, and that poor suitors might be kept for twelve months for redress, too long a period for trivial offences, and secondly that the expense of conducting these small actions would be prohibitive. Demetus at this point did not mention another factor, equally valid, namely the criticism already cited of Great Sessions for multiplicity of suits and actions, which would obviously cause undue delay.

Demetus then suggested remedies for the inefficiencies in the 'base courts', Barthol advocating the transfer of much of the business of Hundred

Courts to the County Courts. Demetus, however, recognised the difficulty of the problem, fearing a possible alienation of sympathy for the Tudor settlement among gentry families who were 'owners' of Courts Leet and Courts Baron, who would feel 'deprived of their inheritance' if these were suppressed. He added that the 'injuries' done in those courts were far less than in Hundred Courts, and there was no annual changeover of officials in Courts Baron, as occurred in the others.[130] Demetus was completely dissatisfied with the running of the Hundred Court, stating that its officials were ignorant of law and justice, 'much like young practitioners in physic who to practise their skill murder many of their patients'. In those courts, he stated further, officials 'still continue without removing, and are somewhat better skilled and practised in their rooms than those that never were acquainted therewith before'.[131] Having said all that, Demetus was obliged to admit that Courts Baron sprang up in places where they never were before, and therefore believed that there should be a reduction in their numbers, which might provide honest and discreet gentry stewards who would administer justice impartially. He also suggested that manor courts should be continued by the Crown, with one only representing them all within a lordship. He even went further to recommend that Justices of Assize in Great Sessions should be made to supervise the working of all these minor courts and to appoint local gentry to cooperate with stewards of lordships or manors to see justice being properly administered, and to lay down orders and prescribe rules for the courts' conduct, to minimise unruliness and vet the competence of clerks who functioned in them. Demetus obviously pleaded for reform of all these courts because he believed that it was necessary to retain a reasonable number of 'base courts' to determine small actions involving poor people, who could not travel to seek justice for small offences, nor incur heavy expenses in higher courts. His description of the husbandman or farmer is quite informative:

> the poorest husbandman [who] lives upon his own travail, having corn, butter, cheese, beef, mutton, poultry and the like of his own sufficient to maintain his house: he makes the apparel of him and his family of his own wool, and seldom uses any money … for seldom buy any of the poorer sort anything for ready money. Corn, butter, cheese, wool and such like the poor man buys of his richer neighbour at days, and commonly their payments are from May to mid-November … Likewise for their iron, salt, oil, linen-cloth, pitch, tar, spice and such like things that are to be had out of towns, the townsman sells the same at days also.[132]

Demetus had relatively little to say about the administration of justice in the urban areas of Wales, but did mention the courts of corporate towns, which were independent of the sheriff's jurisdiction by virtue of the *non intromittant* clauses included in borough charters. Normally, these classes exempted the borough from the jurisdiction of the county Justices of the Peace. He expressed concern about the inadequate officials who functioned in them and their annual changeover, especially the villages, hamlets and even manors, which were still regarded as incorporated boroughs through ancient charters granted by local lords. He referred to the clause in the Act of Union of 1543 by which the Crown retained the right by commission to dissolve those which were unnecessary and to incorporate others considered worthy of borough status.[133] To his knowledge, however, no such action had been taken and no commission had been appointed for that purpose. Since he was aware that many of these courts held pleas 'of great sums' that were beyond the capacity of Judges who functioned in them to administer proper justice, he believed that their numbers, like those of Courts Baron, should be curtailed. All in all, Demetus declared that the judicial system should, in several respects, be reformed by Parliament and all defects rectified, a view which echoed the sentiments expressed by Dr David Lewis and Richard Price of Brecon.[134]

Thus, the long dialogue on the judicial administration of Wales was brought to an end, although other factors were introduced in a later section, chiefly by Demetus, to add to Barthol's knowledge of why the Welsh people accepted Tudor policy so readily, why peace was established, and why and how consequently the country flourished. To strengthen his argument that the country benefited immensely from Tudor administration, he named eight Justices of Assize in the Carmarthen Circuit of Great Sessions who had served well in office.[135] He also added sections underlining his love for his native county of Pembroke and describing the territorial changes in the borders of that county and neighbouring Carmarthenshire, following the attachment in the Act of 1543 of the lordships of Laugharne, Llansteffan and Llanddowror to that county, much to Demetus's disapproval. This led to an exchange about the physical size of Carmarthenshire compared to Pembrokeshire, a comparison of sizes on maps, including that by Christopher Saxton of Welsh counties (1578), which implied that Pembrokeshire seemed to have come off worse than Carmarthenshire in supplying men for military service. Then followed a comparison of the scales of the maps of both counties, which made Pembrokeshire look larger than Carmarthenshire in Saxton's maps, whereas, in fact, it was smaller. Demetus believed that the 'stolen' lordships should be restored, and explained where possible weaknesses lay, on defence or geographical grounds, because of these regional changes.[136]

Introduction

Despite the fact that propaganda often misguides and causes serious misinterpretation, the *Dialogue* does, however, make very interesting history. This discourse by George Owen, who placed constant emphasis on recording what he considered to be historically authentic, would satisfy literate men in government of his own generation, most of them involved in the running of local government and doubtless able to agree or disagree with his version of his own age and its background. He had drawn all his resources together to compile a credible account of judicial government in Wales, and had shown the shrewd Barthol how well the mechanics of government could operate with the support of landed gentry working within a tight governmental structure, headed by the Privy Council and the Council in the Marches.

One weakness in George Owen's treatise is that administrative obligations, at the higher and lower levels, were hardly given any attention. That may have been because of Owen's legal interests, arising from his education in London and his constant litigation. Yet, as Justice of the Peace and county sheriff in his native Pembrokeshire, he was closely involved in supervising the duties of high and petty constables, churchwardens and the workings of the poor law and petty sessions of the peace.[137] Apart from his section on defence problems in Pembrokeshire towards the end of his treatise, there is virtually nothing about the administration of that aspect of government in his county or elsewhere in Wales, especially during the period when the *Dialogue* was compiled, when war with Spain was at its height. There is no examination of the social problems created by the multiplicity of alehouses or of the problems arising from periodic increases in social instability, following plague and economic distress in the 1580s and 1590s.

The gaps in the *Dialogue* raise the question to what extent the work can be regarded as a balanced survey of government per se, since Owen places that word in his title. Government entails the use and application of law, not only to dispense justice in courts of law at whatever level, but also to maintain order and control centrally and locally, whether that be in the parish, the hundred, the county or other division. Owen stressed the success of the Tudor policy, but, excepting references to the social disadvantages arising from the timing of court meetings and procedures, he failed to reveal how effectively that policy was applied among social groupings, especially the urban and lower orders, both of which hardly attract his attention. His propaganda obviously got the better of him, allowing him to use what material he considered relevant to suit his own purpose, which was to applaud the accession of Henry Tudor and heap praises on Tudor legislation. Doubtless, the detailed commentaries on legal institutions and their workings, which cover most of the *Dialogue*, are historically accurate and represent the best which Welsh Tudor historians could offer, but little space is given by Owen to the administration throughout Wales, to regional variation and to an equitable assessment of the content of the two Acts of Union. Surprisingly, no reference at all is made to the imposition of English as the official language for the administration of law and government.[138]

These Acts were more than merely conventional administrative measures to unite Wales with England; rather, they gave a positive expression of the firm alliance which had been achieved between the new middle class in Welsh society and the Tudor Crown. The Acts marked the 'climax of existing tendencies' and were far less revolutionary than past historians have made them out to be. Much of the old system in the Principality and Marches had been retained and allowed to continue under a new governmental regime.[139] The *Dialogue* seems, in part, to be a draft for a further more detailed treatise on the history of his native county, since what Owen has to say about Wales generally is largely centred on Pembrokeshire. That work, however, was produced in manuscript as *The Description of Penbrokshire*, the earliest version of which appeared in 1602–3. A copy which was made of it is now kept in the British Library, Harleian MS 6250.[140]

Viewed from a modern perspective, the chief weakness in the *Dialogue* is George Owen's interpretation of medieval Wales, in particular the post-Edwardian conquest era down to the accession of the Tudors. He continually referred to the Welsh nation as being downtrodden and subjected to the oppressive power of the English monarchy, thereby forcing his own opinions and interpretation of history on Barthol, who, in his responses to Demetus's negative view of the medieval past, found it difficult to conceive how a nation, violated by a dominant neighbour, could recover so rapidly as to accept the Tudor monarchy and English law in the 1530s.[141] Owen failed to realise that social and economic changes led to a greater cooperative spirit between rising new landowning families in the Principality and the Marches and the English Crown, so much so that attempts were made to ease their legal position under the irksome laws imposed upon the Welsh by seeking the greater freedom allowed by English law, particularly in property matters. Alongside, there emerged a Welsh official or administrative class supportive of the Plantagenet kings and their successors, allowing for the period of the Glyndŵr rebellion, at home and abroad, who served as local government officials and military leaders. Despite Glyndŵr's incursions and the severe anti-Welsh laws (1401–2), this new landed order thrived during the fifteenth century, adding to their estates and supporting York or Lancaster in the civil wars, in a long arduous period which saw the decline of Welsh law and an increase in the adoption of English legal procedures.[142] The anti-Welsh laws did not prevent forward-looking and ambitious gentry from progressing as landowners. They possessed an intuitive awareness of the opportunities open to them, and there are examples of some who managed to avoid or manipulate the consequences of the laws and to thrive as Crown and marcher officials in their localities. This 'gregarious and enterprising body of men' played a major role in fifteenth-century politics and were in a position either to maintain peace and good government or to cause disruption and instability. George Owen placed far too much emphasis on the oppression of the English in the post-Conquest period, without realising that some of the most insidious among Welsh gentry were equally prepared to profit from the disabilities of other freeholders and the lower orders.[143]

It is hardly correct to think of Wales, despite periods of social and economic hardships before and after the Plague, as being completely devoid of national self-respect and deprived of a spirit of enterprise. Owen sees the situation in black and white. The 'anarchic' and impoverished later Middle Ages, to him, should be contrasted to the idyllic times under Tudor rule, without realising that Henry Tudor's policy in Wales, assuming that he had one, was aimed principally at strengthening his own powers and building up his financial coffers. Needless to say, he gave the Welsh privileges and enabled the gentry to advance their economic interests, but his policy, particularly in relation to the so-called Charters of Enfranchisement (1505–8), laid much of the basis for what was to become a reality in 1536.[144] Owen, obviously, was in no position to realise this, and his interpretation was essentially governed by the prophetic tradition which had deeply influenced Welsh political thought in the Middle Ages.

This theme leads on to yet another misrepresentation of loyalties and alliances. George Owen interprets the fifteenth century as being an age of strong anti-Welsh and anti-English feelings, particularly in urban areas. Despite the evidence that exists to reveal such animosities, it must also be understood that native kindred strife and competition for land and property were more responsible for social instability than any other factor, a feature to which Sir John Wynn of Gwydir, in his own haphazard way, drew attention in the narrative history of his family and, to a much lesser extent, in the work of Dr David Powel and Rhys Meurig.[145] Owen interprets the national crisis solely in terms of 'oppression' and 'subjection', without realising that the social and economic structures in native and marcher Wales caused more enmity within kindred groupings and the emergent landed gentry. He himself had abundant experience of such ill will in the litigation in which he was involved to safeguard his own interests and extend his reputation as a country squire with local competitors for land and power, and land suits in the courts throughout Wales revealed how eager landholders and landowners of all social orders were to defend their material assets.

The Elizabethan image: governmental authority and control

Compared to the lavish praise bestowed by Owen on her predecessors, Henry VII and Henry VIII, he gave less prominence to Queen Elizabeth I in his *Dialogue*. It was to be expected, of course, that most of his text would be spent in adulation of the early Tudor monarchs, but when it is considered that the 'Elizabethan age' is regarded as one of the most resplendent in British history, it is altogether remarkable that he did not draw attention to her image and give it more prominence when discussing the governmental structure with Barthol. That does not imply that Owen took her reign for granted and that he considered her years on the throne to have been less praiseworthy than those of the two Henrys. He briefly showed his high regard for her when referring to the legacy which she bestowed on the Welsh in supplying one additional Assize Judge in each of the four circuits: 'for the natural love that she likewise bear [bore] unto her said loving subjects'.[146] Owen placed her in the prophetic tradition, as he had done her predecessors:

> This noble Prince [i.e. Henry Tudor] ... so drew the hearts of the Welshmen to him ... whoever since then have borne such natural love and affection to the said King Henry the Seventh, his son King Henry the Eighth and King Edward the Sixth, Queen Mary, and now does bear towards our most sovereign Prince Queen Elizabeth, now living, whom we pray the lord of Lords long and long to preserve to govern ... for over and besides the duty and allegiance that we owe unto her Majesty as our sovereign Prince. There is a certain ardent affection in the hearts of Welshmen towards Her Majesty which makes them inwardly to rejoice that God has blessed our nation ... with a Prince of our own natural country and name.[147]

This commentary is remarkable, in that it associates the Queen specifically with Wales and insists that she was a 'Tudor', a designation not in current use in sixteenth-century England. Owen's statement that Her

Majesty's 'name is Tudor lineally and paternally descended by the said Owen Tudor'[148] was commonly accepted in Welsh, but not English, historical and literary sources.[149]

When referring to her reign Owen gave ample attention to what he considered to be significant developments in Welsh life, such as improvements in society and economy. He attributed them to her long period on the throne, which he regarded as representing the climax of the 'joyful metamorphosis', in his view the most distinctive feature of the middle and later decades of sixteenth-century Wales.[150] Nevertheless, compared to the concept of monarchy which Elizabeth represented to so many artists and writers in England and even on the Continent, he made little use of her image and impact as sovereign ruler in the *Dialogue*. As has been stated above, this 'metamorphosis' was central to George Owen's aim to eulogise Henry Tudor and his son Henry VIII. It was they who engineered the transformation which created a new nation of the Welsh, as Owen envisaged it. The radical change in the quality of life which affected the Welsh people had occurred well before her reign, although it was during that reign that the full fruits of success and achievement were enjoyed. Doubtless, Owen thought highly of his sovereign Queen, since he had compiled material for his *Dialogue* in the days of her greatness, but he referred only briefly to the fundamental changes in religion that occurred in the latter half of the century, the translation of the Scriptures into Welsh and what he, erroneously, regarded as the healthy condition of the clergy and preaching ministry in Pembrokeshire.[151] He had virtually nothing to say about the formation of the religious settlement of 1559 in the new Protestant state and its impact on Wales. The dangers to government and administration of Roman Catholic recusancy in Pembrokeshire and other parts of Wales were also given very little attention, and although John Penry was mentioned, but not by name, Owen dismissed what threat was posed by radical dissenters like him, who had no impact at all on Wales at the time.[152]

Although the advance of Protestantism in Elizabethan times lay beyond his remit, Owen failed to see how relevant church–state relations were to the creation of a strong state, in a period when increasing opposition on the Continent to the new reformed Church caused much apprehensiveness. The realm, as it was known in the Middle Ages, had now become the state, which implied a sovereign government which recognised no superior power – temporal or ecclesiastical – in any aspects of its administration, political, religious or legal. Although ruled by one regal head, it devolved government so that all parts of the state could be efficiently administered according to English law. Wales lay within the English state after 1536, and

The Dialogue of the Government of Wales (1594)

George Owen, in his own way fully aware of that situation, failed in his *Dialogue* to deliver commentary on the usefulness of the state in the more recent history of the Welsh. On the contrary, he continued throughout his conversation as Demetus with Barthol to regard Wales rather simplistically, as a country reinvented with all the trappings of law, administration and religion, all maintained by a growing phalanx of country and urban gentlemen, most of whom were well educated at the universities and the inns of court.[153] George Owen, unlike his creation Demetus, himself partly fell into this social bracket of having obtained legal education in London and having acquired office as sheriff and justice of the peace among others in his region. He had also achieved status as a landed gentleman of good Welsh descent, and had cultivated all the social graces needed to earn respect as a man of means and as head of his household at Henllys.[154] Armed with these attributes, he set forth to put pen to paper to offer his fellow litterateurs a survey of law and government in Wales, now that all traces of oppression had been destroyed: 'Now we see the old castles of Wales ... all in ruin and decay, and ... the houses of the gentlemen and people to flourish and increase which were most commonly burnt once every year in times past.'[155] What essential attributes did George Owen require to establish himself as a typical Welsh Elizabethan squire, and to what extent did the content of his *Dialogue* reveal him as such? He did not, like some of his less modest contemporaries, such as Sir John Wynn, boldly declare his gentlemanly qualities. Indeed, Owen created Demetus as a decorous and retiring country gentleman, unambitious in the political and administrative world around him, but remarkably knowledgeable in the nitty-gritty of legal procedures and administration. Owen doubtless achieved far more than Demetus could ever have done and was well aware of the principles which controlled public service.

That concept of public service assumed a significant role in Owen's interpretation of order in corporate life. Citizenship necessitated an acceptance and observance of the qualities of virtue and justice, for without them, as Elyot stated, 'none other virtue may be commendable, nor wit or any manner of doctrine profitable'.[156] The good citizen was the governor who respected and exercised authority and firm government in the sovereign state, and, as Elyot proceeded, by his example 'men do rise or fall in virtue or vice'.[157] Hence, in humanistic thought, the good man was essentially an upright citizen and public servant. The political culture prevalent in the Elizabethan state was central to Owen's interpretation of Elyot's definition of the just governor. His discourses, as well as those of his literary contemporaries, are regarded as 'the prevailing medium of élite political discourse, one which Renaissance convention recognized as a valid means of counselling the prince'.[158] The powers of the state and institutional government, at central and local levels, were integrated in Tudor political life, and George Owen amply demonstrated this in his studies of the intricacies of legal administration in his native country in its relations with the broader political spectrum.

Of significance is the humanistic literature known as 'courtesy books' which appeared in the sixteenth century, applying classical virtues, primarily Ciceronian and based on Aristotelian teachings in *Politics* and *Ethics*, to the concept of the ideal governor, the individual who, through his descent and upbringing, participated in the *vita activa*. 'The Welsh value distinguished birth and noble descent more than anything else in the world', Giraldus Cambrensis stated in his *Descriptio Kambriae* (1194), and that feature played a vital role in the social make-up of the Welsh gentleman in the Tudor age.[159] Historically, genealogy in Welsh communities arose out of land tenure and social organisation, where blood ties within kindred groupings created the *bonheddig*, which ultimately led to the growth of an indigenous class of gentry. So popular had genealogical activity become in the sixteenth century that deputy Heralds were appointed in Wales and the century became known as the 'golden age of Welsh genealogy'. In Wales, however, unlike England, the bonds of blood were more meaningful than social pride, wealth and ostentation. Whereas in England descent at the top end of the scale was based on the traditional aristocracy, in Wales it stemmed from the roots of the social order of progressive freeholders, who in the later Middle Ages became known as *uchelwyr* (high-born). Genealogists, antiquarians and professional bards maintained a high profile in their occupations in tracing and recording pedigrees, purely as a means of maintaining family status and authority, hence the emphasis placed on them by Tudor gentry, the social climbers of their day. Among them was George Owen, whose family had abandoned the medieval patronymics, and who had built up for himself a nucleus of power based at Henllys in the barony of Cemais. In that context he was adulated by Siôn Mawddwy:

> Os dewr doeth call deallwn,
> Os hael Siors Owains yw hwn;
> Pinagl yw hwn pen gloyw hedd
> Plaid aur ban paladr bonedd.[160]

[If we understand that this is he who is brave, wise and discreet, if this is the bountiful George Owens; he is the pinnacle, the shining summit of peace, a pillar of the golden rank of nobility.]

In such pretentious terms the bard set about, in two couplets, to describe the gentle qualities of his patron, regarding him as a prime figure of gentility.

Not only was Owen a favourite of the bards, but he was also a leading light among genealogists and antiquarians, students of aspects of intellectual life yet again tied to a medieval discipline. This interest of his in the past may well have arisen as much as from his claim to the barony of Cemais and manorial rights as to antiquarianism as a pastime. Be that as it may, he was well aware of his claim to the kind of status that middling gentry enjoyed in England. Sir Thomas Hoby's translation of *Il Cortegiano* appeared thirty years after Elyot's magnum opus, which was described as a training scheme for a ruling class.[161] The emphasis in these works and those of Henry Peacham, Lawrence Humphrey, Roger Ascham and others stressed the need to cultivate virtues, of which justice was the highest, to fulfil the needs of the public servant.[162] Adopting Ciceronian principles led to the laity attaining practical skills, and classical learning combined with the concept of medieval knighthood formed the new social ideal of the gentleman, with education as its foundation. The processes of education and the emulation of good practice would enhance their public skills and intellectual prowess and develop civility through scholarship and law. A good man, it was maintained, was essentially an upright citizen, renowned for his *gravitas*, applying his skills in the interest of the state, distributing his largesse throughout his region and extending his influence among high and low in the interest of peace and stable government. Following the establishment of the Crown's supreme power over the Church in the 1530s, laymen increasingly replaced the old aristocracy and higher clergy in offices of state, and this trend continued, whereby well-endowed country gentry served in the royal court and allied institutions. In view of the increasing authority of the Tudor Crown centrally and regionally, its needs rapidly increased. Dependence was therefore placed on merchants, commercial dealers, lawyers, administrators and the gentry who were prepared to serve the Crown loyally, using the skills obtained at the Universities and Inns of Court, in government, law and administration. Thereby, they increased their authority and influence and were promoted in royal and other noble circles. As representatives of the middle order in society they also had needs, and higher education symbolised their status and that of their descendants. Doubtless, Owen had familiarised himself with a literary genre of this kind, possibly during the time spent at Barnard's Inn, and was in constant communication with educated men familiar with public life and activity.

Resourceful men eagerly sought opportunities to serve the 'commonweal' at the centre or in the localities, and Demetus demonstrated to Barthol how he had been able to adapt himself to fulfilling the needs of the state. Emphasis was placed on cohesive government in the realm, the linking of the Crown, the central component in the mechanism of the healthy state, and the communities. It was Thomas Starkey, in his *Dialogue*, who stated that the King's function in the state was compared to that of the heart in the human body, whereby peace and prosperity were achieved by law enforced by monarchs who had 'their eyes fixed to the Common weal'. Moreover, Starkey, one of the mid-Tudor 'Commonwealth's men', a term now considered inappropriate, examined the role of the skilled and experienced individual administrator in the state or commonwealth.[163] In this context, Demetus's aim, among others, was to illustrate the interaction between local government and its central counterpart and the contribution of experienced administrators to its success. He and his fellow-officials doubtless had thought of the desirability of the new regime, and their decision to serve the Tudor Crown did not merely imply a sentimental attachment to it. Loyalty was certainly not blind and unreasonable. Needless to say, however, the benefits the settlement conferred on the gentry determined their attitude, and since they were the only politically conscious members of the communities they influenced others, particularly their social inferiors, to accept their leadership.[164] It is this optimism and complacency which the historian discovers in the *Dialogue*. In fact, Demetus consistently took a positive view of the Tudor governmental mechanism as applied to Wales, stressing its reform, not abolition.[165] So highly regarded were the Tudors that any abolition of their institutions of government in Wales, regardless of their faults, was never entertained by him. Neither did he question the integrity of the gentry order, which he highly applauded in his native county:

> [So great is] the quietness and love that is among the gentlemen ... that hardly they are found asunder if they be in one town. But always together at meals and meetings in such loving sort that it is joyful to behold. So gentle in speeches, so courteous in behaviour each to other, striving to exceed in Courtesy and kindness the one to the other, no one faction side or quarrel among them.[166]

Such alleged amiability and loving friendship could never have been achieved at a time when the Essex faction, spearheaded by Sir Gelly Meyricke and his allies, ruled the county, following the death of Sir John Perrot, from 1592 to 1601. Earlier, George Owen's own difficult lawsuits concerning his claims to the barony of Cemais did not create amicable relationships between him and some of his fellow gentry. His short but striking description of Sir John Perrot (d.1592) reveals how self-assertive and ambitious local proprietors were in his day:

> being somewhat friended but more feared of the gentlemen and freeholders of the country [he] has, by reason of the rigours which he uses and the heap of retainers that do many times attend him, the most part of the gentlemen and freeholders of the county of Pembroke at his commandment.[167]

Symptomatic of this violent background are George Owen's remarks about the safety of travellers in Wales of his day. The background is familiar; the spirit of marcher resistance to royal power and the overbearing authority of leading families, even generations after the dissolution of the lordships, the continued movement of thieves and illicit traffic over the Severn and elsewhere, and the consequent harbouring of bandits and outlaws, all contributed to the persistence of crime and violence in the border areas. According to Sir John Wynn, venturing outside a house in the northern Principality was considered a serious risk unless the person was securely armed and defended by an entourage. In his comment on mid-fifteenth-century conditions in Eifionydd, for example, he graphically expressed his concerns: 'You are to understand that in those days and in that wild world every man stood upon his guard and went not abroad but in sort and so armed as if he went to the field to encounter with his enemies.'[168] The gentry themselves, in their local ambitions, could and did prove to be equally violent as disturbers of the peace, hence Barthol's fear that he might not be able to travel safely over the notorious Pumlumon mountains, the borders between the three counties of Cardigan, Montgomery and Radnorshire, and between three circuits of Great Sessions, traditional danger-spots.[169] There were other distinctly unsafe areas as well, as reported in contemporary sources, which implied that Tudor government still found it an arduous task to restore complete order. The most remarkable example is the exploits of the dreaded 'Red Bandits of Mawddwy', a group of Merioneth freeholders who mercilessly ravaged the Merioneth–Montgomeryshire borders and resisted Tudor rule.[170] This fear and threat of lawlessness continued well into the early Stuart century, although Owen, in the *Dialogue*, remained complacent, assuring Barthol that it was inefficiency and negligence on the part of local officials and not the inherent physical features of the Welsh countryside that accounted for the persistence of criminal activity on a large scale.[171] Although there was no longer a serious threat of rebellion in Wales in Owen's day, maintaining public order continued to create problems, particularly in years of acute economic tension. These dangers Owen failed to see, or did not wish to see, thereby blurring Barthol's view of the true nature of Tudor government. While he was firmly associated with all that was indigenous in the Welsh social scene in his native shire, his upbringing in an area of Wales closely linked to foreign immigration over the centuries enabled him to identify himself with extraneous features in Pembrokeshire society. Although his view of provincial gentry life was overtly idealised in most places in the *Dialogue*, doubtless he saw in his compeers features which safeguarded what was best in their public status. Doubtless, George Owen saw in the defence of status and authority what he and his peers regarded as prime features of gentility, and in the *Dialogue* Demetus eagerly exposed them to Barthol, so as to instruct him how the Welsh gentry reacted to the demands of government, as imposed by the early Tudors on Wales.[172]

Despite the emphasis placed in didactic literary works on the making of the governor, and the role of virtues such as justice, prudence, liberality and courtesy, no stability could ever be created without exercising the rule of law. The just man was an upholder of law and order, a fitting person appointed not only to keep the peace but also to maintain the spirit of the law, which entailed safeguarding community welfare.[173] Doubtless, 'degree' was a fundamental feature of gentility. Although the gentry varied in their interests and ambitions, they cherished common ideals. As Brian Howells explains:

> the gentry formed a heterogeneous class with diverse interests and tastes ... if there was a good deal of variation and social hostility within the class there was also a sense of degree and of place which gave it a certain unity and cohesion ... the Tudor squires of Pembrokeshire were, as a group, consciously settling themselves from their social inferiors ... governing the countryside.[174]

There was a moral obligation to maintain the well-being of the community, and in the *Dialogue*, although Owen did not specifically state so, there is a constant awareness that peace and good government were essential to protecting the interests of the whole state. Performing public service was the gentleman's chiefest responsibility, and when that became questionable, revealing self-interest, guile and corruption, then his integrity as a royal servant lapsed. 'This is one chief point belonging to the office of the Justices of the Peace', Demetus affirmed:

> wherein a good man may do great good, and an evil man great harm, and verily there are some that either negligently or wilfully suffer many things to

pass their hands with less care than they ought to do if either they remember their duty to their country and Prince or the strict oath they receive for the due and careful exercising of the office.[175]

This assertion draws attention to the major role of the local governor, namely 'to be good', regarded universally as the norm of the moral code governing the life of the upright gentleman.[176] 'Only good men by their government and example', Ascham maintained, 'make happy times in every degree and state.'[177] Being good meant being just and prudent, and dispensing that justice in the name of the sovereign Prince or ruler to all. Hence, Demetus, in his lengthy commentaries, upheld justice to be the highest virtue, and this point appeared at its clearest when he compared the qualities of Justices of the Peace to those which Jethro in the *Book of Exodus* expected his son-in-law Moses to seek in judges appointed by him to rule over the Israelites: 'Provide you among all the people men of courage fearing God, men dealing truly, hating covetousness, and appoint such over them to be rulers'. And he proceeded: 'and the law of England says that these Justices of the Peace should be good men and lawful, and no maintainers of evil'.[178]

Justice was the very essence of civility, a virtue found extensively in all courtesy books, representing propriety and refinement. 'People in Wales', Demetus maintained, 'have greatly increased in learning and civility ... some prove to be learned men and good members in the commonwealth of England and Wales.'[179] This civility he applied to the religious as well as secular aspects of Welsh society. Protestant religious reformers placed their faith in the value of education so as to defeat ignorance, profanity and idleness in the Church. As a good Protestant he regarded the translation of the Scriptures as a blessing to enlighten the hearts and souls of the nation and to instil in the people the truths of the faith:

> and now not three years past we have the light of the gospel, yes the whole Bible in our own native tongue which, in short time must needs work great good inwardly in the hearts of the people, whereas the service and sacraments in the English tongue was as strange to many or most of the simplest sort as the mass in the time of blindness was to the rest of England.[180]

Owen's warm approbation of the new faith and repudiation of John Penry's bitter strictures on the condition of the Church in Wales indicated not only the emphasis which he and his fellow Protestant gentry placed on the consolidation of the Tudor state based on the Reformation changes under Henry VIII, but also the availability in Wales of the vernacular Scriptures and the creation of the national sovereign state.[181] He has been called 'the most authentic surviving voice of the Welsh Tudor gentry', a fitting description of a notable representative of his age.[182]

Notes

[1] *Desc. Pembs.*, pp. xv–xxii. For further information on the background to the Owen family to the thirteenth century see B. E. Howells, 'Studies in the social and agrarian history of medieval and early modern Pembrokeshire' (unpublished MA dissertation, University of Wales, 1956), pp. 132–40; G. E. Jones, *The Gentry and the Elizabethan State* (Swansea, 1977), pp. 21–2, 32–6.

[2] *Desc. Pembs.*, pp. xv–xxii, 308; B. G. Charles, *George Owen of Henllys: A Welsh Elizabethan* (NLW, Aberystwyth, 1973), ch. 10, pp. 170–92; *ODNB*, 42, pp. 199–202. Dillwyn Miles, 'Pembrokeshire antiquarians', *Journal of the Pembrokeshire Historical Society*, 17 (2008), 21–7; R. A. Griffiths, *Sir Rhys ap Thomas and his Family: A Study in the Wars of the Roses and Early Tudor Politics* (Cardiff, 1993), pp. 138–40. Miles's edition of *Penbrokshire* and Charles's monograph supply the detail concerning Owen's career and contribution to late Tudor times in Wales.

[3] Lewys Dwnn, *Heraldic Visitations of Wales*, ed. S. R. Meyrick, I (Llandovery, 1846), pp. xxii, xxiv, 156–7; Charles, *George Owen*, ch. 1, pp. 1–22. For a useful background commentary on George Owen and local government see R. Turvey, *Pembrokeshire:The Concise History* (Cardiff, 2007), pp. 60–73. Owen's intention was to examine critically what had developed in the Welsh legal structure according to the Tudor Settlement (1536–43). See, however, J. H. Baker, 'The dark age of English legal history 1500–1700', in D. Jenkins (ed.), *Legal History Studies 1972* (Cardiff, 1975), pp. 1–2.

[4] This work was William Owen's own version of Sir Anthony Fitzherbert's *Graunde Abridgement* (1514), which was a systematic record of English law.

[5] Charles, *George Owen*, ch. 5, pp. 72–98.

[6] For example, the reference to the 300 soldiers for Ireland and the 75 Spanish captives forced to land on the Pembrokeshire coast in 1597. *Dialogue*, p. 112 [141]. See T. Jones Pierce (ed.), *Clenennau Letters and Papers in the Brogyntyn Collection*, pt. 1, *NLWJ Supplement* series IV, I (Aberystwyth, 1947), p. 39, nos 133–4 (1597). Square bracket entries refer to pages in the modernized version of the text.

[7] J. R. S. Phillips (ed.), *The Justices of the Peace in Wales and Monmouthshire, 1541 to 1689* (Cardiff, 1975), pp. 207–11; PRO Lists and Indexes, IX, *List of Sheriffs for England and Wales* (London, 1963 edn), p. 266; Dillwyn Miles, *The Sheriffs of the County of Pembroke 1541–1976* (Haverfordwest, 1976), pp. 22, 24.

[8] 'Dialogue of the Government of Wales 1594' (*Dialogue*), pp. 4, 24, 37 [81].

[9] Ibid., pp. 25, 37 [82].

[10] For the Welsh descent of the Tudors see Glyn Roberts, 'Teulu Penmynydd', and '"Wyrion Eden": the Anglesey descendants of Ednyfed Fychan in the four-

teenth century', in *Aspects of Welsh History*, ed. A. H. Dodd and J. G. Williams (Cardiff, 1969), pp. 240–74, 178–214.

[11] Cf. David Powel, *The historie of Cambria, now called Wales* [1584] (Amsterdam/New York, 1969), pp. 390–1: 'King Henry the Seventh, who by his grandfather Owain Tudur descended out of Wales, being aided by the Welshmen of Bosworth Field ... knowing and pitying their thraldom and injuries ... granted unto them a charter of liberties, whereby they were released of the oppression'.

[12] John Wynn, *History of the Gwydir Family and Memoirs*, ed. J. G. Jones (Llandysul, 1990), pp. xxxv, 24ff.; Rice Merrick, *Morganiae Archaiographia: A Book of Glamorganshire Antiquities*, ed. B. Ll. James (Barry, 1983), p. 67.

[13] *Dialogue*, pp. 24, 37 [80]. See also Humphrey Llwyd, *Commentarioli Descriptionis Britannicae Fragmentum* (Cologne, 1572), trans. Thomas Twyne, *The Breuiary of Britaine* (London, 1573), fo. 59b.

[14] *Dialogue*, p. 37.

[15] Ibid., pp. 35, 53–4 [94].

[16] Ibid., p. 4 [56].

[17] Francis Jones, 'An approach to Welsh genealogy', *Trans. Cymmr.* (1948), 380–1.

[18] For a detailed study of individual poets whose works reveal changes in emphasis see J. G. Jones, 'The world of poets and patrons: cultural affinities and conflicts', in J. G. Jones (ed.), *Conflict, Continuity and Change in Wales c.1500–1603: Essays and Studies* (Aberystwyth, 1999), pp. 198–245. See also W. O. Williams, 'The social order in Tudor Wales', *Trans. Cymmr.* (1967), pt. ii, 167–78; J. G. Jones, 'Changing concepts of gentryhood in mid-Tudor Wales: some reflections', *Brogliaccio 1 di Lettera*, XIII (1977), 25–37; J. G. Jones, 'The Welsh poets and their patrons c.1550–1640', *WHR*, IX, 3 (1979), 245–77.

[19] P. Roberts, 'Tudor Wales, national identity and the British inheritance', in B. Bradshaw and P. Roberts (eds), *British Consciousness and Identity: The Making of Britain, 1533–1707* (Cambridge, 2003 edn), p. 23; J. G. Jones, 'The Welsh gentry and the image of the "Cambro-Briton", c.1603–25', *WHR*, XX, 1 (2000), 615–55.

[20] Glanmor Williams, 'The Renaissance', in Glanmor Williams and R. O. Jones (eds), *The Celts and the Renaissance: Tradition and Innovation* (Cardiff, 1990), pp. 1–15. See also P. Burke, *Culture and Society in Renaissance Italy, 1420–1540* (London, 1972); J. R. Hale, *Renaissance Europe, 1480–1520* (London, 1971).

[21] Merrick, *Morganiae Archaiographia*, p. 5.

[22] Charles, *George Owen*, p. 7.

[23] Sir Thomas Elyot, *The Book Named the Governor* [1531], ed. S. E. Lehmberg (London, 1975), p. 97.

[24] For background material on this theme see F. Caspari, *Humanism and the Social Order in Tudor England* (Chicago, 1954); R. Kelso, *The Doctrine of the*

English Gentleman in the Sixteenth Century (Massachusetts, 1964); W. P. Griffith, *Civility and Reputation: Ideas and Images of the 'Tudor Man' in Wales* (Bangor, 1995); J. G. Jones, 'Concepts of order and gentility', in J. G. Jones (ed.), *Class, Community and Culture in Tudor Wales* (Cardiff, 1989), pp. 121–57.

[25] H. Llwyd, *Commentarioli Descriptionis Britannicae Fragmentum*, in Twyne (ed.), *The Breuiary of Britayne*, fo. 60b.

[26] W. P. Griffith, *Learning, Law and Religion: Higher Education and Welsh Society c.1540–1640* (Cardiff, 1996), pp. 56, 427–34. For the broader perspective see L. Stone, 'The educational revolution in England, 1560–1640', *Past & Present*, 28 (1964), 41–80; K. Charlton, *Education in Renaissance England* (Cambridge, 1965), pp. 131–95; J. Simon, *Education and Society in Tudor England* (Cambridge, 1979 edn), pp. 291–368.

[27] John Leland, *Itinerary in Wales, 1536–1539*, ed. L. Toulmin Smith (London, 1906). John Leland (*c.*1503–52) was appointed Antiquary Royal in 1533, and between 1536 and 1542 he travelled extensively to gather information from the records of dissolved monastic libraries. T. D. Kendrick, *British Antiquity* (London, 1970), pp. 45–64, 134–67; M. McKisack, *Medieval History in the Tudor Age* (Oxford, 1971), pp. 1–25; *ODNB*, 33, pp. 297–301.

[28] Kendrick, *British Antiquity*, pp. 45–64; Richard Carew of Antony, *The Survey of Cornwall*, ed. F. E. Halliday (London, 1953); William Lambarde, *A Perambulation of Kent*, ed. R. Church (Bath, 1970); Glanmor Williams, *Reformation Views of Church History* (London, 1970), pp. 33–45.

[29] *Dialogue*, p. 4 [56].

[30] *Penbrokshire*, II, pp. 425–509; III, pp. 127–286, 287–360. See Charles, *George Owen*, pp. 136–9 for further details.

[31] George Owen, *The Taylors Cussion*, ed. E. M. Pritchard (London, 1906), intro., pp. v–xviii. The 'Vairdre' Book was a manuscript containing a collection of antiquarian notes compiled by George Owen. It was owned by John Lloyd of Y Fairdre in the parish of Llandysul. *Desc. Pembs.*, pp. xlvii–xlix; H. Owen, 'The Vairdre Book', *Archaeologia Cambrensis*, IV, 6th ser. (1904), 143.

[32] John Penry, 'A Treatise Containing the Aequity of an Humble Supplication' (1587) in *Three Treatises Concerning Wales*, ed. D. Williams (Cardiff, 1960), pp. 33–41; D. R. Thomas, *The Life and Work of Bishop Davies and William Salesbury* (Oswestry, 1902), pp. 37–44 (Bishop Richard Davies's certificate of the state of his diocese 1569); Glanmor Williams, *Wales and the Reformation* (Cardiff, 1997), pp. 290–9, 301–2.

[33] Charles, *George Owen*, ch. 8, pp. 146–59.

[34] For background see Francis Jones, 'An approach to Welsh genealogy', 383–4, 375–7; R. G. Gruffydd, 'The Renaissance and Welsh literature' in *The Celts and the Renaissance*, pp. 23–30; Glanmor Williams, 'Sir John Pryse of Brecon', *Brycheiniog*, XXXI (1998–9), 49–63; D. C. Rees, *Tregaron: Historical and Antiquarian* (Llandysul, 1936), pp. 99–105.

[35] NLW Llanstephan MS 133,780. Other odes were composed by Siôn

Mawddwy in honour of George Owen, MS 133, 756, 777; Charles, *George Owen*, p. 112.

[36] Jones, 'An approach to Welsh genealogy', 378–86; J. G. Jones, 'Robert Holland a *Basilikon Doron* y Brenin Iago', in J. E. Caerwyn Williams (ed.), *Ysgrifau Beirniadol*, XXII (Denbigh, 1997), pp. 161–88; J. Peter and R. J. Pryse, *Enwogion y Ffydd*, I (London, 1878), pp. 100–2; R. G. Gruffydd (ed.), *A Guide to Welsh Literature c.1530–1700* (Cardiff, 1997), pp. 178–80.

[37] Jones, 'An approach to Welsh genealogy', 407–9; J. G. Jones, 'Griffith of Penybenglog: a study in Pembrokeshire genealogy', *Trans. Cymmr.* (1938), 136–41; J. Conway Davies, 'Letters of Admission to the rectory of Whitechurch', *NLWJ*, IV (1956), 93–8; *Desc. Pembs.*, pp. xxxii–xxxvi.

[38] Jones, 'An approach to Welsh genealogy', 382–3; E. D. Jones, 'George Owen Harry', *The Pembrokeshire Historian*, 6 (1979), 58–75..

[39] NLW, MS 13,687; CCL, Phillipps MS 2,35; Charles, *George Owen*, pp. 122–3 and the map, as a pull-out, at the end of the volume.

[40] Jones, 'An approach to Welsh genealogy', 378–9.

[41] NLW Llanstephan MS 38, 1, 36, 37–8, 41, 55. This concept of the 'gwladwr', the provincial or county governor and 'moral leader of his community', reflects bardic interpretations of men of Owen's milieu. For fuller discussion of such concepts see R. Kelso, *The Doctrine of the English Gentleman in the Sixteenth Century* (Massachussetts, 1964), ch. 5, pp. 71–110; J. G. Jones, *Concepts of Order and Gentility in Wales, 1540–1640* (Llandysul, 1992); W. P. Griffith, *Ideas and Images of the 'Tudor Man' in Wales* (Bangor, 1995).

[42] NLW Llanstephan MS 38, 1, 16, 20, 24, 25, 27, 28, 29, 30, 31. Euros Jones Evans, 'Noddwyr y beirdd yn sir Benfro', *Trans. Cymmr.* (1972–3), 146–51. Surprisingly, no elegies in his honour have survived.

[43] Evans, 'Noddwyr y beirdd yn sir Benfro', 149; NLW, Llanstephan MS 38,176 and MS 133,756; D. J. Bowen, 'Graddedigion Eisteddfodau Caerwys 1523 a 1567/8', *Llên Cymru*, II, i (1952), 134; D. J. Bowen, 'Ail eisteddfod Caerwys a chais 1594', *Llên Cymru*, III, 111 (1955), 155–60.

[44] HMC, *Report on Manuscripts in the Welsh Language*, ed. J. Gwenogvryn Evans, I (London 1898), pp. 293–5.

[45] Evans, 'Noddwyr y beirdd yn sir Benfro', 134; *DP*, II, p. 502 ('Kemes Tracts') 'Citherae argenteae dispositio, ad istam pertinet Baroniam, quasi ad mansionem principis, quem in absencia Domini ad Monasterium suum custodienda traditur.' ['The disposal of the silver harp belongs to this Barony as to the Palace of the Prince which in the absence of the Lord is delivered to the Monastery of St Dogmaels for safe custody'.]

[46] D. J. Bowen, 'Graddedigion Eisteddfodau Caerwys 1523 a 1567/8', 134.

[47] Desiderius Erasmus, *The Colloquies of Erasmus*, ed. Craig R. Thompson (University of Chicago Press, 1965); Craig R. Thompson, 'Translations of Lucian', in *The Complete Works of St Thomas More*, vol. III, no. i (Yale University Press, 1974), xxii–liii. Although Thomas Starkey's *A Dialogue between Reginald Pole and Thomas Lupset*, which was written *c*.1532–3, was

not published in Owen's time, and the original manuscript probably not available to him, it still remains a work typical of the dialogues which appeared in the sixteenth century. See Thomas Starkey, *A Dialogue between Reginald Pole and Thomas Lupset*, ed. K. M. Burton (London, 1948). Christopher St German, who wrote *The Dialogue between a Doctor of Divinity and a Student*, was regarded as the most erudite of Tudor lawyers. *ODNB*, 48, pp. 609–11. Owen may also have been familiar with Sir Thomas Smith's *A Discourse of the Commonweal of this Realm of England*, the earliest version of which appeared in 1549, and his *De Republica Anglorum* (1569).

[48] Robert Recorde published the first English textbooks as dialogues on elementary arithmetic and algebra, including *The Grounde of Artes* (1543) and *The Whetstone of Witte* (1557); Howell A. Lloyd, '"Famous in the field of number and measure": Robert Recorde, Renaissance mathematician', *WHR*, XX, i (2000), 254–82.

[49] J. H. Elliot, *Europe Divided 1559–1598* (London, 1968), pp. 262, 268, 272. When Antwerp later fell to the Spaniards on 17 August 1585 it led Elizabeth I to declare war on the side of the Netherlands. P. S. Crowson, *Tudor Foreign Policy* (London, 1973), pp. 222–4.

[50] For further discussions of the hardened anti-Spanish attitudes in England see W. S. Maltby, *The Black Legend in England: The development of Anti-Spanish Sentiment 1558–1660* (Duke UP, 1971), esp. chs 5 and 6, pp. 61–87.

[51] C. Koeman, *The History of Abraham Ortelius and his Theatrum Orbis Terrarum* (1964). This work was translated into English as *Epitome of the Theater of the Worlde* in the same year. Humphrey Llwyd's *De Mona Druidium Insula* (1568) was published in the *Theatrum*, and his map of Wales (*Cambriae Typus*) and of England and Wales both appeared for the first time in Ortelius's atlas in 1573. D. Huw Owen, *Mapiau Printiedig Cynnar o Gymru/Early Printed Maps of Wales* (Aberystwyth, 1996), [2–5], [9]. R. Geraint Gruffydd, 'Humphrey Llwyd of Denbigh: some documents and a catalogue', *Transactions of the Denbighshire Historical Society*, 17 (1968), 99–101; T. M. Chotzen, 'Some sidelights on Cambro-Dutch relations', *Trans. Cymmr.* (1937), App. D, 137–43. Llwyd dedicated his *Commentarioli Britannicae Descriptionis Fragmentum* to Ortelius; Charles, *George Owen*, p. 102.

[52] *Dialogue*, pp. 14–16 [63]. It was probably Sir Richard Clough of Denbigh, merchant and Sir Thomas Gresham's factor in Antwerp, who introduced Ortelius to Llwyd's work. F. J. North, *Humphrey Lhuyd's Maps of England and of Wales* (National Museum of Wales, 1937), pp. 12–13; R. Gwyndaf Jones, 'Sir Richard Clough of Denbigh c.1530–1570', pt. 2, *Trans. Denbs. Hist. Soc.*, 20 (1971), 72–5 (esp. 73).

[53] *Dialogue*, p. 16 [64].

[54] Ibid., p. 16 [64]; *Desc. Pembs.*, intro., p. 1; Owen, *Taylors Cussion*, p. vi.

[55] *Dialogue*, p. 20 [67].

[56] Ibid., pp. 21–31 [68–76].

[57] C. A. J. Skeel, *The Council in the Marches of Wales: A Study in Local Government during the Sixteenth and Seventeenth Centuries* (London, 1904), ch. 1, pp. 18–48; Penry Williams, *The Council in the Marches of Wales under Elizabeth I* (Cardiff, 1958), pp. 7–15; G. E. Jones, *The Gentry and the Elizabethan State*, ch. 3, pp. 42–59.

[58] T. B. Pugh, '"The Indenture for the Marches" between Henry VII and Edward Stafford (1477–1521), duke of Buckingham', *English Historical Review*, LXXI (1956), 436–41.

[59] R. R. Reid, *The King's Council in the North* (London, repr. 1975); F. W. Brooks, *The Council of the North* (Historical Association, 1966).

[60] Williams, *Council in the Marches*, pp. 15–24; Michael A. Jones, 'Cultural boundaries within the Tudor state: Bishop Rowland Lee and the Welsh settlement of 1536', *WHR*, XX, ii (2000), 227–53.

[61] St. 34–35 Henry VIII c.26; *Statutes*, p. 102.

[62] *Dialogue*, p. 13 [68].

[63] T. Churchyard, *The Worthines of Wales* [1587] (London, 1776), pp. 85–6.

[64] Ibid., pp. 80–1; A. H. Dodd, *Studies in Stuart Wales* (Cardiff, 1971 edn), p. 50.

[65] NLW, Brogyntyn MS 6,56b; E. D. Jones, 'The Brogyntyn Welsh manuscripts', *NLWJ*, VI (1949–50), 225–6, 242 (English trans. by E. D. Jones); Dodd, *Studies in Stuart Wales*, p. 50.

[66] Williams, *Council in the Marches*, pp. 259–60; *CSPDom., 1581–1590*, CLIX, i, p. 98.

[67] *CSPDom., 1547–80*, CVII, 4, 4(i), p. 514; D. Mathew, 'Some Elizabethan documents', *BBCS*, VI, i (1931), 76. Cf. views of lawlessness, especially the misuse of *cymorthas*, referred to by Richard Price of Brecon in a letter to Lord Burghley in 1575. H. Ellis (ed.), *Original Letters Illustrative of English History*, III (2nd ser., London, 1827), pp. 41–4.

[68] Mathew, 'Some Elizabethan documents', 76.

[69] D. Ll. Thomas (ed.), 'Gerard's Second Discourse', *Y Cymmrodor*, XIII (1899), 161; *CSPDom., 1547–1580*, CVII, x, p. 514.

[70] *Dialogue*, pp. 21–2, 66, 73, 115 [68–9, 104, 110, 144].

[71] Williams, *Council in the Marches*, pp. 114–15, 123; G. Scott Thomson, 'The origin and growth of the office of Deputy-Lieutenant', *Transactions of the Royal Historical Society*, V, 4th ser. (1922), 150–66; J. Ballinger (ed.), *Calendar of the Wynn of Gwydir Papers 1515–1690* (Cardiff, 1926), no. 154 (21 Sept. 1595); Historical Manuscripts Commission, *Calendar of the Marquis of Salisbury Manuscripts* (Hatfield House MSS), IX (London, 1902), pp. 313–14 (20 August 1599); J. G. Jones, 'The defence of the realm: regional dimensions c.1559–1604', in J. G. Jones, *Conflict, Continuity and Change in Wales c.1500–1603: Essays and Studies* (Aberystwyth, 1999), pp. 113–53. For documents relating to the exercise of the office of Deputy Lieutenant in Caernarfonshire see T. Jones Pierce (ed.), *Clenennau Letters and Papers in the Brogyntyn Collection*, pp. 152–9. See also *CSPDom., 1581–1590*, CLXXIX, 51–4, 58, pp. 248–9, which reveals that plans for appointment to the office

were being made by Sir Francis Walsingham, Secretary of State and chief Elizabethan spy-catcher, in 1585. Deputy Lieutenants, who assisted Lord Lieutenants (one of which was appointed in each shire for life soon after war broke out with Spain in 1585) in local military organisation, served one shire only, and two usually functioned in each of them.

72 Ralph Flenley (ed.), *A Calendar of the Register of the Queen's Majesty's Council in the Dominion and Principality of Wales and the Marches of the Same, 1569–1591* (London, 1916).
73 For a list of Instructions issued by the Privy Council to the end of Elizabeth's reign see Williams, *Council in the Marches*, pp. 362–3. For examples, see also Flenley, *Calendar of the Register*, pp. 163–5, 200–2, 219–21.
74 NLW, MS 2377; *Desc. Pembs.*, p. 138.
75 *Dialogue*, p. 21 [68].
76 Ibid., p. 22 [68].
77 St. 34–35 Henry VIII c.26; *Statutes*, p. 108.
78 *Dialogue*, p. 23 [69].
79 For the broader background see Penry Williams, 'The attack on the Council in the Marches, 1603–1642', *Trans. Cymmr.* (1961), pt. i, 1–22.
80 *Dialogue*, p. 24 [70].
81 Ibid., p. 24 [70].
82 See E. A. Rees, *Welsh Outlaws and Bandits: Political Rebellion and Lawlessness in Wales 1400–1603* (Birmingham, 2001), pp. 191–207; *Council in the Marches*, chap. IX, pp. 229–45, 314–25.
83 Mathew, 'Some Elizabethan documents', 76–7; *Original Letters Illustrative of English History*, ed. Henry Ellis, III (2nd ser., London, 1827), p. 42.
84 *Dialogue*, p. 27 [72].
85 Ibid., pp. 32–4 [77–9].
86 St. 18 Elizabeth I c.8; *Statutes*, pp. 152–6.
87 *Dialogue*, p. 41 [84].
88 Ibid., pp. 94–7. Owen's view of the state of law and order is contrary to that expressed by Dr David Lewis. Mathew, 'Some Elizabethan documents', 75–7.
89 *Dialogue*, pp. 114–15.
90 Ibid., p. 96; Williams, *Council in the Marches*, pp. 282–3.
91 St. 27 Henry VIII c.26; *Statutes*, pp. 81–2.
92 *Dialogue*, p. 43. For broader views on the connection between 'Law' and 'morality' and the standards and attitudes adopted by those who practised law and pronounced judgement in the courts see Cynthia B. Herrup, 'law and morality in seventeenth-century England', *Past and Present*, 106 (1985), 102–23.
93 *Dialogue*, p. 43.
94 Ibid., p. 44.
95 Ibid., pp. 49–50.
96 G. E. Jones, *The Gentry and the Elizabethan State*, pp. 57–8.

97 For the background see *Cal.CQSR*, I, *1541–1558* (Caernarfon, 1956), intro., pp. xxvii–xxxiv; J. G. Jones, *Law, Order and Government in Caernarfonshire, 1558–1640: Justices of the Peace and the Gentry* (Cardiff, 1996), ch. 2, pp. 30–72; T. H. Lewis, 'The Justice of the Peace in Wales', *Trans. Cymmr.* (1943–4), 120–32.
98 *Dialogue*, p. 53; St. 27 Henry VIII c.5; *Statutes*, pp. 67–9.
99 *Dialogue*, p. 53 [93].
100 Ibid., p. 55.
101 St. 34–35 Henry VIII c.26; *Statutes*, p. 113.
102 *LPFDom.*, X (1536), 453, p. 182.
103 St. 18 Henry VI c.11; *SR*, II (1377–1504), p. 309.
104 *Dialogue*, p. 54 [94].
105 Mathew, 'Some Elizabethan documents', 76; *CSPDom.*, *1547–1580*, CVII, 4, 4(i), p. 514.
106 Although George Owen, who himself served for many years as a magistrate on the Pembrokeshire bench, was well aware of the internal workings of the Court of Quarter Sessions, he was careful not to portray Demetus as being a magistrate himself. Consequently, he was able to adopt a balanced view of proceedings.
107 *Dialogue*, p. 52 [93].
108 Ibid., p. 57 [96–7].
109 Ibid.
110 Ibid., p. 55.
111 Ibid., p. 56 [96].
112 Ibid., p. 55 [95].
113 Ibid., p. 56 [96].
114 Ibid., p. 58 [98]. Interesting comparisons can be drawn with the judicial activities in other counties. For, example, see Louis A. Knafla, *Kent at Law 1602: The County Jurisdiction: Assizes and Sessions of the Peace* (London, 1994), intro., pp. vii–vvi, xxv–xxvi, xxx.
115 *Dialogue*, p. 62.
116 'Keeper of the Rolls of Quarter Sessions, usually the senior magistrate'. *Cal.QSR*, I (1541–58), lxxxiii (note i); *Statutes*, p. 113 (cl. 53–4).
117 *Dialogue*, p. 61 [100].
118 Ibid.
119 St. 34–35 Henry VIII c.26. *Statutes*, p. 113.
120 *Dialogue*, p. 67 [104–5].
121 Ibid., pp. 70–5 [107–11].
122 Ibid., p. 70 [107].
123 Ibid.
124 Ibid., p. 71.
125 Ibid., p. 73 [110].
126 Ibid., p. 76 [113].
127 Ibid., p. 78 [115]. St. 27 Henry VIII c.26; *Statutes*, pp. 106–7.

[128] *Dialogue*, p. 82 [118].
[129] Ibid., p. 85 [120].
[130] Ibid., p. 86 [121].
[131] Ibid.
[132] Ibid., p. 83–4 [119].
[133] St. 27 Henry VIII c.26; *Statutes*, pp. 106–7.
[134] *Dialogue*, p. 89; *CSPDom., 1547–1580*, CVII, no. 4, 4(i), p. 514; Mathew, 'Some Elizabethan documents', 76; Ellis, *Original Letters Illustrative of English History*, III, pp. 42–4.
[135] *Dialogue*, pp. 94–8 [128–9].
[136] Ibid., pp. 101–2 onwards, for a full discussion of George Owen's views of territorial changes affecting Pembrokeshire and Carmarthenshire in the Act of Union 1536.
[137] For more general information on these lower officials see *Cal.CQSR*, lxxvi–lxxvii; Jones, *Law, Order and Government in Caernarfonshire*, passim.
[138] St. 27 Henry VIII c.26; *Statutes*, p. 87 (cl. 20). No objection was raised to the 'language clause', but the poets subsequently made indirect references to it in their comments on gentry attitudes towards native culture in the late Tudor and early Stuart periods. Peter R. Roberts, 'Tudor legislation and the political status of "the British Tongue"', in G. H. Jenkins (ed.), *A Social History of the Welsh Language: The Welsh Language Before the Industrial Revolution* (Cardiff, 1997), pp. 130–1; D. J. Bowen, 'Y cywyddwyr a'r dirywiad', *BBCS*, XXIX (1981), 453–73; C. W. Lewis, 'The decline of professional poetry', in R. G. Gruffydd (ed.), *A Guide to Welsh Literature c.1530–1700*, III (Cardiff, 1997), 239–74.
[139] *Cal.CQSR*, xxviii–xxxiii; Glanmor Williams, *Wales and the Act of Union* (Bangor, 1992), pp. 27–49. For a full discussion of the implications of the 'union' legislation see P. R. Roberts, 'The "Act of Union" in Welsh history', *Trans. Cymmr.* (1972–3), 49–57.
[140] Charles, *George Owen of Henllys*, pp. 189–90. For a fragment of a continuation of the *Description of Penbrokshire* see B. G. Charles, 'The second book of George Owen's *Description of Penbrokshire*', *NLWJ*, V (1947–8), 265–88; *DP*, I, xv–xvi.
[141] *Dialogue*, pp. 90–1 [126–7].
[142] *Cal.CQSR*, lx–lxvi; Roberts, *Aspects of Welsh History*, pp. 314–18; J. Beverley Smith, 'Crown and community in the Principality of north Wales in the reign of Henry Tudor', *WHR*, III, ii (1966), 165–71; Ralph A. Griffiths, 'Wales and the Marches', in S. B. Chrimes, C. D. Ross and R. A. Griffiths (eds), *Fifteenth-Century England, 1399–1509* (Manchester, 1972), pp. 152–65.
[143] For the anti-Welsh laws of Henry IV (1401–2) see *Statutes*, pp. 31–7. For Anglo-Welsh relations in the later Middle Ages see Roberts, 'Wales and England: antipathy and sympathy, 1282–1485', in *Aspects of Welsh History*, pp. 295–318, and Griffiths, 'Wales and the Marches', in *Fifteenth-Century England*, pp. 152–65; R. A. Griffiths, *Sir Rhys ap Thomas and his Family: A*

Study in the Wars of the Roses and Early Tudor Politics (Cardiff, 1993), intro., particularly pp. 135–8.

[144] Smith, 'Crown and community', 165–70.

[145] Wynn, *History of the Gwydir Family and Memoirs*, pp. 30, 37; Powel, *The historie of Cambria* [7–8]; Merrick, *Morganiae Archaiographia*, p. 67.

[146] *Dialogue*, p 41 [84].

[147] Ibid., p. 37 [81]. Cf. Owen's reference to the Queen in his *Description of Pembrokeshire*: '… our most gracious Sovereign Lady Queen Elizabeth, whose long and peaceful government was, and may be, a mirror, or rather an admiration, to all princes'. *Desc. Pembs.*, p. 202.

[148] *Dialogue*, p. 38 [82].

[149] See C. S. L. Davies, 'A rose by another name: why we are wrong to talk about "the Tudors"', *The Times Literary Supplement*, 13 June (2008), 14–15. For the Welsh background see Glanmor Williams, 'Prophecy, poetry and politics in medieval and Tudor Wales', in *Religion, Language and Nationality in Wales: Historical Essays* (Cardiff, 1979), pp. 80–6; Glanmor Williams, *Harri Tudur a Chymru/Henry Tudor and Wales* (Cardiff, 1985), pp. 75–109; G. A. Williams, 'The bardic road to Bosworth: a Welsh view of Henry Tudor', *Trans. Cymmr.* (1986), 7–31.

[150] *Dialogue*, p. 57.

[151] Ibid., pp. 56, 99. See note 180.

[152] Ibid., p. 99.

[153] Ibid., pp. 56–7. Cf. Demetus's overtly lavish eulogy identifying Wales with England, stating that no part of England had 'flourished in one hundred years as Wales had done' since the reign of Henry VII.

[154] The family on the male side traced itself to Philip Fychan, living at Henllys Isaf in the parish of Nevern in the latter half of the thirteenth century. Henllys was regarded as a citadel of bardic activity.

[155] Ibid, p. 57. Cf. Sir John Wynn of Gwydir's references to house-burning, owing to kindred animosities, in fifteenth-century Eifionydd. Wynn, *History of the Gwydir Family and Memoirs*, pp. 22, 33, 45–6.

[156] Elyot, *The Book Named the Governor*, p. 159.

[157] Ibid., p. 165.

[158] John Guy, *Tudor England* (Oxford, 1990 edn), pp. 410. See also pp. 408–13; Kelso, *Doctrine of the English Gentleman*, pp. 70–2, 76–9.

[159] Gerald of Wales, *The Journey Through Wales and The Description of Wales*, ed. Lewis Thorpe (Penguin Books, Harmondsworth, 1980), p. 251.

[160] NLW, Llanstephan MS 38,176; D. J. Bowen, 'Graddedigion Eisteddfodau Caerwys', 134.

[161] Fritz Caspari, 'Sir Thomas Elyot', in *Humanism and the Social Order in Tudor England*, pp. 79–109.

[162] Henry Peacham, *The Compleat Gentleman* (London, 1622); Lawrence Humphrey, *The Nobles or of Nobilitye* (London, 1563); Roger Ascham, *The Scholemaster* (London, 1570).

Introduction

163 Thomas Starkey, *A Dialogue between Cardinal Pole and Thomas Lupset, Lecturer in Rhetoric at Oxford*, in J. M. Cowper (ed.), *England in the Reign of King Henry the Eighth*, Extra Series 12 [*Early English Text Society*] (London, 1871), pp. 46–8, 50–1, 157, 164; W. R. D. Jones, *The Tudor Commonwealth 1529–1559* (London, 1970), pp. 19–20. For a more critical view of the 'Commonwealth men' as an action group see G. R. Elton, 'Reform and the Commonwealth's men of Edward VI's reign', in *The English Commonwealth 1547–1640*, ed. P. Clark et al. (Leicester, 1979), pp. 23–38.

164 J. G. Jones, *The Welsh Gentry 1536–1640: Images of Status, Honour and Authority* (Cardiff, 1998), ch. 3, pp. 95–132.

165 G. E. Jones, *The Gentry and the Elizabethan State*, pp. 63–5.

166 *Dialogue*, p. 98 [130].

167 *DP*, II, p. 511. For further details on gentry conflicts in late sixteenth-century Pembrokeshire and social features in general in south-west Wales see B. E. Howells, 'Studies in the social and agrarian history of medieval and early modern Pembrokeshire' (unpub. MA dissertation, University of Wales, 1956), pp. 162–78; B. E. Howells, 'The Elizabethan squirearchy of Pembrokeshire', *The Pembrokeshire Historian*, I (1959), 17–40; H. A. Lloyd, *The Gentry of South-West Wales 1540–1640* (Cardiff, 1968).

168 Wynn, *History of the Gwydir Family and Memoirs*, p. 37.

169 *Dialogue*, pp. 92–3; E. A. Rees, *Welsh Outlaws and Bandits: Political Rebellion and Lawlessness in Wales, 1400–1603* (King's Norton, 2001), pp. 218–31.

170 For this theme see J. G. Jones, 'Lewis Owen, sheriff of Merioneth, and the "Gwylliaid Cochion" of Mawddwy in 1554–55', *Jnl. Merioneth Hist. and Record Soc.*, XII, 3 (1996), 221–40; J. G. Jones, *Gwylliaid Cochion Mawddwy* (Darlith Glyndŵr, Machynlleth, 1994); Lewys Dwnn, *Heraldic Visitations of Wales*, ed. J. R. Meyricke (Llandovery, 1848), II, pp. 336–7 [Robert Vaughan of Hengwrt's account of the assassination of Lewis Owen].

171 *Dialogue*, pp. 92–3 [126–7].

172 Howells, 'Studies in the social and agrarian history of medieval and early modern Pembrokeshire' (unpublished University of Wales MA dissertation 1956), p. 188; Jones, *Concepts of Order and Gentility*, pp. 10ff.

173 Elyot, *The Book Named the Governor*, pp. 159–60.

174 Howells, 'Society 1536–1642', in *Early Modern Pembrokeshire, 1536–1815* (Haverfordwest, 1987), pp. 32–8. Howells, 'Studies in the social and agrarian history of medieval and early modern Pembrokeshire', p. 188.

175 *Dialogue*, p. 58 [98]; Kelso, *Doctrine of the English Gentleman*, pp. 76–8.

176 Kelso, *Doctrine of the English Gentleman*, p. 70.

177 Ibid.

178 Exodus 18: 21; *Dialogue*, p. 53 [93].

179 *Dialogue*, p. 56 [96].

180 Ibid., pp. 56–7. In these words Owen echoes the praises of William Morgan's labours by several litterateurs, such as Thomas Jones, a Gwent cleric, Huw

Lewys, Maurice Kyffin, Dr John Davies of Mallwyd and several professional poets. Ceri Davies (ed.), *Rhagymadroddion a Chyflwyniadau Lladin, 1551–1632* (Cardiff, 1980), p. 127; R. G. Gruffydd, *'Y Beibl a Droes i'w Bobl Draw': The Translation of the Bible into the Welsh Tongue* (London, 1988), pp. 30–83. The background to Morgan's career and translation is adequately traced in Glanmor Williams, *Wales and the Reformation*, ch. 13, pp. 338–60, and Eryn M. White, *The Welsh Bible* (Tempus, 2007), chs. 1 and 2, pp. 17–52.

[181] *Dialogue*, pp. 56–7, 99 [96, 131].

[182] Glanmor Williams, 'Prophecy, poetry and politics in medieval and Tudor Wales', in *Religion, Language and Nationality in Wales*, pp. 85–6.

The Dialogue of the Government of Wales (1594)

GEORGE OWEN OF HENLLYS, PEMBROKESHIRE[1]

Preface

Gentle Reader, for the most part of this last year, my private study which I use rather for my recreation than for any toil I take therein was in reading and searching out the ancient state of my native country of Wales wherein I endeavoured especially to learn how the same country was first brought subject to the hands of diverse English lords as in the end it was and to the Crown of England in sort as now it is; as also in noting how and in what sort and with what laws and Governors the same has been ruled from time to time since the Conquest, wherein I might see and perceive the miserable and lamentable estate of that poor afflicted nation and country in former time as well in subduing of the country by fire and sword and the continual thrall thereof for many years by the misgoverned Governors of each several province, country or lordship thereof rather endeavouring themselves to live upon the spoil and fleece of the poor people than to see them well governed and their oppressions redressed.[2] Therein also appears the happy reforming of the said government in the time of Henry the Eighth by reducing the same into shires and in providing sweet and wholesome laws for the government thereof that comparing the present government of Wales with the government of the rest of this realm I find ourselves now in far better estate than any other part thereof governed with more ease and less charge.[3] Which things by me being noted as I passed by in reading thereof I collated the same together which, for the more easy understanding, I have done it dialogue wise in sort as you see which, when I had done, I added thereunto some few things such as in my simple opinion I thought might be reformed and for the which I have heard as well the reasons of those that were learned as the complaints of those that were grieved therewith.[4] And although I well know that diverse matters spoken of herein are too high and too weighty for me to presume to handle or deal withal, yet, seeing they remain as griefs forgotten and thought upon but of few, I have been so bold as to put the same drawn briefly as remembrances for others to view and that are more fit to deal further in hereafter when opportunity shall serve and that they shall see cause. Which things also being well considered should and ought to move us upon the knees of our hearts to thank the living God that has so mercifully provided for our deliverance out of ancient thraldom and frame ourselves more agreeable to his will and to hold our obedience towards our Prince with a more willing and firm heart, by whose means we are thus peaceably governed comparing our former oppressions with our present happy estate:[5] beside the matters aforesaid there is partly touched the manner of the first subduing of the country of Wales by the English lords. All which matters I have but touched as briefly as I might whereby it may be perceived that my meaning was not to handle those matters to the full nor to discourse so largely as the same required: but referring the same to others of better skill than myself I have laid them but as notes for their better remembrances as before I have said. The other part of my notes which I have gathered by reading which is the order of conquering and subduing of Wales, and how and by what English lord each country and lordship was first subdued and taken from the ancient owners thereof, I have now in hand.[6] Which work for that it is a far more tedious labour and which, without search of some matters of antiquity not to be found in this country and conference with some skilful in those antiquities, I am not able so to perfect as I have determined to do and as (if I may have time and opportunity) by God's grace I hope to accomplish.

The Dialogue of the Government of Wales (1594)

A Dialogue of the present government of Wales *anno domini* 1594. Wherein as well the ordinary proceedings of justice in most of the courts there is briefly handled, what matter each court determines, as also some defects not provided for when Wales was first brought to be shire-ground, and now fit to be redressed by Parliament, together with some inconveniences that may be reformed by the Judges and Ministers of those courts.[7]

The speakers' names are Barthol, a Doctor of the Civil law [and] Demetus, a Pembrokeshire man.

THE CHIEF MATTERS THAT ARE HANDLED IN THIS BOOK ARE THESE.

Of the Court of the Council of the Marches.

That it is a Court of Justice and trial of causes.
That it has the authority of the Star Chamber and Chancery.
Their authority is by Articles from Her Majesty.
What matters they most commonly hear and determine.
The four terms at the Council when they begin and end.[8]
Whether the same court be necessary or not for the government of Wales.
Of the smallness of charges awarded in that Court.
Complaint of the multitude of frivolous suits there and the causes thereof.
Of the multitude of Attorneys there.
Of the multitude of unnecessary processes at the Council.
Smallness of charges awarded there is the cause of many frivolous suits.
Smallness of charges awarded to the Plaintiff causes the defendant wilfully to delay the [*cause or*][9] suit.
That the multitude of processes in causes at the Council breeds too much delay before the defendant can be brought to answer.
Of the speedy trial that the said Court yields after appearance.
The good order observed there for suing forth of process there.
The inconvenience in holding plea of all manner of suits there.
How the multitude of frivolous suits might be redressed.
The description of the nine courts of Westminster.
Wales more bound of late to the Kings of England than any other province of England for their good laws.
The hard laws of Henry the Fourth against Welshmen.[10]
The cause why King Henry the Fourth hated Welshmen.
The rising of Owain Glyndŵr against Henry the Fourth who then usurped the Crown of England.

The Dialogue of the Government of Wales (1594)

The great happiness that came into Wales by coming of King Henry the Seventh to the Crown of England.

That King Henry the Seventh was a Welshman by descent and birth, that he was born in Pembrokeshire, and landed there when he achieved the Crown of England.

That his father's bones do rest there in great reverence and estimation.

That he gave in charge to his son Henry the Eighth to have special care of his native country of Wales.

Of the great care that King Henry the Eighth had of his father's commandment, and of most pleasant [*and easy*] laws which he provided for the same.[11]

That there is a Common Pleas, King's Bench and Chancery in every shire in Wales.

Justices of Assize and Great Sessions in every shire in Wales.[12]

The great and large authority of the Justices of Assize in Wales.

The subjects in Wales equal in freedom with the subjects of England, and now are of the Parliament of England.[13]

The great care that Her Majesty that now is had in providing two Justices for every circuit in Wales.[14]

A description of the Great Sessions in Wales and the officers thereof.

Of a shift and slight whereby prisoners and offenders do escape punishment at the Great Sessions unknown to the Judges.

Whether the Justices of Assize in Wales be sworn.

A fault imputed to the Justices of Peace that guilty prisoners escape.[15]

The Justice of Peace excused for that fault which is laid elsewhere.

Another fault whereby thieves do escape punishment.

Complaint of the husbandmen for the unfit time that those Sessions are sometimes kept in.

Of two ancient Terms that were kept in Wales yearly, by Hywel Dda's laws,[16] and how well those Terms were placed for the ease of that country.

That those two Terms had 67 days more than the four Terms at Westminster now have, and yet no hindrance to the husbandmen.

Of the Chancery Court before the Justices of Assize in Wales, and of the great benefit that would ensue thereby if some defects there were reformed.

That the Protonotaries of the circuits in Wales dislike of that Chancery before the Justices.

That the Protonotaries are nothing or very little hindered by the same.[17]

A description of the Quarter Sessions.[18]

Of the great care that the laws have in appointing Justices of the Peace and what manner of men they ought to be.

That it is fit the Statute for the Ordinances of Wales were reformed touching Justices of Peace and Sheriffs.

How that fault in the Statute could not be remedied at the first when Wales was brought to be shireground as now it may.

How felons escape oftentimes by the negligence of the Justice of Peace in their examinations, especially for robberies and burglaries.

Defect in the Quarter Sessions by lingering pleas upon recognizances[19] forfeited.

Of the keeping of the Quarter Sessions out of time.

Of Base Courts, and of the County Court;[20] of the worthiness thereof above all other Base Courts, and of the great decay of the same in Wales of late and why.

Of the High Sheriff and his authority and charge.[21]

Of the inconveniences that Sheriffs and Escheators[22] in Wales are not sworn at home in the country as Sheriffs of England are.

A description of the Sheriff's office and duty.

That the Sheriffs in Wales are charged with the gathering of estrays,[23] and not the Escheators.

Of the great benefit and ease that the Sheriffs and all the people of Wales receive by the Exchequer which they have in their country, and with what ease the Sheriffs do pass their accounts in Wales.

Of the inconvenience that Collectors of the Subsidies[24] in Wales are forced to account at London, seeing that all the rest of Her Majesty's revenues are paid into the Receiver's hands here in the country.[25]

[Whether it were beneficial; for Wales that all base courts were dissolved and all suits brought to the Great Sessions before the Justices of Assize.]

[The multitude of Base Courts breed much inconvenience.][26]

The disorders of Sheriffs' Hundreds.[27]

[*That all actions should be brought from the Hundred Court to the County.*][28]

(The Sheriff is Judge in the County and Hundred Courts, and how and when those courts are usually kept.[29]

The inconveniences of the Hundred Courts newly erected.

Multitudes of actions in those Hundred Courts.

Wales divided into thirteen shires.

No Court Baron[30] or Leet[31] kept where the said ancient Hundred Courts were.

Three and twenty ancient hundreds in Wales before the Statute of 27 Henry the Eighth.

Dividing of nine shires of Wales into new hundreds.

No suitors in any of these new hundreds whereby any Hundred Courts may be kept.

That a writ of false judgement lies not in the new Hundred Courts for want of suitors to certify the record.

Sheriffs in Wales cannot prescribe to keep these Hundred Courts.

When and at what time first Sheriffs began to keep Hundred Courts in these new hundreds in Wales.

Some Sheriffs fined for keeping these Hundred Courts.

Some hundreds newly annexed to English shires.

The Hundred Courts suppressed in Monmouthshire by whom and when.)

[*Exclamation against the Sheriffs' Bailiffs.*[32]

Whether it were better that those Bailiffs should continue in their office for a time or be removed yearly as they are.

Of the inconveniences that is found by the yearly changing of officers and of certain complaints thereof made in old time.

Of the multitiude of Courts Baron and of the inconveniences thereof.

How the enormities of these courts should be redressed best for the ease of the country.

How the multitude of suits in these Base Courts do grow.

Of the inconvenience that would ensue if all these small suits were brought to the Great Sessions.

That it were fit that the Justices of Assize should have the oversight and controlment of those Courts Baron, and for the examining of the officers for their skill and sufficiency before they exercise their offices.

Of courts in corporate towns and the great disorders that do and may happen by the unlearned Judges of the same.

Of Leets and Sheriffs' Turns.[33]

How the alteration of laws in Wales, by reducing the same into shire-ground, was received of the people without tumult or rebellion and why.

Of three chief happiness and blessings of God bestowed upon Pembrokeshire.

Of the great happiness that happened to that country by the first coming of the Lord Keeper to be Chief Justice there.[34]

Of the great love the said Lord Keeper bears to his old circuit in Wales, and of his love showed to them at the yielding up of his office.

How much Pembrokeshire is bound to God, for his goodness above the rest of Wales, with a warning for them to be thankful therefore.

The praise of the towns of Tenby, Pembroke and Haverfordwest.
That Pembrokeshire is but a little shire, and of the injury it received by taking away of Laugharne, Llansteffan and Oysterlow[35] *from the same, and of the inconvenience thereof.*]
Inconveniences found by yearly changing of officers in Wales.[36]
Of the multitude of Courts Baron and the enormities in them.
The causes of the great number of the actions in Courts-Baron and Hundred Courts in Wales.
These Base Courts very necessary for the subjects as the state of Wales stands.
Of the inconveniences that would ensue if all small suits were brought to the Sessions.
Courts Baron do daily increase in Wales.
That it were fit the Justices of Assize should control the officers of Courts Baron.
Of courts in corporate towns in Wales and of the inconveniences that may happen by the unskilful Judges thereof.
Of Leets and Sheriffs' Turns.
How the alteration of laws in Wales by King Henry the Eighth was received without grudging or rebellion.
That Pembrokeshire was in old time won by Strongbow and planted with Englishmen and continued English to this day, and why it is called Little England beyond Wales.[37]
That although the King's writ did not run into Wales, yet was the same directed into Pembrokeshire of ancient time by the Common Law of England.[38]
Of the great wrong done to Pembrokeshire by taking diverse lordships from it and adding the same to Carmarthenshire.
Pembrokeshire in all taxes and levies of men at as high a rate as Carmarthenshire, being far greater than it.
That Pembrokeshire by Mr Saxton's map seems to be bigger than Carmarthenshire although it be far lesser.[39]
That the error and mistaking thereof is in the difference of the scales of both shires, and the reasons why the said scales were made for to differ.
That these lordships newly taken from Pembrokeshire and put to Carmarthenshire were in ancient time part of Pembrokeshire.
Diverse reasons to prove it were convenient that those lordships should be restored back again to Pembrokeshire.
A short recital by Mr Barthol of such abuses as the Judges of diverse courts in Wales might of themselves reform and amend.

The like recital of diverse matters fit to be reformed by Act of Parliament in the government of Wales.

GOD WELL you good gentleman:[40] you have chosen yourself a sweet and pleasant solitary place in a fair cold shade. It is like to prove hot this day when the sun comes to any height.

DEMETUS: Sir, you are welcome. You find me like a sloven wallowing on the grass.[41] I drew myself into this solitary place to the end to shun company, while I might in hast run over this little written pamphlet which I borrowed of a gentleman of my acquaintance.[42] I perceive you are a stranger by that you have lost your way by coming into this thicket, and where few that are acquainted with the ordinary way do resort. I pray you from whence come you and what is your name?

BARTHOL: Gentleman, I am a stranger indeed both in this country and in this realm also. I was born at Frankfurt in Germany and my name is Barthol.[43]

DEMETUS: I pray you what occasions should bring you into this country, and how long have you been in England?

BARTHOL: I have been in England almost three years; I first landed at St Ives in Cornwall: my business seems not so necessary to others as pleasant to myself. The cause of my coming into England was to see this worthy island, whose praise is so much founded beyond the seas; the like has been my trade into other countries of Europe for the space of these eight years past, ever since the sacking of the worthy town of Antwerp,[44] where my abode was, and where in times past I have been of some good account by reason of my profession. And if I might be so bold with you, I would be glad to know your name also.

DEMETUS: My name is Demetus. I am anciently descended of the country of Pembrokeshire, as you may well perceive by the analogy of both our name. For this country in ancient time was called Demetia, as you shall read in the ancient histories of the same.[45] And now if I may, without offence, I pray you Sir what was your profession while that famous town of Antwerp flourished?

BARTHOL: I was a lawyer, and from my youth have spent my time in the study of the Civil Laws in diverse of the universities of

Germany,[46] until I attained to the degree of a Doctor in that faculty, and ever since have practised until the ruin of my said country. And for that I could not endure to behold and see the tyranny and bondage laid upon that unhappy soil, I having before gained a competent mass of wealth, and my wife and two sons, which God had sent me, being at one instant cruelly murdered with the Spanish sword,[47] for very sorrow I determined with myself to lead a pilgrim's life, and to content myself with the portion which I had already gotten, dividing the same into so many parts as I supposed my sorrowful life might endure years, I take each portion for a year's revenue; and for my trade of life, for that I am naturally comforted with the view and travel of strange countries, I have chosen to wear out the later part of my days in travelling of strange lands, and to see with eye, that which in my youth I greatly delighted to read, little thinking that ever it should have fallen to my lot to be an eyewitness to many things that then I viewed in my private study. But such is the fickle state of man's pilgrimage, that little knows he in his youth what will befall him in his age.

DEMETUS: It seems unto me, and diverse others that enjoy the pleasant fruit of quietness, that you have chosen to yourself a most painful penance, much like the pilgrimage of the former worlds, which was counted of them for great merit. But I hope you are not of that resolution, for unto us that have our quiet rest at home, our journey here hence to the Council of the Marches, or the city of London seems unto us most grievous and painful, so that if the pain that you have voluntarily taken upon you, were enforced unto us, we should more complain thereof, that Ovid does of his banishment in his doleful works *De Tristibus*.[48] But I pray you what do you chiefly regard and note in these your travels to the end you may leave some fruit thereof to the posterity, and wherein are you most solaced in the same?

BARTHOL: In truth, good gentleman, I have been always as I said delighted in the pleasant study of cosmography,[49] and in my youth spent much time therein, although I never made open profession thereof, but it so delighted me, that being wearied with other studies, it was unto me a sufficient recreation, whereby I grew acquainted with the state of most foreign countries; so that I perfectly understood the situation of most realms, cities, famous rivers, and most notable places of each region. I also was acquainted who first inhabited the lands, who built the chief cities and the famous universities. I also learned what Princes had ruled each province in old time, and how the present Princes achieved the same, and what wars and conquests each country had sustained. I also was very desirous of the old and present estate and government of each state and land, and by what laws they were governed; and diverse other things I learned by the historical and geographical description of countries, a study which greatly delighted my humour.[50]

DEMETUS: Truly Sir you and I, as I ween, were both born, as the Astrologians say, under one planet or constellation; for our natures are much of one, and truly I could, it seems to me, be content to join with you in your laboursome journeys, were it not that my charge of house, wife and children force me to ride at anchor here in this poor country where God has lent me a poor living, being placed and cast, as it were, in the end of the world in an odd solitary corner fit for a hermit.

BARTHOL: You are in a good country and a quiet.[51] I have heard much good speeches of this country of Pembrokeshire, and heard it called Little England beyond Wales. I have been in it these three weeks last, and did greatly rejoice to hear the English tongue spoken after so long a journey through Wales, where in few places saving in good towns, or of some gentlemen in the country, I could not hear one word that I might understand:[52] yet truly I have found throughout Wales as courteous and gentle people as in any country that ever I travelled, whose courtesy and gentle entertainment made me the more sorry that they might not understand how thankfully I accepted the same at their hands. But whereas you ask me what things I chiefly note in my travels; I am very inquisitive in each place where I come of such things as I have read of the place; and such other things as I can obiter[53] learn of any of the country worth the noting, I register briefly in my writing tables. Also any famous castle, city, town, fort, trophy,[54] or other thing that I see worth the questioning, I learn as much thereof as I may. But the matter wherein I take most pains is to learn by what laws, and by what orders, customs, judges, justices and officers each country is governed: In this I take the more pains, for that I have always professed law, and am better able to judge thereof than of any other things in any travels. And of this I have a brief of the government of Germany, being infinite in number. Also in France I noted the several proceedings in law of the provinces[55] of Vermandois, Picardy, Normandy, Brittany, both Haut and Basse,[56] Maine, Anjou, Touraine, Poitou, Limousin, Auvergne, Gascogne, Toulouse, Dauphiné, part of Burgundy, namely the French County, and diverse other provinces, whose government, although under one supreme Prince and one law; yet do I find great difference in the order of their courts and proceedings in justice, the one differing very far in form from the other, which I have particularly noted, beside other antiquities, and present matters of each of these provinces. And the like have I endeavoured since my coming into England of every particular country and shire, but to no great purpose. For that I find but one manner of proceeding in law in all parts, which is a very great good and readiness to the subject, for I perceive they all fetch their law out of one place at Westminster, where all suits, in a manner, of the whole realm have their beginning and ending, saving for ease of the Juries, which try all things were in England. They have Commission of *Nisi Prius*, as they term it,[57] twice every year in the country where the matter lies to try the same, and this is, as I do guess, for the ease of the Jurors and witnesses.[58]

DEMETUS: I perceive by your speech that I shall have great delight in your company. Will it please you to take your rest upon this bench in this cold shade which I have caused to be made in this solitary place for this purpose; it seems you are almost weary by going. And let me understand, first, I pray you, of your estate since you came into England, and what countries have you passed here. And what things have you found worth the noting, and afterwards I will make bold with you to learn more strange matters out of foreign countries.

BARTHOL: Gentleman, I have almost passed all England over. My first landing was, as I said, at St Ives in Cornwall, where, at my first coming I thought I had been in Wales by reason of the strange language which I found in diverse places there, differing from the English tongue, which I well understand, until it was told me that it was Cornish.[59] Then I remembered myself how I had read, that a remnant of the ancient Britons, the most ancient inhabitants of this Isle of Britain, remained there, and that (which now I perceive to be true) there is great affinity between the Cornish speech and the ancient British tongue, which yet remains in this country of Wales, which they call now the Welsh tongue. And having passed through Cornwall, I came into the next shire (for I perceive England is divided into shires) called Devonshire, and into the fair city of Exeter, and so from thence through Dorsetshire, and so into Wiltshire, and to the city of Salisbury; and then to Hampshire and to Winchester: and so through Sussex into Kent, and to Dover, and to the cities of Canterbury and Rochester, and from thence to the famous city of London, where I made my abode for three months, where I found many of my acquaintance, who wondered to see each other, especially to see me, that was wont to ride in my long gown, accompanied with three or four men and a troupe of clients following me, and now to be clad in a short cloak and this little walking-staff in my hand, who serves me now for my foot-cloth nag, it was more strange unto them than grievous unto me. After I had spent sufficient time in London, I took my journey towards York, another ancient city of this land, and on the way, omitting many famous cities and towns, I visited the famous university of Cambridge, and the good city of Norwich. From York, where I made three weeks stay, I passed through the city of Durham to the town of Newcastle [upon Tyne], and through the county of Northumberland to the strong and only garrison town of England that I could see, Berwick [upon Tweed],[60] whence shortly after I entered into Scotland and passed as much thereof as I could with safety, and so returning into England at the north sea coast at Carlisle and passing through Cumberland and Westmorland I came to the town of Lancaster, and passing through Lancashire and Cheshire I came to the ancient city of Chester where I found many antiquities that delighted me. And after a few days I departed; and no sooner was I out of town, but I perceived I was in Wales; and so enquiring in what shire I then was, it was answered it was Flintshire, from whence I went to the sea coast of St Asaph and to the town of Denbigh and through the fair valley of Dyffryn Clwyd, which for the beauty and pleasantness thereof, led me willingly out of my way, so that I was forced to retire in a manner backward into Caernarfonshire, and so the shire and isle of Anglesey, and there hence back again into Caernarfonshire to the said town of Caernarfon, and so through the rough country of Merioneth to Montgomery, and stepping somewhat aside to Radnor, I drew again northward to the upper part of Cardiganshire to Cwmwd Deuddwr, Cwm Ystwyth, Aberystwyth and Llanbadarn and so along some part of the sea coast, and then I crossed over to Newcastle Emlyn and so to Carmarthen, and from thence to this little England, Pembrokeshire, where indeed, if that I saw not the sea environ the same in a manner about, I should have thought that Wales had been in the middle of England, and that the cosmographers had erred in placing Wales on the one side of this Isle of England, for the most part of this country, both in speech and order of buildings, diet, fare, and entertainment does so far differ from the rest of Wales that I have recited unto you, and does so imitate England in all points, that no man would judge it to be any part of Wales. And therefore was it not without good cause called *Anglia transwalina*.[61] But Sir, I have wearied you in reciting these my long journeys of England, Scotland and Wales, which, although the time in reciting the same may seem long and tedious unto you, yet the travel and meteing out of each of these places by the foot was nothing laboursome or painful unto me.[62]

DEMETUS: Mr Barthol you have made a very long voyage about this noble country of England, and no doubt a man of your wisdom, diligence, and experience has found great matters to delight you withal, worth the remembering. But I pray you, what is your greatest defect in your journeys here in Wales, and what do you most want that might give you contentment?

BARTHOL: All this journey through Wales, it has not as yet been my chance to meet with any gentleman or other, that could instruct me of the state of government of the country: as to show by what ordinary Judges or chief officers the noble Queen of England does govern this her dominion or country of Wales.[63] For I perceive, by that I have heard, that it differs somewhat in administration of laws from England although governed by the selfsame laws; and therefore I would be instructed therein for my learning's sake. And you Mr Demetus, for so I perceive your name is, as I guess by your speech, if it were not too much tedious unto you, might greatly further me therein. You may say I am too bold to move you thus far.

DEMETUS: Mr Barthol, it shall not be tedious unto me to pleasure any gentleman, especially a stranger and a traveller as you are, with anything that I may. My skill is not such as to the full I might satisfy your expectation, neither were it fit for me, being a gentleman, leading my life in the country, and not professing the study of the law, to take upon me any such matter, but only so far as my skill shall serve, to pleasure you I would be glad. But for you being skilful, as I perceive you are, in the Civil laws, learning some part of me, and as much of another, by such fragments may join together the whole body of your contentation. And therefore you shall understand, that the chief and supreme governor of all the Principality and Marches of Wales is the Lord President of the Council established in the Marches, who is chief of the said Council; which Council does consist of the said Lord President as chief,[64] of one Chief Justice, who is always chosen of some learned man in the laws of this land; and also diverse others learned in the laws and some other gentlemen of great worship and in commission there.

This Council, although it bear the name of Council, is not so much occupied in matters of Council as it is in hearing and determining of matters of right. For it is now used and grown to be an ordinary Court of Justice for every man to sue in; and is much like in authority to the court called the Chancery in Westminster, which is a court of equity to mitigate the rigour of law in diverse causes.[65] The authority and jurisdiction of this Council is not certainly known: for they are to judge and determine of such matters as the Queen of England shall authorise them from time to time by way of Instructions, and their authority is not certain. But most commonly they deal for all manner of misdemeanours, as assaults and affrays, riots, routs, forcible entries, briberies, extortions, *cymorthas*,[66] exactions, and all manner of outrages and misdemeanours committed within their commission. And therein they resemble much in authority the high and honourable Court of Star Chamber at Westminster.[67] They also deal in mitigating, as I said before, of all extremities and rigorousness of the

Common Law of this land, as extreme dealings upon penal bonds and such like. It also determines detaining of evidences where there is no remedy at the Common Law. It examines the title of lands depending upon the same. It takes order for the speedy trial and pleading of matters at the Common Law. Also it holds plea for debt without speciality, detaining of goods or chattels: it forces evil-dealing tutors to yield account to fatherless infants of their goods and debt. It examines witnesses to remain on record *ad perpetuam rei memoriam*;[68] and which is most beneficial of all other matters, it takes speedy remedy for restoring or stalling of possessions of lands or tenements, which otherwise would be long ere they might recover their lawful possessions by ordinary course at Common Law. It also punishes the vices of incest, adultery and fornication. And generally it is the very place of refuge for the poor oppressed of this country of Wales to fly unto. And for this cause it is as greatly frequented with suits as any one court at Westminster. Whatsoever the more for that it is the best cheap court in England for fees: and there is great speed made in trial of all causes. For they divide their sittings for matters in hearing into four Terms, agreeable to those for England in number, though not agreeable in time. For the first Term in the Marches begins the Monday next after Twelfth Day,[69] except the said Monday be so near Twelve Day as men cannot conveniently travel from home to the Council, and then it begins the Monday following. The second Term is held in Lent, clean contrary to the order in England, for it begins the first Monday in Lent. Concerning the inconvenience of this Term I will declare my mind unto you hereafter. And whereas there is a term after Easter in England, here in the Marches they have none; for from Easter until Trinity Sunday they have no sitting.[70] But the Monday after Trinity Sunday they begin their third Term. The fourth and last Term begins the Monday next after the Feast of All Saints,[71] and every of the said Terms, by a later order taken and used by the Council there, endures a month: so that it ends always on the fourth Saturday after the beginning thereof. Thus they divide their Terms. All those of the Council that are in commission do not continually sit, but certain of them; and those are such as it pleases the Lord President to appoint. Also they have allowance of six shillings eight pence a day each Councillor that is learned in the law during the time of his sitting, and their diet of the Queen's charge for them and certain of their men. This court is it which, at the beginning, brought Wales to that civility and quietness that you now see it, from that wild and outrageous state that you shall read of. And although some think it an unnecessary court at this present, considering the obedience that Wales is brought unto, and fitter to be dissolved than continued, doubtless they are far mistaken therein, unless there were some other court of like authority erected for punishment of diverse the offences aforesaid, and for redressing of diverse of the causes before recited. For let that house or Council be dissolved but for a few years, and no place erected to seek redress in diverse of those things, those that live now most quietly and think that court unnecessary should first feel the smart and want thereof.[72]

BARTHOL: As you say indeed, I have heard men of opinion that it might well be spared, as the state of Wales now stands, and that the Queen's Majesty might greatly benefit herself by dissolving thereof, by saving the charges in maintaining a Lord President and Council, and a great number of officers there to her own coffers; and yet the country of Wales to be as well governed as it is now. I have heard that Her Majesty has been moved to that end, and that bills have been preferred in Parliament to that effect in times past. And surely I myself, being inquisitive, as I passed through the country, of the good liking of the people to that Court, have heard many complain how they have been sued there for very trifling causes, such as no court of any authority or credit would hold plea of. Also they have grievously complained of the great charges they have been at, some in prosecuting suits wherein they have recovered, some in answering frivolous and unjust suits, whereof they have been, at the full hearing thereof, dismissed, and that they have recovered but very small costs, after the spending of great sums of money; and this I should hear of most that have been suitors in that Court. And truly these two, in effect, were the chiefest causes that I could hear any complain of in general of that Court.

DEMETUS: In truth, Mr Barthol, it appears that you are very diligent in enquiring of these things; and surely the greatest fault of that

The Dialogue of the Government of Wales (1594)

	Court is the receiving of many trifling and frivolous causes or suits not fit to be heard of so honourable a bench as that should be and is, and also the awarding of so small costs, both which are causes of much trouble both to the whole country of Wales, and to the Judges of that court also.
BARTHOL:	It were great pity that these defects were not reformed, rather than so honourable a court should be defamed, and termed a trouble, and held for unnecessary, seeing indeed it is so necessary a court, as the simple dissolution thereof might be the dissolving of the great quiet and ease of the whole country of Wales, which I have heard to be one of the quietest parts of this land for good and quiet government. But better it were that these defects were reformed, than like an evil physician, for that some part is grieved, to kill the whole body. But how do you think fit that those defects might be redressed?
DEMETUS:	Before the physician should take in hand to cure the malady, he ought to know the cause of the grief, which in the one is the granting of so small charges, the remedy whereof lies only in the discretion of the Judges of the Court, in whose power it lies to augment the same by their discretions. And surely it is often times seen that it is necessary, that the charges of some courts, especially where criminal causes are heard, should exceed; for thereby diverse frivolous suits are stopped, that would be attempted for every trifling cause, especially supposed misdemeanours; which always proceeds of hatred and envy between men; and upon any small conceit of displeasure had, every mean man, being moved with choler, would in their heat seek after some colour of misdemeanour to exhibit his complaint for to put his adversary to trouble and charges, which surely many would do if it stood them not in great charges. And this cause, as it is thought, stops many frivolous suits from the honourable Court of Star Chamber, which, if the fees thereof were not so great, would be over-pestered with many frivolous suits, grounded more upon malice than good matter. The causes of the other complaint, which is the multitude of frivolous and causeless suits, as I do guess and conjecture, among other, are two. The one is the multitude of Attorneys[73] belonging to that Court, more than should seem necessary that such a court should have. For whereas there are admitted in the High Court of Star

Chamber but two or three Attorneys, and in the High Court of Chancery but six Attorneys, yet does there belong to this Court of the Marches 24 Attorneys, besides diverse Attorneys Peers, which they call Clerks, admitted, who, in the absence of the Attorneys have an Attorney's place and authority.

BARTHOL: Surely that Court is well applied that yields food to so many Attorneys, and this confirms your former speeches, that that Court is as greatly frequented with suitors as any court in England.

DEMETUS: The other cause which breeds so many frivolous suits there, is that which I have lately touched before, the small charges awarded to the defendant upon the hearing of those frivolous suits. For a busy person that is given to molestation, perceiving that for a little money he may frame his bill, and procure forth his process, will, for a very trifling cause, vex his neighbour, and make him ride a 100 miles to answer his malicious suit; and this he will do of evil will, when otherwise he cannot annoy the man, and perchance hoping for some composition rather than a man would travel so far; or when the worst comes he is sure to pay but a noble[74] or ten shillings charges, when he has caused his adversary to ride 100 miles, and spend £5 in the journey. This is a great satisfaction to a malicious stomach, which thing, if it were reformed, and that it would please the Council to consider partly the goodness or badness of the cause and partly the countenance and charge of the party vexed, and award his charges thereafter. It would make these frivolous suits to be fewer, and the plaintiff would be well advised ere he would procure any such suits, and the defendant would be the more willing to answer. Whereas now an honest Welsh yeoman, being molested wrongfully by a litigious person, considers with himself in this sort: that first he shall be driven to travel a 100 miles from home, he shall spent £4 or £5 in this journey besides his travel, loss of time, neglecting of his thrift at home; and yet in the end he hopes of good success in the cause, for that he assures himself that there is no just cause of suit against him. But before he shall come to clear himself, the suit will stand him in £10, and then he shall be dismissed with 40 shillings charges. Here he has the victory and lives by the loss.

On the other side the busy plaintiff upon the first process

offers to discharge him for 20 shillings or little more or less, which things being considered, the honest man thinks it more wisdom to buy his quietness with 20 shillings, than to purchase 40 shillings with £10 expenses besides his travel; and many a 20 shillings is gotten by this means in Wales, and all for the causes aforesaid.

On the other part, if the plaintiffs, in their good and just suits recovered, might have their reasonable bill of charges allowed them, having consideration to the distance of his dwelling, the number of journeys he has been forced to make in person, and the long delays the defendant has procured in the suit, and that his charges should be indifferently rated thereafter, it would make the defendants also more willing to yield to other men their right without suit; whereas now the defendant, knowing he may detain a man's right from him a long time, for any suit in that Court, and pay but a very little costs when the matter passes against him, makes him the more obstinate and wilfully to offer the wrong, which otherwise he would not do. And these two causes indeed make that Court to be evil spoken of, and make much trouble to the country of Wales, in so much that I myself have heard diverse wise men of my country say that they had rather sue and be sued in the Chancery at Westminster than in the Court of the Marches for the causes aforesaid.

One other great inconvenience and hindrance there is in that Court of the Marches not yet spoken of, which greatly delays the plaintiff, which is, the number of unnecessary process more than is thought necessary, or is used in the Star Chamber or Chancery in Westminster, or any other court yields. For the first process at the Council of the Marches, which we call a Commandment, is in nature of a *subpoena*[75] which, being disobeyed, the plaintiff must sue forth the second process, which they call a Contempt, at which if the defendant do not appear, then must he sue forth the third process, called a Proclamation, upon which if he do not appear, then goes forth a Sequestration, which is the fourth process, and then if the defendant disobey, goes forth the Attachment, which is the fifth process of that Court. Whereas in the Star Chamber and Chancery at Westminster, the Attachment is the second process. And at the Council after that upon the Attachment is returned *non est inventus*,[76] then goes forth a Placard infinite so that a whole year and more is spent before a man may be brought to answer by ordinary process of that Court. And in the opinion of diverse men many of these processes might be cut off as needless and unnecessary, which is a marvellous great hindrance to the suitors in that Court. But this inconvenience will not easily, at least willingly, be reformed, for it were a great loss to the Secretary of the Council in his fees for the same process. And it is thought, that was the first cause of inventing so many processes in that Court, and so I have heard some men of judgement reason; for other cause or reason they could not gather; which only delay excepted, it is the speediest court for trial of causes of all the courts of England, which is a great benefit to the suitors, and greatest joy to the plaintiff. For at the first the defendant answers, the plaintiff replies, the defendant rejoins without process and joins to commission forthwith upon the first appearance. So that I have known suits commenced, answered, examined and heard in less than half a year, which is a far greater expedition than any Chancery Court in England besides does yield.

And one good order I must commend that is used and duly observed in that Court praiseworthy before all the courts of Westminster, for whereas out of all or most of the Chancery and English courts at Westminster, or elsewhere in England, a man may have forth process without any bill in court, whereby many *subpoenas* and other process are sued forth in England to the great trouble and molestation of the people; whereby many are forced to travel for very small causes: yet in this Court of the Marches no process may be had forth, but first the bill must be framed, perused, the matter therein allowed and signed by some of the Council's hands, which only is a warrant to make forth such process upon the same bill and no other, and the same endorsed upon the back of the bill, and the day of the said endorsement laid down, which endorsement might likewise be subscribed by some of the Council's hands before the process will be had forth [whereas now the defendant knowing he may detain a man's right from him a long time, for any suit in that Court, and pay but a very little costs when the matter passes against him].[77] And in this

The Dialogue of the Government of Wales (1594)

point it excels the Chancery at Westminster or any other court that I know. There is an order much like thereunto in the Star Chamber at Westminster; but of late days not so straightly observed as it is in the Court of the Marches.

BARTHOL: I have heard that that Court receives all or most manner of matters into it, both matters determinable in the Common Law, matters of equity,[78] capital and criminal causes of life and member as I have heard it termed in England matters of the Court Christian[79] both civil and criminal.

DEMETUS: Indeed, that is thought to be another inconvenience in that court to examine all manner of causes, and it were better and more fit that the causes determinable in that Court were limited, to be fewer in number, and such special causes to be selected, as were most for such a bench to hear, and such as were most enormous to the country.

BARTHOL: You have made a very large discourse of the Council of the Marches which I perceive by your speeches, some defects being reformed, is so necessary a court for the quiet government of that country, as without the same Wales would be turned into her former chaos of troubles. Your speech of the multitude of frivolous and unnecessary suits makes me to remember a well governed and great state of Germany; where there are three several courts for the determining of criminal causes and matters as misdemeanours and suchlike, in which the higher court holds plea for the most heinous matters, the middle court holds plea for more inferior matters, and the smallest matters of all are referred to the inferior court. Each court differs in charge and pain; the higher the court the greater the pain, and the more the charges; and as you yourself said, all these criminal causes, which you call here in England misdemeanours, do proceed from the root of hatred and malice: therefore, ever the party pursuant seeks the greatest pain and molestation for his adversary; so much is mankind given to revengement, and therefore in that state I speak of, most commonly, let the misdemeanour be never so small, yet will it be first attempted to the highest court, which if the defendant allege ought not to be handled there for the exility of the cause, if it were true, then this course is taken. First, some of the Judges of that court are selected out (for there are many Judges in each of those courts which they call

Chambers) which selected or chosen men are called Committees of the Cause, which Committees shall call before them both parties, and examine them touching the heinousness of the fact and cause of suit, and upon their report the court will either retain it as a cause worth the hearing, or dismiss it as frivolous and followed of vexation: and this I perceive is often used in the Star Chamber at Westminster, a very good use indeed. But in the said state of Germany, if these Committees cannot find out sufficient matter to ground a true report, then are letters written down by the state to the chiefest men next adjoining to the place where the parties dwell, or offence was committed, to certify the state of the cause; by which means those courts scarce in a whole year do trouble themselves with one frivolous or unnecessary cause; and in my simple opinion, if some of these courses were taken before the Council of the Marches, it would breed great ease to the country, and great quietness to the Court. But then were not that great troupe of Attorneys able to live by that Court, as now they do, who benefit by every of those poor suits.

DEMETUS: Surely Sir, if it would please the rulers of that Court to take any of these you have spoken, or the like courses, doubtless it would turn to the great good of this poor country, and those that are now living and their posterity should be bound to pray to the living God to bless them and theirs with all His good blessings.

BARTHOL: I would think it very fit and convenient that some good gentleman of worship should acquaint that honourable man that now is Lord President,[80] and the rest of the Council with these defects, which in my conceit are very small and easy to be redressed. And no doubt their careful duty to their commonwealth and country would move them with speed to devise a reformation herein. And now, methinks, you have taken much pains in this discourse touching the said Court of the Council in the Marches.[81] But I understand and partly know that you have diverse other governors and courts of justice in every shire, besides the said Lord President and Council.

DEMETUS: So is there indeed, which, unless you be very well acquainted with the courts in Westminster, I shall be forced to take the greater pains to make you understand the orders and authorities of these here in Wales. And therefore let me understand how you are informed touching the courts you find in Westminster Hall, which is also called Little England for that out of most parts of England you shall find some there.

BARTHOL: I find in Westminster Hall divers courts; as first at the lower end of the Hall at my coming in there is on my right hand that Court called the Common Pleas,[82] wherein is handled mere law, and which Court holds all manner of pleas real, as you call it for land, and all actions mixed, as Trespass and suchlike, and Plea of Debt, Detinue, Covenant and other like, which court holds itself so strictly to the precise course and words of the law, that it will not digress anything from the rigour thereof. Close beneath the said Court of Common Pleas up a stairs, there is a court of the Prince's revenues called here the Exchequer, but in our law *Fiscus Principis*.[83] There is the receipt of the Queen's Revenues paid there all accountants yearly make accounts and payments of all things due to the Prince, and this is the chief care and office of that Court. It also holds plea touching the Queen's inheritance and revenues and diverse other matters.

Within the said Exchequer on the left hand there is the Exchequer Chamber which holds pleas of greatest importance as occasion serves.

On the upper end of Westminster Hall is the court called the Chancery,[84] a court judging all things in equity called also a Court of Conscience[85] mitigating the rigour of the Common Law of the land and providing remedies where the Common Law is defective and gives exceptions where reason and equity allows. The Chief Judge here is the Lord Chancellor of England or Lord Keeper, the Master of the Rolls[86] in his absence, and certain doctors of the Civil Law sit there as assistants which are called Masters of the Chancery. This court is likened in authority to that of the praetors in ancient time amongst the Romans.[87]

Over against the Chancery, on the other side of the Hall, is the court called the King's Bench,[88] where capital crimes are examined, as treason, murders, robberies, felonies and other crimes committed against the Crown. It also holds pleas as the Common Pleas, yet with more equity than that and more arbitrary power, and less tied to the strict principles of the law; and here the Lord Chief Justice of England and his associates are Judges.

At the lower end of Westminster Hall right against the Exchequer, there goes up another pair of stairs where the honourable Court of Star Chamber[89] is held, wherein are criminal causes (life excepted) heard, such as are very heinous, as perjury, forgery, notable riots, routs, outrageous assemblies, cozenage[90] and suchlike. This of all the courts that ever I saw in Europe excels for honourable judges, and deliberate hearing of causes, for here sits the Lord Chancellor or Lord Keeper,[91] which are both one in authority, the Lord Treasurer, both the Lord Chief Justices, the Lord Chief Baron, then the Lords of the Privy Council, then any Lord of the Parliament may sit in judgement there, also the spiritual lords may (and some must) be present especially my Lord's Grace of Canterbury who most commonly sits in judgement there. There is a very honourable presence to decide any cause. And therefore matters of small importance come not there to be heard, besides the Court is very chargeable to sue, and therefore trifling causes do not trouble the Court. And during my abode in London I had great delight to be present in this Court where I have heard causes heard with such gravity, and sentenced with such equity that I, having travelled most of the countries of Europe, this only made me to admire, such was the majesty of the Court, where I noted on course contrary to all the rest of the courts of England, that every of these honourable persons that there sit in judgement after full debating of the cause at large, gives his sentence particularly,[92] declaring what he thinks of the cause as well of the proof as of the quality of the offence, and lastly the Lord Chancellor or Lord Keeper, collecting of all their opinions an equal sentence, strikes the stroke, and gives the final sentence.

There is near unto this Court of Star Chamber the court called the Duchy Court,[93] about the which for that is not a court belonging to one province, and of the authority of diverse of the other courts I will spend no time about it.

There is above the upper end of Westminster Hall, beyond the King's Bench, two other courts, that is the Court of

The Dialogue of the Government of Wales (1594)

                Wards[94] and the Court of Requests.[95] In the Court of Wards is determined only matters belonging to the Queen's Wards, an unknown court in other countries. It seems to me that it is of great affinity to the Exchequer.

DEMETUS: So it is indeed, for it was in old time a part of the Exchequer and severed by King Henry the Eighth.

BARTHOL: These wardships are the greatest inconvenience of England, and I have heard it called the slavery of England. But of this not here to be spoken of.

                The other court called the Court of Requests, for aught that I could learn, differs not much from the Chancery, and are in a manner one; it was told me that this Court is greatly augmented of late years.

                And thus in effect I have briefly recited unto you my knowledge of those nine courts of Westminster Hall as much as I could learn.

DEMETUS: You have done very well being of so small standing in England, and now that I perceive you are well acquainted with the authority of those courts,[96] I shall with the less pains inform you of the whole government of Wales as it presently stands, whereby you shall perceive how much that nation is bound to the Kings and Princes of England for the great care they of late years have had to that poor country more than to any other of their dominions or provinces of England.

BARTHOL: That were very strange, and I thought the contrary, and that of all parts of the realm it was the least regarded and worst provided for by laws, for I remember that I have read laws made by King Henry the Fourth most unnaturally in my simple opinion against Welshmen, not only for their punishment, but also to deprive them of all liberty and freedom, and to bar them from all civil education.[97] That they should not dwell or be brought up in any city or town, that they should not be inheritable in any town, or bear any office of credit or trust were it never so mean, and diverse other laws loathsome to recite, which laws doubtless at that time were provided of some hatred that the said King had conceived against the whole nation.

DEMETUS: True it is that Henry the Fourth greatly hated the Welshmen, the cause was for that he being an usurper, and had deprived Richard the Second, the lawful King of England, from the

Crown,[98] they would never yield their obedience to him, but still withstood the usurper and wrought him much woe and fought against him all his lifetime.

Also in his time Owain Glyndŵr did take arms whom our chronicles do register for a notable rebel, whose quarrel for that he was condemned of treason (as it is said) I will not seem to defend, seeing the poor friendless man had none to move in Parliament the reversing of his attainder as diverse of the self-same faction and quarrel have had obtained.[99]

But this may be said of him, if all the nobility and commons of England had been of Owain Glyndŵr's mind and suppressed Henry the Fourth, fought on the defence and restored Richard the Second, their lawful King, then had not that civil and bloody dissention between the houses of Lancaster and York have plagued England so long; then had the life of many a duke, marquess, earl, baron and many a valiant knight and many thousands of good English subjects been saved, but no more of that, God's will must be fulfilled.[100]

BARTHOL: Indeed, I have read in the English chronicles of a notable traitor and rebel of a Welshman called Owain Glyndŵr, and I was persuaded he was some notable traitor.[101]

DEMETUS: Judge you if he that seeing his lawful Prince suppressed, imprisoned, deprived of his Crown and realm, would stretch forth his force to withstand the usurper, whether he were worthy to be registered for a traitor? But for this the whole nation grew into marvellous great hatred and endured the rigour of those hard and unreasonable laws of King Henry the Fourth, until God, the consolator of the comfortless, looking down upon the oppression of this poor nation, as he did upon the heavy burdens of the children of Israel under the whip of the merciless taskmasters of Egypt, sent unto us a Moses that delivered us from bondage;[102] for whereas by reason of those rigorous laws which were provided against the Welshmen to keep them poor, to deprive them of good education and make them uncivil and brutish, there grew about the time deadly hatred between them and the English nation insomuch that the name of a Welshman was odious to the Englishmen, and the name of Englishman woeful to the Welshman;[103] and when they were thus in most distain, it pleased the Lord of his mercy to send us a Prince of our own nation and born in our country to govern both England and Wales; I mean that worthy and grave prince Henry the Seventh, who, for his wisdom is termed in histories of foreign nations a second Solomon.[104] This noble Prince, achieving the Crown of England and being lineally descended from the ancient British Kings of this land, so drew the hearts of the Welshmen to him, as the leadstone does the iron, whoever since then have borne such natural love and affection to the said King Henry the Seventh, his son King Henry the Eighth and King Edward the Sixth, Queen Mary, and now does bear towards our most sovereign Prince Queen Elizabeth, now living, whom we pray the Lord of Lords long and long to preserve to govern England and Wales, that there has not been found in England any country or province more obedient in heart, than this country of Wales has been and is to the progeny of the said King Henry the Seventh that has governed here after him in this land; for over and besides the duty and allegiance that we owe unto Her Majesty as our sovereign Prince there is a certain ardent affection in the hearts of Welshmen towards Her Majesty which makes them inwardly to rejoice that God has blessed our nation (who was so long oppressed by the hatred of diverse of the Kings of England) with a Prince of our own natural country and name.[105]

BARTHOL: I am no good herald. I never knew that Her Majesty was descended of the ancient British blood which is the most ancient progeny of this land, neither did I know so much that King Henry the Seventh was a Welshman by descent and birth.

DEMETUS: Yes, verily, for he was the son of Edmund Tudor, earl of Richmond, son of that worthy gentleman Owen Tudor lineally descended of Cadwaladr, the last King of England of the ancient British line, and also most certainly known to be descended of the late Kings and Princes of Wales, since the conquest of the Normans.[106] Also, the said King Henry the Seventh was a Welshman born, and that in this country of Pembroke, in the castle of Pembroke,[107] whereof and of diverse other things touching the same we of this present country do greatly rejoice, as that he first landed here in Milford Haven[108] when he achieved the crown of England;

where he found the hearts and hands of this nation and his native soil ready to aid and further him, and surely we the poor people of Wales want only but wealth to show our enflamed hearts towards Her Majesty whose name is Tudor lineally and paternally descended of the said Owen Tudor who is now (woe is us therefore) the last of the said name now living.[109]

We also of Pembrokeshire reserve as a treasure the bones of that famous Prince Edmund, earl of Richmond, father to the said Henry the Seventh in our ancient and famous cathedral and sometimes metropolitan church of St David's,[110] which was set and translated thither by us Pembrokians out of the Friars of Carmarthen upon the suppression thereof where the same was first entombed with as great joy and triumph as either were the bodies of Jacob or the bones of Joseph carried out of Egypt to the land of Canaan,[111] where the said bones of Edmund Tudor are yet reserved in as great honour and estimation (but not in such superstitious account) as ever were the bones of any saint or martyr adored and reserved for relics among the Papists in the times of blindness.[112]

Thus King Henry the Seventh, making trial of our fidelity, love and obedience, gave in charge as it is thought to his son Prince Henry that he should have a special care for the benefit of his own nation and countrymen the Welshmen, which King Henry the Eighth, not forgetting after long trial of the faith and fidelity of that his country people towards him, in the 27th year of his reign made much beneficial laws for the good government of the country as that he showed his affection to be more towards that country than to any part of this realm.[113] The sweetness of which good and pleasant laws our fathers that are dead, we that are living, and our children that are to come, do, have, did, and daily shall taste of, such as you shall perceive no part of this realm enjoy, with the like ease, so little charge being poured into our bosoms, and sent home to our doors, whereas all other parts of England, be they never so far distant, are forced to fetch at London with greater travel and expenses.[114] And now, after my long digression from my purpose, I will return to satisfy your request craving pardon for wandering thus far from my purposed method and your expectation, but this I thought good to acquaint you withal being a stranger in the state of our country.

The Dialogue of the Government of Wales (1594)

BARTHOL: Sir, I yield you as great thanks for this as for the rest for it is not from my purpose most of your sayings, and truly it has greatly delighted me. But now, if it would please you to proceed with your determined purpose.

DEMETUS: With a very good will and the better will because I see you so attentive to hearken and note each matter that methinks I see the same enter and imprint itself in your mind and settle there as at home.

But to my purpose, to that which King Henry the Eighth provided for us and our good in the seven-and-twentieth year of his reign by act of Parliament he divided the whole country of Wales into thirteen shires whereof one is called Monmouthshire he made English in all respects of laws and subject to the courts of Westminster, because the same was the nearest part of Wales to London and might with least cost and labour travel thither every term.[115]

But for the rest of Wales, being 12 shires, he provided for every three of them, a Common Pleas, a King's Bench, a Chancery, and an Exchequer, and that at home in every shire.[116]

For there is in every shire a Great Sessions or Assizes held every year twice, which endures for six days each time, and for the keeping of the said Sessions by the said statute there was appointed a Justice of Assize for every three shires which yearly rides those circuits to minister justice to the King's subjects of those parts.[117] And this Justice in his circuit has great authority and jurisdiction, yes, far greater than the Lord Chief Justice of England, or the Lord Chief Justice of the Common Pleas, for he is to enquire, hear and determine of all treason, petty treason, murders, robberies, felonies, riots, routs, extortions, embraceries[118] and all other offences and evil deeds of what nature, name or quality soever the same be, within his commission, and to hold all manner of pleas of the Crown in as large and ample manner as the Lord Chief Justice of England, and other the Justices of the King's Bench, and also to hold all pleas of assizes, and other pleas real, personal, and mixed in as large and ample manner as the Chief Justice of the Common Pleas in England, and before him are all fines levied and recoveries[119] past, and not at Westminster; which Justices have belonging to their office a judicial seal as has the Common Pleas at Westminster, which Justices have large fees and allowances for their diet at the Prince's cost, such care had the noble Prince King Henry the Eighth for the quiet governing of his loving subjects.

And besides made his said subjects of Wales equal in all respects in freedoms and liberties to the rest of his subjects of England and made them free and gave them place and voice in his High Court of Parliament in England.[120] Which Justices of Assize continued alone in sort aforesaid in Wales until the 18th year of our most sovereign Lady Elizabeth who then, for the natural love that she likewise bore unto her said loving subjects, considering that the life, lands, goods and possessions of her loving subjects of Wales was to be tried and decided before the Justices of Assize there and not elsewhere, and that there arose demurrers[121] and great questions in law before them to be determined, and therefore thought fit to associate another Justice learned in the laws to every of the afore-named Justices so that ever since all matters are judged by two Justices in each shire of Wales in sort as you now see.[122]

The said King Henry the Eighth ordained also a Sheriff in every shire to be chosen of gentlemen of the country, and the same to be removed yearly as in England.[123] Whereas before in divers parts of Wales of ancient time there were Sheriffs for term of life, and those most commonly strangers in the country who sought more to enrich themselves by the office than to see justice ministered indifferently to the people, to the great grievance and heart-burning of the people.[124] Also, he ordained Escheators,[125] and Coroners to be chosen of the inhabitants of each shire,[126] and also whereas by the laws of King Henry the Fourth no Welshman might be Justice, Steward, Constable of Castle, or Chamberlain, or other officer, now they are franchised to have Justices of Peace in every shire of their own countrymen, and in conclusion has made the country of Wales equal in all respects for freedoms and liberties with the realm of England.[127] This has so tied the hearts of Wales to the said King Henry and his posterity as never before did any Prince by any manner of merit towards his subjects procure the like.

But now to our ordinary Court of Great Sessions. In the said Sessions the inhabitants of Wales commence all their suits, real, personal and mixed, and there have their original writs,[128] for unto every of these three shires is there erected a Chancery and an Exchequer, as I said before, out of which Chancery are sued all original writs sealed with a Chancery seal ordained for the purpose, and in the Exchequer before the Auditor and Receiver, who, with the Chamberlain, are the Barons[129] there, do most officers account as the Sheriffs, Escheators and such-like as shall be spoken of more hereafter.[130]

Also there is a Protonotary belonging to every three shires which comes twice a year to the country with the Justices of Assize, which Protonotary makes out all judicial process under the seal and *teste* of the said Justice.[131] He also enters all pleas, process and issues, and makes up the records as the Protonotaries in the Common Pleas at Westminster so that you may well perceive that no subject of Wales needs to ride to London for any right but has law and justice sent home unto him in his own country: And I would you were at some of the Assizes in Wales to see with what care and deliberation matters are heard and examined. There I dare assure you I never saw at any of the bars[132] at Westminster or in the English circuits such deliberate hearing of causes, as is used here at our Assizes in Wales. It passes my skill to express that which I have often seen in debating and opening of causes, at our bar causes are so deliberately examined and so much time spent in searching out of all doubts, and in the end the pith and substance so collected by the Judges that never jury passes from the bar without sufficient resolution which way the right lies, neither need they to stay any long time to debate upon their evidence the causes are, for the most part, so well handled at the bar and by the Bench.

BARTHOL: I have been oftentimes at all or most of the Benches at Westminster. I have been in my journeys at diverse Assizes in England. I have been in most of the public forms or places of justice in Germany, Italy, France, Spain, Bohemia, and this last week I was at your Assizes at Haverfordwest, where I duly attended for my learning's sake every sitting where I found to be true as much as you say and much more: and surely of all the places of justice for gravity, prudence and majesty of Judges, and for solemn, grave and deliberate hearing of causes, I will and must extol and reverence that honourable assembly of Lords in Star Chamber, and without offence be it spoken, for grave and deliberate hearing of causes I give the next place to your circuits in Wales, a happy country that is so governed by such laws and magistrates, a blessed Prince that so provided for so loving subjects, and happy people that were governed with so careful and gracious a Prince. There, among other things, I saw poor prisoners answer for their lives and tried, wherein I saw the Judges deal with such care of justice joined with mercy, as I would wish to see in all places; there saw I the guilty condemned with pity, and the innocent delivered by justice, rich and poor, the like care and pains was used for both; so that I perceive that all offenders and transgressors are tried at home in your own country by your own people, it seems you dwell here in a happy country that are judged by such gracious Judges.

DEMETUS: Yes Sir, we are happy indeed for good Justices ever from the beginning furnished with famous men, it proceeds more of God's goodness than of our desert of His Majesty that he blesses this soil with such men. But put me in remembrance hereafter of this and I will recite unto you diverse blessings of God upon the shire of Pembroke more than the rest of Wales both in this we now speak of and other also. But one thing I would demand of you; I perceive you are a diligent observer of all matters you desire to know, did you in the proceeding against those prisoners which you spoke both in the indicting of them, and at their trial, perceive any defects which breed inconvenience, and whereby some offenders might escape by a sleight?

BARTHOL: No truly, I could never discern any such matter but justice must take place; only one thing I have heard in England but whether it be true or not I shall learn of you, that your Justices of Assize in Wales are not sworn as Justices of England be for execution of their office.

DEMETUS: I know not how it was in times past but I have heard indeed some gentlemen of account complain that the Justices of Assize in Wales who judged their lives, lands and living were not sworn; but I heard this year that the good Lord Keeper, that now is perceiving the said inconvenience, does use now to minister them an oath, and surely it seems they are sworn

	for they cleave unto right and justice with a marvellous zeal, which makes me to judge they are sworn. But my meaning is not of any such matter, but did you perceive any way to shift a felon out of trouble, the matter being apparent in court and yet to blind the eyes of the Judges that they should never espy the shift, but wonder why so innocent a man should be bound to answer before them?
BARTHOL:	No truly, I would gladly learn not to the end to practise the same but how to eschew or redress it if occasion were *Quia bonum est omnia scire, sed non tamen omnibus uti.*[133]
DEMETUS:	Although it be somewhat tedious, yet will I intreat you to hear it with patience, and thus it is brought about, when the offence is first perceived and the offender taken, while the matter is fresh there is hot prosecution of the cause and the offender brought before some Justice of Peace in the country who, by his intelligence and pains in examining of the offender and the witnesses, and two or three days perchance spent therein, the matter is sufficiently brought to light, the prisoner bound to answer, the party to prosecute, and the witness to give evidence, all being first laid down in writing, now has the Justice of Peace done his duty sufficiently, as much as is required at his hands; but now *Pars rea*[134] which we in our law call the prisoner, perceiving the Sessions to draw near falls to talk for an end to be had with the party pursuant, and in the end agrees with him so, that the prosecutor will stop the cause as much as he may, yet is he bound to prosecute and to give evidence, which he will do very faintly, but to have his recognizance[135] and *pro forma*[136] prefer a bill to the jury and as for evidence after composition he can give none or else such faint matter as it will be to small purpose; thus he drives most part of the week the bill being with the jury and no evidence given in the middle of the week, or towards the latter end perchance, the gaol is perused and the prisoner called, and Judges demand wherefore he was committed, answer is made that it is for such an offence and that there is a bill in against him with the Great Inquest,[137] the Judges with this pass over to another, thinking that something will be found against him before the end of the week, and so there is no more said till the end of the week towards Saturday that the gaol is delivered, then the offender is called again and the

Judges ask what the Jury did in the bill that was preferred against him, who answer as true it was, they could do nothing for want of evidence, and then is the offender discharged by proclamation, and there is an end of that trouble, all this while the examination, the deposition of the witnesses being delivered into court before the Justices of Peace, as he is commanded and bound to do, lie still in the dock and never once perused nor look upon where would sufficient matter appear to condemn the offender if so much pains would have been taken as once to have perused the same. And so is the pains and toil of the Justice of Peace lost for want of looking on which, if they would peruse then could the party pursuant have done no good in stopping of the cause but needs must the truth have appeared.

BARTHOL: Methinks that the Justice of Peace is much to blame in that he does not acquaint the Justices of Assize with such matters.

DEMETUS: The Justice of Peace, having done his duty sufficiently in bestowing great pains to bolt[138] out the truth at the beginning and having delivered in the examinations of the court thinks himself discharged, and lays the burden on the Judges who then are to look and take care thereof as the Justice of Peace was while the case lay under his hand: and also the Justice of Peace many times has great business of his own all the Sessions or else is clapped[139] in to be of the Great or Second Inquest and so is occupied that way which if the party pursuant compounded[140] perceive he will be sure to direct his bill to the other inquest, and also some Justice of Peace, being of a modest nature, will be loath to move the Justices privately of any such matters least they might think or conceive that there were some malice or hatred between him and the party, and lightly the party will have some man or other to incense[141] the Justice that the matter is followed more of malice than good matter, and few men that are in those troubles are so destitute of friends, but will make some or other to intreat with the Justice of Peace not to inform the Justice of Assize of the matter, persuading him that he has done his duty faithfully and sufficiently and that he may be content and let the fault lie where it is, and thus by one means or other Barabbas is delivered.[142] I have of late known one or two turned loose and escaped through the nets by these and the like means.

BARTHOL: It were fit the Justices were acquainted with these sleights that they might be prevented, but in whom lies this fault seeing you seem wholly to excuse the Justice of Peace who is most privy and best acquainted with the cause, and what fault is, it is unknown to the Justices of Assize.

DEMETUS: The fault chiefly, in my opinion, lies in the Queen's Attorney[143] who should look to these matters more narrowly, for to that end he has a fee of Her Majesty, and if the Justices of Assize themselves would take some care and pains either themselves to peruse the examinations that are returned into the Court before them or else if that seem tedious or that their business will not permit the same, to appoint some gentleman to do the same and briefly to recapitulate the substance of the proof of each matter, and to deliver the same unto the Justices who by the same might daily call and enquire what the juries do upon the bill and if need were to hear the evidence given openly at the bar, then there would not so many felonies be concealed.

Also the perusing of the gaols in the beginning of the week and to be thoroughly informed by the examinations would greatly prevent this practice.

Besides there is another shift which I would wish were looked into and prevented, by the which many great thieves escape, and that is by the undervaluing the theft or things stolen, if it be such things as the value or near the value is not notoriously known then, after composition[144] with the party as is aforesaid, it shall be found under the value; by this means I have known a brazen pan which, within half a year before cost ten shillings, valued to eight pence, linen clothes which were worth 20 shillings valued to ten pence and as many new nets as cost eighteen shillings valued to eleven pence, and thus felonies may decrease in value and yet not decay. The Justices of Peace may be much in fault of this as I will hereafter declare in a more convenient place, but most of all the Juries do offend in this, and in my opinion the Queen's Attorney ought chiefly to look to these things.

BARTHOL: You have spoken much in praise and commendation of the Great Sessions, and of the great good and sweetness that is found thereby, but as my use is in all such things when I have learned all the commodity[145] goodness and pleasure of anything, then do I enquire next what are the discommodities and griefs that are found thereby for *Commoditas omnis sua fert incommode secum*.[146] I pray you what discommodities or inconveniences are found by these Sessions or Assizes if any be, and what sort of people are most grieved therewith.

DEMETUS: Mr Barthol, the inconveniences and griefs that arise by keeping of the said Sessions are not many nor grievous, and if any complaint be, it is by the husbandmen of the country for the keeping thereof in the busy time of harvest, and in Lent which is the busiest time of sowing in Wales, for Wales, being for the most part tilled with oats, the chiefest time of sowing is in Lent, and then again commonly the Justices come in the latter end of August or September which most years is the middle of corn harvest in Wales, for that harvest is there more late than in England, and therefore these two times of the year are most troublesome to the husbandmen.

BARTHOL: What times of the year then are most convenient for keeping of those assizes in this country?

DEMETUS: It appears by the ancient laws of Hywel Dda, King of all Wales,[147] who lived in the year 940, by the which laws all Wales generally was governed until the same came in subjection to the Englishmen, and in most parts of Wales the same law was in force till the seven and twentieth year of King Henry the Eighth that Wales was reduced to shire-ground; by the same law there was but two times of sitting or Terms for law in the year, the one from the ninth of November till the ninth of February, the other from the ninth of May till the ninth of August, so that they had to spare three weeks in August, all September and all October, in which time they had done all their harvest, sowed all their wheat and rye. Then, likewise, had they to spare three weeks of February, all March, and April and part of May in which space they had sowed all their oats and barley. So they had in their winter Term 92 days and in summer Term 92 days which was very convenient for the country of Wales, for then had they the chiefest time reserved for applying their thrift about tilling the land and yet sufficient time reserved for administration of justice, for those two Terms had 67 days more than the 4 Terms now used in England have; and therefore, as I glanced before at the Term which the Council of the Marches does

	keep in Lent it is thought unfit for the country, and better to be held at some other time of the year.
BARTHOL:	And why is this time of Lent more inconvenient for the keeping of the Assizes or Sessions here in Wales, than in England, for in England the circuits never miss, but are kept in Lent and yet there is no complaint that ever I heard?
DEMETUS:	They in England have no such cause, for there is great difference between the state of both countries, for in England most of their tillage is wheat, rye and barley, and in Lent there the husbandman is not occupied about the tillage of any of these, and therefore Lent is the idlest time of the year with the husbandman in England, and then he may best spare his service of all times in the year: And the Assizes in England hold but three days, but in Wales (as even now I have declared) the most tillage is of oats, which is sown in March and April yearly; therefore the Sessions and Terms in Lent altogether hinders the Welshman's sowing, and you cannot find any time in all the year (corn harvest excepted) that the husbandman in Wales is more busily occupied than in Lent. And this makes the poor husbandman there so much complain of the keeping of the Sessions, and holding of the Term at the Council of the Marches in Lent as they do.
BARTHOL:	Truly you have satisfied me well touching the order and state of those two courts which I take to be sufficient for the whole government of Wales, for in these two courts there is determined all matters of law and equity, for that I think there needed no more courts for the whole government of the whole country of Wales saving these, and yet I perceive you have diverse other Courts of Justice besides the said Council and the Great Sessions and diverse other officers.
DEMETUS:	Yes verily that we have as you shall perceive before I end, but I am glad you are satisfied touching the order and authority of our Assizes with so few words. I thought to have troubled you more, and especially in one thing very material and beneficial for the inhabitants which I have omitted, which is that the said Justices of Assize in their several circuits do hold and keep a Chancery Court for determining matters in equity[148] between party and party by English bill in sort as does the Chancery in London or Council of the Marches, which is a very great good and ease to the country, and especially to the poorer sort

	that are not able to sue in those High Courts for their right, and this Court is to the great good and quiet of the country, and would be more especially if good and orderly proceedings were better observed by the proctors and advocates[149] as you term them in that Court, the want whereof has been the overthrow of many causes there.
BARTHOL:	This is very material and a chief matter which you had almost omitted, and I expected when you would have spoken of it, for the last day of your Sessions I was present when your Justices sat upon these causes, and as I remember they sat not all that week till then.
DEMETUS:	That is a thing that poor suitors complain of that the Justices do not bestow more days in hearing those causes, two or three sittings in a week, which they might well do if it were their pleasures, especially now being two Justices[150] which, if they would, it would work great ease to the country and stop many suitors which are forced against their wills to sue before the Council of the Marches to have the more speedy dispatch of their causes, for two or three days hearing of a cause in a year is very little, and long it will be ere it come to hearing, which two defects the disorderly proceeding and pleading of the Attorneys, and the few days of hearing of the Judges, if it were redressed doubtless it would grow to be a great Court, and work much ease to the country.
BARTHOL:	I have heard that the Protonotaries dislike with these courts for that they draw unto them many suits which otherwise of necessity should be commenced at the Common Law, and thereby their office decays.
DEMETUS:	Truly nothing at all for those that dislike to commence their suits in the Chancery before the Justices, for the causes aforesaid are forced thereby to go to the Council of the Marches, and there spend themselves rather than they would commence suit at the Common Law, and this they do chiefly to avoid the great delay and partly the great charges the Common Law yields.
BARTHOL:	I perceive your law admits no appeal, and what if a man be injured and has wrongful sentence pronounced against him in the Great Sessions, has he no remedy or redress for the same?
DEMETUS:	Yes truly, for if he be injured by a wrongful sentence, or erroneous proceeding against him, which we call false judgement

	or error, in real or mixed actions the same is to be reformed by the Justices of the King's Bench at Westminster, and in personal actions by the Lord President and Council of the Marches.
BARTHOL:	Now I pray you, will you proceed with your purpose and declare what court is next in authority for government to this Great Sessions.
DEMETUS:	The next as I take it is the Quarter Sessions,[151] which is held four times every year, by the Justices of Peace of every shire; this is a court wherein chiefly matters of the peace, and diverse felonies, and diverse other misdemeanours are heard and determined by the said Justices of Peace whereof there are diverse in every shire.
BARTHOL:	It seems to me there are more of these kind of officers or Justices in Wales and England than of any other one kind of Justices; for passing by diverse gentlemen's houses it was told me that a Justice of Peace dwelled there, and it seems that they are the chiefest gentlemen in every shire that bear that office.[152]
DEMETUS:	So they are or ought to be, and in appointing of those Justices our law of England seemed much to imitate the counsel of Jethro, the Priest of Midian in the 28th [chapter] of Exodus to his son Moses, in choosing of the Judges under him to Judge over the people of Israel,[153] touching what manner of men they ought to be, where he says *Provide autem de omni plebe viros sapientes et timentes Deum, in quibus sit veritas, et qui oderint auaritiam, et constitue ex eis Tribunos et centuriones et quinquagenarios et decanos qui Judicent Populum*; which is, Provide you among all the people men of courage fearing God, men dealing truly, hating covetousness, and appoint such over them, to be rulers over thousands, rulers over hundreds, rulers over fifties and rulers over tens, and the law of England says that these Justices of the Peace should be good men and lawful, and no maintainers of evil. Year 1 Edward the Third, cap. 16,[154] and by a statute in the 18th year of the same King it is said they shall be of best reputation in the countries with some learned in the laws;[155] and by the statute 34 Edward 3 cap. 1 it is said there should be assigned in every country one Lord and with him three or four of the most worthy men in the county with some learned in the

law;[156] whereby it appears that they ought to be good men, lawful men, no maintainers of evil, best of reputation in the countries, learned in laws and most worthy men in the county wherein they are appointed, which six qualities if they have they are equivalent to those Judges which Jethro wished to be appointed to rule over the Israelites:[157] which Justices of the Peace are chosen of the best sort of gentlemen of the shire by the Lord Chancellor or Lord Keeper; whereas before the said statute of Henry the Eighth we in Wales had no such officers, nor any one man almost of our nation that bear any authority in the commonwealth. But such officers as we had in Wales were, for the most part, strangers of other countries living on the spoil of the poor afflicted Welshmen, keeping them under as did the Egyptians the Israelites. But as touching these Justices of the Peace of Wales, there is in the said statute of 34 Henry the Eighth a defect very convenient at this present to be reformed; which is that Justices of the Peace and Sheriffs in Wales may exercise their office although they may not dispend £20 a year land nor yet be learned in the laws,[158] whereas in the time of Henry the Sixth it was found that men of small substance and living were crept into the commission of the peace in England, which were not able to govern and were had in contempt of the common people, and made a gain of their office, as the statute mentions, and therefore in the 18th year of the said King, cap. 11, it was ordained that none should be Justices of Peace in any shire in England, except he might dispend twenty pound land a year or were learned in the laws,[159] and twenty pound land at that time is worth now five times £20, at least, by reason of which first recited statute for Wales, we do find the same inconvenience now in Wales that was in England in the time of Henry the Sixth for with us diverse men of mean living are climbed up to the bench by whom, as the said statute says, the people will not be ruled, and (if they be not belied), now and then offend in taking unlawfully *Quia necessitas cogit turpia*,[160] which inconvenience I would some good gentlemen of Wales would consider of, for the good of their country, and procure to be reformed by Parliament speedily.

BARTHOL: Now, it seems to me, you are repugnant to yourself in your former speeches, for whereas before you extolled the great

The Dialogue of the Government of Wales (1594)

care and natural love and affection that King Henry the Eighth bore unto his subjects of Wales above all other of his realm of England, especially in providing for them more careful, provident and better laws to govern themselves withal, and by your reason now it seems that he was careful what magistrates should govern you there, when he should make laws, which in effect is that any man, be he never so simple of condition, so ignorant of learning, so void of honesty and credit, small of reputation in his country, should be a Justice of Peace, and ruler of his subjects there. Methinks that those two cannot concur and hold together that he should so love and affect that country and yet provide that that should be governed by blind and ignorant Judges to execute the laws which you said were ordained by him for such great benefit of the people, how can your skill reconcile these two points to stand?[161]

DEMETUS: Very well, and with sufficient reason such as shall content you, if you will but hear a little and consider the cause, circumstance and time thereof, how Wales was then and how it is now; and first you must know that from the time of William the Conqueror until the time of Henry the Seventh, which was for the space of 420 years and odd, the Kings of England, as well by open hostility and wars, as by providing of extreme and intolerable laws, sought continually the subversion, ruin and impoverishing of the said nation, as appears by the continual invading of them with wars, destroying of their country dispossessing them of their ancient and lawful inheritances, whereof the histories of our country, the multitude of castles built by the Englishmen throughout Wales are sufficient testimonies, and lastly worst of all other the laws of Henry the Fourth against them makes it most manifest that their decay was sought every way both by peace and wars, insomuch that the Welshmen, being the poor and small remnant of the ancient noble Britons, were brought into such poverty and thraldom and with such rudeness by reason they might not bring up their youths in civil towns, that when King Henry the Eighth came to redress those enormities and to establish good and wholesome laws among them, and to give them magistrates of their own nation, I mean Sheriffs and Justices of the Peace in every shire, he then was fain and forced to take and admit such to be Justices of Peace as were to be found in the country, for then there was not sufficient number to be found in many shires of Wales that might dispend £20 lands or were learned, for most gentlemen could neither write nor read for they were clean barred from all manner of learning and good education.[162] But since the time of Henry the Seventh and Henry the Eighth that we were emancipated, as it were, and made free to trade and traffic through England, the gentlemen and people in Wales have greatly increased in learning and civility for now great numbers of youths are continually brought up and maintained at the Universities of Oxford and Cambridge and in other good schools in England where some prove to be learned men and good members in the commonwealth of England and Wales.[163] Some worthy labourers in the Lord's vineyard, many of them have proved excellent in the Civil Laws, some in Physic and other laudable studies, wherein they are found nothing behind other nations; many good grammar schools in diverse parts of the country are now to be found throughout Wales, whereby the country is grown and shortly like to be as civil as any other place of this land; besides, the people being governed by these late established wholesome and good laws before recited, have wonderfully thriven by husbandry, the country is grown to be much more tilled, and enclosures in most parts full, and the country people with great diligence apply their labour, many countries heretofore desolate now well inhabited. No country in England so flourished in one hundred years as Wales has done since the government of Henry the Seventh to this time, insomuch that if our fathers were now living they would think it some strange country inhabited with a foreign nation, so altered is the country and countrymen, the people changed in heart within and the land altered in hue without, from evil to good, and from bad to better. The Lord continue his goodness towards us and make us thankful; and now not three years past we have the light of the gospel, yes, the whole Bible in our own native tongue which, in short time must needs work great good inwardly in the hearts of the people, whereas the service and sacraments in the English tongue was as strange to many or most of the simplest sort as the mass in the time of blindness was to the rest of England,[164] whereby the people have grown to be of great wealth, the gentlemen of great livings, so that in a country, when it came first to be shire-ground, where there was scarce two gentlemen that could in lands dispend twenty pounds apiece, there are now in the said shire to be found some that do receive yearly five hundred pounds, some three hundred pounds and many one hundred pounds good lands, so that now there is no shire in Wales but is able to yield sufficient number of gentlemen that may dispend £100 a year good land, to be Sheriffs and Justices of the Peace in the shire, and besides diverse of them of good skill in most points, sufficient to discharge the room and calling, this has our country of Wales attained by the blessing of God in sending them Princes of their own nation to govern them. This confirms my former speeches, that we of Wales are bound and must need love our said Princes, with a more natural affection than the rest of this realm, for that they of England do not know the sweet that we of Wales do feel, by that is before written, for they never tasted of the sour as the Welshmen did continually for the space of 400 and odd years. This I say does make our hearts to leap for joy, when we hear the names of these our loving Princes recited, being more like fathers than Princes to the poor Welshmen. Now we see the old castles of Wales, from whence in old time issued out daily our destroyers and disinheritors, all in ruin and decay, and on the contrary the houses of the gentlemen and people to flourish and increase which were most commonly burnt once every year in times past. This is a joyful metamorphosis for Wales, and now again to my purpose.[165]

Now I say we in Wales find this clause in the said statute of 34 Henry the Eighth breed us some inconvenience as the like defect did in England in the time of Henry the Sixth and therefore, as I said before, it might well be reformed by the good means of some of the best sort of the gentlemen now being admitted to be of the Parliament of England.

Now I hope Mr Barthol you are resolved that that noble Prince King Henry the Eighth, that worthy Moses of Wales,[166] did not of malice to the nation insert nor of careless negligence permit the said clause touching Sheriffs and Justices of Peace in Wales to be of such smallness of substance and living, but was forced thereto upon great and deliberate care and considerations had of the present poor estate of the country at that time. But now the cause of that inconvenience being taken away I would wish the inconvenience itself were also removed.

These Justices of the Peace are great furtherers in the bolting and searching out of felonies and misdemeanours daily committed in the country, and they are to see that the offenders be forthcoming before the Justices of Assize to answer the matter, and that the parties pursuant[167] be bound therein to prosecute and give evidence against the prisoner, and to see that all proofs and examinations be ready and orderly laid down in writing against the trial of the prisoner. This is one chief point belonging to the office of the Justice of Peace, wherein a good man may do great good, and an evil man great harm, and verily there are some that either negligently or wilfully suffer many things to pass their hands with less care than they ought to do if either they remember their duty to their country and Prince or the strict oath they receive for the due and careful exercising of the office, but for that I mean to speak thereof elsewhere, and that it is not pertinent to my course I handle now I will omit.[168]

BARTHOL: Wherein I pray you do you find the said Justices of Peace defective and negligent in their office?

DEMETUS: I could recite unto you many examples, but those wherein they most offend and whereby greatest annoyance arises I will note a little as I pass. Partly I have touched one point thereof already where I declared unto you how diverse felonies escape punishment[169] before the Justices of Assize where things stolen of great value are valued under twelve pence by the inquest that indicts the prisoner, for when there is no remedy but that the fact is made apparent then all the shift[170] is to value the thing under the value, and so make it petty larceny, a shift oftentimes used, and therein the Justices of the Peace are very negligent unless they do enquire of the value of the theft as well as of the circumstance of the fact, and to lay down the value of the same in the examinations of those that know the thing what it was worth when the same was stolen, and that upon their oaths, and then could not so many felonies escape through the hole as they do.

In like sort as they may offend in omitting the value of the theft so may they do as greatly in not exactly examining the circumstance of the fact, and thereby omitting the chiefest matter of all, as when a house is robbed to omit to examine whether the fact was in the night for then it is burglary, an offence more heinous than a common theft or felony in our law of England. Also to examine whether anywhere in the house and put in fear for therein again is a great difference for in the one case by the law of this land he shall have his Book[171] to save his life for once if he can read, but not so in the other.

In like manner in examining of all felonies stealing of anything to inquire whether the same was stolen or taken from the person of a man, or in the highway, or otherwise for therein is great difference touching his saving by the Book as I have said now.

BARTHOL: You have noted very good observations and matters methinks necessary to be observed in examining of those offences, I hear by you that those Justices of the Peace do keep Sessions four times a year, which you call Quarter Sessions I think because they are held quarterly, I pray you what matters are determined there and what proceedings is used in those courts?

DEMETUS: The most matters that are heard there are matters of the peace, for there those that are bound to the peace are called to appear and if occasion so serve they are bound over and so continue until they conform themselves to live in peace. Also, there are indictments of diverse kinds, felonies presented and found by the Juries there, and from thence they are returned over in the Great Sessions before the Justices of Assize to take their trial, for so we commonly use for offences of any importance. There also men are indicted for any manner of trespass and assaults, affrays, riots, routs, unlawful assemblies, embraceries, maintenance;[172] there also they take order for alehouses and allow and disallow those whom they think fit and punish unlawful games, take order for servants' and labourers' wages and covenants, and a multitude of other matters are referred to the hearing and examining of those Justices of Peace both in their Sessions and out of their Sessions tending to the good and quiet government of the country.

BARTHOL: I thought there had been no more need of any more courts for the government of Wales saving the Council of the Marches and the Great Sessions, but I hear you recite such matters of the Quarter Sessions without the which no country might be well ordered, and I perceive they deal with no small number of matters there; but I would gladly learn is all proceedings in those courts in good order or is there anything worthy of reformation (I told you before)?; this is a question which I make in most matters, especially such as we are in hand withal.

DEMETUS: There is nothing so well settled but something might be reformed, especially there is no Court of Justice but something will be amiss, and in this the Quarter Sessions, although I have no dealing therein,[173] yet have I, as a looker on, noted some things that might be amended as upon recognizances[174] there for the peace, and appearances if any be forfeited upon the *scire facias* granted forth,[175] the matter is delayed by frivolous and dilatory pleas until some general pardon come, and thereby the Queen's Majesty is defeated of the forfeiture.

BARTHOL: And in whom is the defect as you think?

DEMETUS: A great part thereof is for want of the Queen's Attorney there, or some deputy for him to solicit and follow those advantages and forfeitures for Her Majesty's use, and yet I have heard that the Clerk of the Peace[176] in the Sessions of the Peace is the Queen's Attorney by his office, and if he be then does he discharge his duty but ill for most commonly he is made acquainted with these delays and *particeps criminis* therein.[177]

There is another fault which is oftentimes seen by keeping of these Sessions of the Peace commonly called the Quarter Sessions out of due time; for the statute of 2 Henry the Fifth, cap. 4[178] has limited four special weeks wherein the said Sessions ought to be held quarterly, that is to say, the first week after the Feast of St Michael, and the first week after the Epiphany and in the first after the close of Easter, and in the first week next after the translation of St Thomas the Martyr[179] (*which always is the seventh of July, although our common almanacs do misplace it, and thereby causes great errors*),[180] for the performance hereof the Justices of Peace are especially sworn that they shall hold their Sessions according to the form of statutes: notwithstanding the same is not as precisely observed as careful men of their oaths would do. And this law seems to be granted with great reason, for that to that Quarter Sessions diverse persons are bound to answer as well for the peace as otherwise, and therefore it was necessary that the very weeks and times of keeping the same were known, otherwise men might forfeit their recognizance for non-appearance or else be driven to attend and expect the keeping of the same Sessions and so neglect their private trades and affairs, whereby they might be greatly hindered, especially those that trade by sea and far from home by the land, wherefore it was very conveniently provided by the Parliament that the said Sessions should be kept at times certain, that all men that are to answer or prosecute there, might know their times and so to dispose of their private affairs, that the one might not be a hindrance to the other, and therefore it were well done that care should be had hereof and not to be wilfully neglected.

BARTHOL: You have well said, and although this point is not received for so necessary a matter, yet would I wish men of discretion to have a special care hereof for the reasons you have alleged, but chiefly seeing they are specially sworn to that point above all other things belonging to their offices, but have you anything else to say of the Sessions of the Peace?

DEMETUS: No more that I do mean to trouble you withal at this time, but would all I have said already were reformed.

BARTHOL: I pray you have you now ended with all ordinary courts of Wales, or is anything more to be said, and if you have ended what other matters have you of like effect, to instruct me withal touching your government here in Wales?

DEMETUS: Many other courts there are in Wales which, in their force and kind, do determine causes although not of that authority as those that I have recited, and those that we call most commonly Base Courts; the chiefest of all these courts, in my opinion, is the County Court[181] which is a court held monthly by the Sheriff of the shire for determining of small matters under the value of forty shillings, I mean debts, trespasses, detaining of goods and trespass on the case and suchlike. It also holds plea for replevin of cattle and takes order for restoring of distresses wrongfully taken.[182]

In some courts are Knights of the Parliament and Coroners elected and chosen by virtue of writs directed to the Sheriff out of the Chancery at Westminster. The Sheriff and the suitors of the court, that is, all the freeholders of the shire, are Judges there; this ought to be the chiefest and greatest Base Court in the shire, but it is become the meanest of all other courts in Wales by reason of other baser courts than itself usually kept by the Sheriff, which they call Hundred Courts, for in every hundred there is one of these courts kept.[183]

BARTHOL: Mary[184] Sir that I expected all this while to hear you have spoken nothing of one of the greatest officers of every shire, the Sheriff which I perceive to be one of the chiefest account of all the rest, for I see him preferred before all degrees of persons under lords and earls, I marvel why you over-passed him all this while.

DEMETUS: My course and method of speech to you was such as that I had no cause to speak particularly of him till now, for your questions to me, and my answers to you were touching officers of administration of justice, and for the ordinary proceeding of causes before them here in Wales. And this office of Sheriff, although he be the chiefest man in account within the shire, and the Prince's Lieutenant, yet is he not chiefest in the matter we have in hand for he is rather a minister than a Justice to execute the precepts and commandments of the aforesaid Justices of Assize, Justices of Peace and other inferior officers, and of himself is Judge of no court to minister justice save of the aforesaid Base Courts; which I shall impart unto you more at large hereafter. This Sheriff is an anniversary officer, and changed every year, and is nominated by the Prince herself yearly by advice of her Privy Council, and the Lord President of the Marches, Justices of Wales and others the nobility attending her royal person. He has his patent[185] yearly under the great Seal of England, and a writ of aid, as they term it, and takes his oath before the Lord President of the Council of the Marches or Justices of Assize of Wales by *Dedimus Potestatem* to them directed,[186] wherein the Sheriffs in Wales do find themselves more grieved than the Sheriffs in England touching the taking of their oath, for that therein they are forced to more trouble and charge than Sheriffs in England and the Queen thereby worse served, which is this: the Sheriffs in England have writs of *Dedimus Potestatem* to some nobleman, Knight or discreet gentleman at home in the county to receive their oath and to take recognizance of them with sufficient sureties[187] to Her Majesty's use for answering the Queen's debts and duties which are by him gathered whereby the Sheriff is not forced to travel out of his country, and also in the country at home is able to procure very sufficient gentlemen of good ability to be his sureties; whereas the Sheriffs of Wales are forced to sue forth their *Dedimus Potestatem* to some of the Justices of Assize of Wales most commonly who dwell no nearer than Shropshire or Gloucestershire, being a hundred miles distant from diverse parts of Wales, whereby the Sheriffs are forced to ride far from home out of their country to their trouble and charge being always about Christmas when the ways are most deep, the weather most foul and the day at the shortest, and for their sureties, although they might and would find sufficient gentlemen in their country that would willingly be bound for them as well for the due execution of their office, as to yield a true and just account before the auditors.[188] Yet loath they are to travel so far from home at that time of the year, whereby the said commissioners that so take the Sheriff's recognizance, are forced to take simple sureties to Her Majesty's use, as most commonly the host where Mr Sheriff lodges, or some of the Sheriff's men or suchlike, or else to be without any whereby damage might ensue to her Majesty saving that most commonly they are chosen of such honesty and sufficiency that it has not been often seen or heard, that the Sheriff's bonds[189] have been called in question. But yet it may in time so fall out that it may come in question, and Her Majesty hindered, all this would be remedied, if order were taken for granting the *Dedimus Potestatem* to sufficient gentlemen at home in the country, where sufficient sureties might be had with ease.

 This inconvenience has been lately moved to the late Lord Chancellor and other of Her Majesty's Privy Council[190] who have thought it very reasonable that it should be redressed. But that the words of the statute made for the ordinance of Wales anno 34 Henry the Eighth cap. 26 is so strict in this point that the Sheriffs of Wales shall make and take oaths and acknowledge recognizance such as is used in England before the Lord President and Justices of Wales[191] or one of them by virtue of *Dedimus Potestatem* to be directed for the same; by which words the *Dedimus Potestatem* must be directed to the Lord President and Justices of Wales or to some of them and to none other, and therefore it must be remedied in the Parliament and not elsewhere, as answer has been made upon these motions.

And the inconvenience is not only troublesome to the Sheriffs of Wales alone but, which is more grievous, the Escheators of Wales are, by the words of the statute aforesaid, tied to the like inconvenience for taking of their oaths and acknowledging their recognizances as the Sheriffs are, which Escheators are chosen most commonly of a meaner degree of gentlemen than the Sheriffs are, and such as greatly complain that they are forced to such travel and charge for so mean and fruitless an office for they are forced likewise to receive their oaths by commission before some of the Council of the Marches or Justices of Wales as is aforesaid of the Sheriffs, which were also a thing very fit to be reformed, and would breed ease yearly in every shire of Wales, and the Queen would be better and more willingly served; for the charge and trouble of taking the oaths of these Escheators is not without great hindrance to the men, and the office itself yields no profit which makes them complain; and therefore surely methinks the Knights and Burgesses of the Parliament might do well to consult hereupon and to seek redress hereof, which would breed both the ease and benefit of their country and also the better security to Her Majesty.[192]

Now I have told you one inconvenience united to the office of our Sheriffs in Wales, I would briefly describe part of his duty. He is the chief officer of trust and credit in the shire; he does execute all process out of the Exchequer, Common Pleas, Star Chamber, Court of Wards, Court of Requests to him directed; out of the King's Bench there runs no process into Wales, saving writs of error, which are directed to the Justices of Assize, and process upon statutes and recognizances acknowledged there.[193] The Sheriff also is to execute all process out of the Great Sessions, Quarter Sessions and from the Coroner, Escheator and other officers and commissioners, he returns all Juries for trial of all causes between party and party, and for trial of life and death he names and returns the Great Inquest[194] and Second Inquests. In the Great Sessions and Quarter Sessions he keeps and has the charge of the gaol and all manner of prisoners; he is to do and serve all executions whatsoever, be it of goods, lands, life or limb, he is to do all. He must execute all lawful process, precepts and commandments of the Lord President and Council of the Marches and from the Justices of the Peace; he is, as I said before, the only minister and officer to execute all lawful mandates, writs, process and commandments, and to end with few words he is Bailiff of the whole shire and the shire is termed in law his Bailiwick. The Sheriff is charged with collections of all the Estreats[195] sent unto him of the Great Sessions, Quarter Sessions, Counties, Hundreds and Sheriffs' Turns, and all other issues, fines and amerciaments due to the Queen's Majesty whatsoever within his Bailiwick, and is to account therefore. Also in express words by the said statute of 34 Henry the Eighth made for the ordinance of Wales the said Sheriffs are charged to answer the Prince of all felons' goods, and goods of outlaws, waifs, strays, forfeitures and all escheats whatsoever,[196] for the words of the statute is that the King shall be answered thereof by the hands of the Sheriffs, and yet it is seen that the Escheators do intrude themselves and intermeddle with gathering of strays which should seem by the said statute to be the Sheriff's duty and charge and not the Escheator's.

BARTHOL: I have during my being in London heard grievous complaints by those that have been Sheriffs in England touching their accounts in the Exchequer, how they are hardly handled and pass the time with much toil and labour to their great cost.

DEMETUS: Among other the manifold benefits that we in Wales receive by our proper laws so graciously provided for us, by our dear and dread sovereign King Henry the Eighth we enjoy one great ease in that which you now speak of touching on Exchequer in Wales, for we by the same law (as I before somewhat touched) have an Exchequer appointed for every three shires in Wales, and the Queen's Majesty's Auditor and Receiver of Wales, and the Chamberlain are the Barons thereof.[197] Before them even here at home do our Sheriffs in Wales, Escheators and customers[198] pass through their accounts with such ease and small fees, as it seems unto them no grief at all, where they are so well used that few depart discontented. Before them also do all the Queen's Majesty's tenants pay their rents and farms. Her Highness is content to send her officers home to us unto the country to receive her revenue which is a greater benefit than most men do consider. One only kind of accounting does most trouble us in Wales, which is the Collectors of the Subsidies[199] in Wales, who are forced to pass their accounts in the Exchequer at Westminster to their great trouble and charge, and as beneficial were it to Her Majesty to have the same paid to her Receiver here in the country, with the rest of Her Highness's revenues of this country, as to receive the same at Westminster, and truly I think if the Knights and Burgesses of Wales in Parliament when such subsidies are granted would consult together, and have the same moved in Parliament it would easily be obtained, it would be great ease to the country at all times hereafter.

BARTHOL: Methinks you have not spoken all this while of a more material matter nor that might be brought to pass with more ease, if the gentlemen of your country would endeavour themselves thereto.

DEMETUS: So it is in my conceit an easy matter, and now that I have shown you that the Sheriff is chiefly a minister to execute the commandments of other her Majesty's officers, and where and in what things he is charged, now will I briefly touch the office of Justice committed to him which is but small, for he is only a Judge but in one Base Court, and that is the County Court which I have mentioned before (but of late years the Sheriffs of Wales have usurped and of their own authority newly erected)[200] and certain Hundred Courts, wherein he judges of such matters as before I have said, and there his Bailiffs are the ministers. I said before the Sheriff keeps his County monthly, which Court, of all the Base Courts of the shire, should be the chiefest, and these new erected Hundred Courts are held every fortnight in every hundred, but as I have heard of those that are learned in the laws of this land it is without any warrant or authority that they keep the same so.

BARTHOL: I remember when you began first to speak of Sheriffs you said this County Court was the chiefest Base Court of the shire, and it was decayed because of the Hundred Courts

The Dialogue of the Government of Wales (1594)

which, as you say, now are kept without good authority. I pray you, let me learn the cause of this and what you think of these courts, whether they be necessary in the commonwealth or not,[201] for I have heard some say that if all the Base Courts as touching plea of actions and trial of causes were dissolved, and all matters tried before the Justices in the Sessions, it were much better and more ease for the country, for as I have heard there is a multitude of those Base Courts in this country far more than you have spoken of as yet, and that these are held by ignorant persons and unjust, and the poor people greatly molested thereby; and that which is worse, great perjury committed in them. And that the dissolving of them all would breed great ease and more justice. There are few of these courts in England, and why should there be so many and so noisome in Wales I would gladly learn.

DEMETUS: Doubtless there are too many of these Base Courts and in all or most of them too much oppression, chiefly by reason that they are held and kept by ignorant and unjust men as you have said. But whether the bearing with the great and manifold oppressions that are daily used in them as they now are kept, or the utter dissolving of them were to be wished, for the commonwealth of Wales, is a question worthy of disputation, and therefore, for your satisfaction, I will open unto you first the abuses in all those courts as they are now used. Then the inconveniencies that would follow by the utter dissolving of them, and lastly you shall hear my simple opinion how the malady might be cured and the patient preserved alive. I mean how the abuses might be taken away and so much as is good of those courts to be preserved, but this will require a long discourse and therefore I must request your patience.

BARTHOL: You bring me a bed, as they say, while you feed me with such matter, it is the chiefest thing I desire to know, you cannot please me better. I pray you proceed with your purpose.

DEMETUS: I will first begin with the County Court held monthly for that is the chiefest court, for it extends over the whole shire, wherein are least abuses to be found, for that it deals with fewest matters, for the same is so decayed that you shall scarce have a dozen persons at a County Court, and this court of all others would I wish to continue, and to be preferred before the rest, for in this court the Sheriff himself, the two

Coroners and the gentlemen and freeholders of the shire are Judges, and if these Hundred Courts, which are most exclaimed upon, were dissolved by the Sheriff and the plaints brought to the County there would not so many injuries and oppressions be done as now there are, for in the Counties the High Sheriff is commonly present himself, who always is of discretion, judgement and skill more than meaner men. Here also commonly are the Coroners present and other gentlemen would often resort thither, were the same maintained as it ought to be, where every poor man might have better right than in the Hundred Court before the deputy Sheriff, or most commonly before the deputy's deputy where little reckoning or account is made of the Judge, if there be any, as many times you have no Judge at all; also the County Court is commonly kept in some good town or village where entertainment may be had for gentlemen that come thither. Where the Hundred Courts are always held before the deputy Sheriff, being of less estimation than the High Sheriff is, and that commonly in some odd or obscure place or blind alehouse in every hundred where no man of account will resort. There is the deputy Sheriff or, as I said, his deputy Chief Judge, the Bailiff of the hundred quarter-master, his deputies, great doers, the Clerk of the Court, a Controller, the Attorneys unruly, the plaintiff exclaiming, the defendant disobedient, and all out of order, and yet there is a multitude of suits and suitors twenty times more than in the County. I have been present at a Hundred Court (where I often resort to see their fashions, and where I have heard 140 actions of debt and trespass[202] called in one court day, all under 40 shillings, some 20 shillings debt and under, and some 2 shillings, and yet most of all these due); here shall you see diverse petty-gentlemen that can do much among the meanest sort of people, commonly maintain matters openly in court and embrace the Jurors to pass with their friend or client, whether with the right or against it they force not, here have I seen Jurors pass against their evidence, being as apparent as the daylight at noon by the means of these barrators[203] and maintainers,[204] and if the actions were brought into the County Court, then would not these mean gentlemen once show their faces, or offer to speak before the High Sheriff, Coroners and other gentlemen that would be there, and then should the poor be better able to defend himself, In these Hundred Courts, because they are kept before mean persons, and in odd corners, it is very common to have actions recovered, the parties being never summoned nor attached. The first notice that he shall have will be a *Capias ad satisfaciendum*.[205] After judgement the party must needs to the gaol or make satisfaction there is no remedy for with us in Wales the writ of False Judgement shall be no *supersedeas*[206] for so is our law by special proviso in the statute.[207]

And therein it seems that this point was omitted by negligence of the makers of that law as of likelihood some things among so many provisos might escape, which now at this present might well be reformed, the inconvenience thereof now showing itself. For whereas King Henry the Eighth, having regard to the poverty into which Wales was brought in former time, His Majesty endeavoured therefore to devise laws in such sort as his subjects in Wales might have the use thereof with the least pain and toil, and best cheap, and therefore among other ordained that errors and false judgements given in personal actions in the Great Sessions,[208] which is the chiefest and highest Court in Wales, should be redressed before the Lord President and Council of the Marches in Wales, which Court, as I have before declared, is the best cheap court for the fees, and best expedition of suits of any court in England. And yet, in those Base Courts I now entreat of, if any erroneous judgement be given (as God knows there are too many) then is there no such necessary proviso that the same may be redressed before the Council of the Marches, or elsewhere, saving that the party must sue his Writ of False Judgement[209] at the Common Law before the Justices of Assize which is so chargeable for the fees and so long ere it may be brought to pass that it is never worth the following. For such base sums as are recovered in these Base Courts, and yet many of those small errors, being put together, make a great oppression of the poor, and great and grievous are the complaints touching those erroneous proceedings in those courts, and it must be thought that seeing King Henry the Eighth had that care, that for personal actions in a court of so high authority as the Great Sessions is that the errors there should be redressed with such ease, speedy trial and small charge, doubtless if his Majesty had been remembered of the errors that might happen in these Base Courts, he would have provided as easy a redress for the same, if not more easy. For it is thought that the fittest place for the examining and redressing of those errors in those Base Courts were before the said Justices of Assize by English bill,[210] in their Chancery Court, where it might be done with good justice and small charge, and therefore this is another thing worthy to be redressed by Parliament.

BARTHOL: What is the reason that the mad people do so haunt this Hundred Court, and forsake the County where they might assure themselves to have better justice? I marvel at that folly.

DEMETUS: The only cause, as I guess, is the speedy recovery they hope to have, for the said Hundred Courts are held every fifteen days, whereas the Counties are held but once a month, but some suitors in the Hundred Courts make many times more haste than good speed, for let their causes be never so good or apparent some times it will pass against them. These Hundred Courts, I would wish they were forborne, and all the matters brought into the County Courts for the causes afore-recited which would turn greatly to the quiet of the country, the ease of the Sheriff and his deputy from posting[211] every day in the week to one hundred or other to keep those obscure disordered courts. I do here omit to tell you the great disorders and extortions committed by the annual *cymorthas* of those the Bailiffs of every of those hundreds.[212] I was reading in the middle of their commonwealth, even in this little pamphlet which you see here in my hand when you came to me [*Wherein I find their outrageous extorting and cunning shifting partly touched and laid down. But not half to the purpose as they use it.*][213] (And it is a lamentable thing to think how the poor people of Wales are unjustly molested by colour of these unlawful and new erected courts, being held without warrant or authority.

BARTHOL: And are not those Hundred Courts held by the Sheriffs in Wales warranted by law? I well remember that in most parts of Wales as I travelled, I have seen great assemblies of people together, and it has been always told me that it was the Sheriff's Hundred held there.[214] It is strange that all the

The Dialogue of the Government of Wales (1594)

DEMETUS: Sheriffs in Wales should err in a matter so grievous to a commonwealth; how comes it to pass that they are so kept if there be no warrant for the same?

DEMETUS: Surely Sir, I shall tell the cause and the error whereby these courts were first begun, and how the same are hitherunto continued, first, as I told you, King Henry the Eighth in the 27th year of his reign, having a purpose to have his Dominion and Principality of Wales to be governed by the selfsame laws as the realm of England was, did divide the country of Wales into thirteen shires and ordained laws for the government thereof,[215] as near the laws and administration of justice used in England as the state of Wales could then permit; and afterwards in the 34th year of his reign did ordain further institutions and ordinances for the government of Wales, among which it is ordained that the Sheriffs in Wales should keep their Counties monthly, and their Hundred Courts for pleas under 40 shillings as is used in England, and that the King should have fines, issues, amerciaments and forfeitures lost and forfeited in the said Counties, Hundred Courts and Turns to his own use;[216] by which words as the best opinions are, was not meant, nor does erect any new Hundred Courts, where none was used before; but that such Hundred Courts as were before the making of the said statute should be kept by the Sheriffs after such form and fashion as Hundred Courts were kept in England, and that the words and meaning of the statute is, not to erect new Hundred Courts in every hundred of Wales, but only to reduce the form and manner of keeping those that were ancient Hundred Courts before the said statute to be kept as Hundred Courts in England are and were kept.

BARTHOL: Were there Hundred Courts kept in some parts of Wales before the said statute, and in some places none?

DEMETUS: Yes, verily, for in the shires of Anglesey, Caernarfon and Merioneth, and in part of Flintshire there were ancient Hundred Courts called in the ancient British tongue commotes kept every fifteen days in every hundred by the Sheriffs' Bailiffs made in the twelfth year of King Edward the first who, when he had conquered Prince Llywelyn, the last Prince of North Wales of the British line, he divided that part of Wales, which the said Prince Llywelyn possessed, into shires, and ordained Sheriffs and writs and process after the course of the Common Laws of England;[217] and that the Bailiffs of the commotes,[218] which are the Sheriffs' Bailiffs, in every hundred in those shires, should hold their courts and do justice to the people. But now by the said statute of 34 Henry the Eighth, the King would have the Sheriffs themselves to keep those Hundred Courts and not the Bailiffs,[219] and that after the form as hundreds are kept in England which, by the opinion of the best lawyers of our time, was the meaning of the words of that statute, and ever since the Sheriffs of those shires have kept those Hundred Courts and not the Bailiffs, as they did before the said statute and for a long time after the said statute of 34 Henry the Eighth; none other Sheriff in Wales kept any Hundred Courts but the sheriffs of these four shires only; for within these shires where the said ancient hundreds are kept, there is no manor nor Court Baron kept or held, nor Leet kept and unto these ancient hundreds, being in number 23 viz in Anglesey six, in Caernarfonshire ten, in Merioneth four, and in Flintshire three. There are of ancient time suitors that owe suit and hold their lands by the Queen's Majesty by doing suit to these hundreds, whereas there is not one suitor that owes suit to any of the rest of the hundreds in Wales; and by the law of this realm there can no Hundred Court be kept without suitors, but all new hundreds newly divided since the said 27th Henry the Eighth were compacted and made of diverse lordships and manors, some being Her Majesty's and some the inheritance of noblemen and gentlemen who have Courts Baron and Leets of ancient time belonging to each of them, and the freeholders of those manors do hold their lands by doing suit to the Courts Baron of the manors, and so do they to this day; and now since the erecting of these new Hundred Courts, the said freeholders and their tenants, inhabitants within the said Hundred Courts, are called and compelled to do suit and answer to these Hundred Courts to their trouble and vexation whereas they owe no suit to the same. They are also called to do suit to the Sheriff's Turns, twice every year, whereas their lords have Leets in the manor wherein they dwell.[220] To which Leet they are and were time out of mind tied to answer by reason of their residency and now are doubly vexed by answering to the Lord's Leet, and to the sheriff's Turn whereas by the laws if this land no person that dwells within the precinct of any Leet and by reason of his resiancy is tied to do suit to the same, ought to answer at any Sheriff's Turn.

BARTHOL: Is your law clear that no Hundred Court can be kept but where there are suitors that owe suit to the same Hundred, and if the law be so and that you are able to prove that to these Hundreds which you call new there belong no suitors? Methinks this thing of itself were able to overthrow those Hundreds by the judgement of the law only without more ado; but how will you prove that these are new Hundreds, and that there are no suitors belonging to them, seeing it is a thing of so long continuance as this is?

DEMETUS: These two things are easily made manifest without any great proofs for the statute of 27 Henry the Eighth, which divides Wales into shires says that immediately after that Parliament, there should go forth commission under the Great Seal to certain persons to divide the shires of Carmarthen, Pembroke, Cardigan, Monmouth, Brecknock, Radnor, Montgomery, Glamorgan and Denbigh into so many hundreds as to them should seem convenient whereby it may appear plainly[221] that there was no hundreds in these shires before; and for the other shires viz. Anglesey, Caernarfon, Merioneth and Flint, there is no speech of dividing those into hundreds for that there were ancient hundreds in them before the said statute, otherwise they should have been named with the rest to be newly divided; and further to confirm and prove that the said commission went forth and that the shires so named were divided into hundreds and the same returned into the King's Chancery at London, it is made manifest by the Statute of 34 Henry the Eighth, where it is said, that the limitation of hundreds late made by virtue of the King's commission, returned into the Chancery shall stand and be of force,[222] by which it appears plainly that there were no hundreds in these nine shires before the said statute of 27[th Henry the Eighth], and then it must follow that there were no hundreds, there could be no suitors belonging to those hundreds.

BARTHOL: And what is the reason that there must be suitors to a Hundred Court, and is it so requisite in all other courts?

DEMETUS: Our law of England holds that in all Base Courts as County, Courts Baron and Hundred Courts, there must of necessity be two suitors at the least or else there can be no court kept, for they are Judges of the Court, and where there are no suitors, there can be no court; another thing is, where there is no suitor there lies no writ of false judgement, for any erroneous proceeding therefore in a writ of false judgement it is a good return to say there are no suitors in that court who must certify the record.

BARTHOL: It will be said that Sheriffs may prescribe to keep those Hundreds, and how will you answer that?

DEMETUS: They cannot prescribe, for these yearly Sheriffs that now we have are not ancient officers but newly erected by the said acts of 27 and 34 of Henry the Eighth,[223] and their authority also grounded by the said statutes, and therefore they can claim no more authority than is given them by those statutes. Another matter is that stops them from prescription, they have no certain estate in their office but are changed yearly and a tenant-at-will and Sheriff, or such like officer, that has no certain estate in his office, cannot prescribe in any by our law of England, so that prescription will not help them in this case.

BARTHOL: When began they to keep those Hundreds, was it immediately after the statute of 34 of Henry the Eighth or since, and what is the reason that the Sheriffs are so greedy, to keep those Hundred Courts, and what remedy is there to force them to leave them of?

DEMETUS: As I learn by men of years, there were no Hundred Courts kept in these shires till the latter time of Queen Mary or in the beginning of this Queen's reign that the Sheriffs of these parts, seeing those of the three shires of north Wales keep their ancient Hundred Courts in every of their hundreds, and imagining that the former words of the statute would warrant them so to do, by example or rather ill sample began to do the like, and finding therein a gain are loath to forego the same, especially for that they sell their bailiwicks at higher prices, by reason that the Bailiffs have hereby a colour to extort and poll the poor people the more, and therefore will buy their offices the dearer at the Sheriff's hands.[224] How to force them to forego the same, it is hard to say; for there has been diverse attempts offered. For the Council of the Marches, a few years past, sent down strict commandment to all the Sheriffs of

Wales, that those Hundred Courts should be given over and some Sheriffs, have been grievously fined before the said Council for keeping of them, and some Sheriffs as those of Brecknockshire, have given over the keeping of these courts and so have they been forced in diverse hundreds in Montgomeryshire and Glamorgan upon complaints made against the Sheriffs. And the opinion of the learned is, that by *Quo Warranto*[225] these courts are to be overthrown and that an action of Trespass lies against the officer that takes any goods or distresses for any matter recovered in those unlawful courts so does an action of false imprisonment for any that is imprisoned upon any recovery had in the same courts, and these are some means for people to relieve themselves from these oppressions.

BARTHOL: Methinks that you omit one material point not spoken of as yet that greatly concerns this matter; methought you find the words of the statute were that the Sheriffs in Wales should keep their Hundred Courts as is used in England, do the Sheriffs keep Hundred Courts in every hundred in the shires in England as you say the Sheriffs do in Wales. Methinks that it is a thing material to be learned?

DEMETUS: No certainly, for I have been diligent in searching for this and I find by those that have been under-sheriffs and best known of this matter that there are no Hundred Courts held by the Sheriffs in every hundred in England as is used in Wales, for in the shires of England next adjoining to Wales as Herefordshire, Worcestershire and Shropshire, the sheriffs do not keep any Hundred Courts at all. But where any courts are kept, the same are kept by the lords of the hundreds, or else have them in fee-farm[226] from the Queen or in lease, and the Sheriffs do not intermeddle with keeping of any of those Hundred Courts; and if there be any Hundred Courts kept in any other shires in England by the Sheriffs, the same is in some ancient hundreds that have suitors belonging to the same hundreds as I said before of the 23 ancient hundreds of north Wales; and in those hundreds where the Sheriffs of England do keep such hundreds, there are no Courts Baron nor Leets kept to vex the people with double suits as they do here in Wales, and these Hundred Courts in England are very rare and but very few shires to be found, for in a shire that has four and twenty hundreds, it is much if there be two such hundreds in the shire that the Sheriff keeps any Hundred Court and that but once every three weeks, and these be ancient hundreds annexed to the body of the county where the Sheriffs time out of memory, for many hundred years past have used to keep such courts; and yet will our greedy Sheriffs of Wales keep a Hundred Court in every hundred within their shires, and where there was never any kept before, as though there were such courts kept in every hundred in England, as some will not stick[227] ignorantly to affirm, which has made me diligent in learning out the truth as I have before declared. And that which is more, the shire of Monmouth,[228] being a new made shire out of Wales but yet guildable[229] under the English laws at Westminster and served by the Judges of Westminster who ride the English circuit, it being divided into six hundreds at such time as the other eight shires where the Sheriffs there do not keep any Hundred Court within any of the said hundreds in that shire, besides there was by the said acts of Parliament three new hundreds and out of the country of Wales and annexed to Herefordshire viz. the hundreds of Huntingdon, Wigmore and Ewyas Lacy,[230] so were the hundreds of Oswestry and Clun new made and annexed to Shropshire, besides diverse other lordships annexed to other hundreds of Hereford, Shropshire, Gloucestershire, and yet do not the Sheriffs of any of these shires offer to erect or keep any Hundred Courts in any of these places.[231]

BARTHOL: This seems strange for methinks they have as good warrant so to do as the rest of the Sheriffs, especially the Sheriff of the shire of Monmouth should do as the rest do, it being a new shire as the rest are.

DEMETUS: Indeed, I have heard of ancient men of the country that the Sheriffs of Monmouthshire, hearing that the Sheriffs of these parts had begun to keep these Hundred Courts did follow the like example there, but that the Lord Chief Baron, then riding that circuit, and other learned men finding fault therewith and finding it was not the meaning of the Parliament to erect any such new courts where none was before, forced the Sheriffs to relinquish the same, so that those Hundred Courts were kept there but for one year only. And now, for these forty

The Dialogue of the Government of Wales (1594)

	years, there has not any such Hundred Courts been held within that shire. But the Judges of this country have not had such care for these shires within their circuit, and therefore the Sheriffs, seeing they are borne withal, they still prosecute the same, the rather for the unlawful benefit of their Bailiffs, and other inferior officers who, with all greediness by colour of these courts, pill and poll[232] the poor people, I was reading in the middle of their commonwealth in this little pamphlet when you came unto me first as I told you before.)[233]
BARTHOL:	I was about to have asked you what pamphlet you were reading with such earnest attentive mind as I found you at my first coming.
DEMETUS:	It is a matter not altogether from the purpose that we have in hand. It is a little dialogue between Bryto and Phylomatheus touching the government and reformation of Wales,[234] but chiefly it notes the disorders and abuses thereof, but trouble me not now any further touching the same! But when we have ended this matter we will begin and read over this pamphlet; remember me when we have ended, least I forget it, for there is opened very much bad dealings.
BARTHOL:	I will not overslip such matter, but proceed you forward.
DEMETUS:	These Bailiffs use very great polling of the subjects yearly for they are changed yearly, and not suffered by the law of this land to continue in office above a year, and then must anew come in his place, who will follow the steps of his predecessors, and as much as he can of his own invention beside, they use to scrape and gather £20 or £30 and some of them much more in a year, so that it is thought a very great living to get a bailiwick, and they pay thereafter for it some £10, some £20 to have it for a year. All this must be made in the office, and his charges borne besides, and somewhat for his pains, or else it is a very ill bargain, and whereas the laws of this land do provide that they shall be removable yearly I know not what the reason should be, or what the mischiefs were in old time (for it is an old law) by suffering them to enjoy the office for many years or for life. But sure the mischief of our time is worse by changing of them, for now there is every year a hungry Bailiff placed who thinks to fill himself by fleecing others ere the year go about, and by that time his polling is ended there succeeds him another as needy as he, whereas if

they had it of continuance when they had well satisfied themselves, they would be the easier pleased and not continue greedy for ever, and I think the granting of these bailiwicks by patent for life by the Prince which now lately is begun, will prove beneficial to the country. Of this changing of officers yearly did the villein[235] of Germany complain to the senate of Rome, likening them to the hungry flies that fed upon the galled horse back wishing rather to keep the full-bellied fly still, then to receive new hungry flies to suck his blood continually. Of this change of English officers in Wales did Prince Llywelyn ap Gruffudd complain to King Edward the First by the Archbishop of Canterbury how that the King, often changing his officers in Wales, when some by polling had enriched themselves, others more hungry should be sent in their place afresh to fleece those whom the others had shorn as his words are.[236] And now because I would not be tedious I will leave there for so much. And to the rest of the Base Courts which we call Courts Baron; whereof there is in this country of south Wales an innumerable company for every manor or lordship, be it never so simple and small has now a Court Baron whereof you shall find a dozen in some parishes, but in the three shires of north Wales, it is not so. Diverse of these are also kept every fifteen days and held by stewards, for the most part ignorant men, unskilful (though wilful) in the law. These hold plea also of personal actions under 40 shillings as largely as is said of the County and Hundred Courts. [Where also much wrong and oppression is likewise in diverse of them];[237] diverse gentlemen are lords of these manors, but most are in Her Majesty's hands, which are ruled by as ignorant Judges (I mean deputy Stewards) as the rest are in these Courts Baron;[238] there is much injury done by ignorant and wilful stewards; I would I might live to see these enormities reformed in my poor country.

And now that I have told you part of the inconveniences and disorders of these courts, which I wish to be reformed, now shall you hear would ensue if these Base Courts were utterly dissolved. As you say, you have heard some of opinion, and no place left to sue for these small debts and wrongs which are under 40 shillings but before the Justices of Assize in the Sessions. And for the better understanding hereof you must know partly the trade of living that most of the poorer sort of people have to live by in Wales; and partly is to be considered the nature and disposition of the people. First, as touching the trade of life, the poorest husbandman lives upon his own travail, having corn, butter, cheese, beef, mutton, poultry and the like of his own sufficient to maintain his house.[239] He makes the apparel of him and his family of his own wool, and seldom uses any money, but those that want such necessaries are driven to buy altogether in a manner at days; for seldom buys any of the poorer sort anything for ready money. Corn, butter, cheese, wool and suchlike the poor man buys of his richer neighbour at days, and commonly their payments are from May to mid-November, for all that while is the country of Wales full of fairs; then are their cattle, sheep, lambs, swine, wool and other matters in prise so that he that has any of these to sell all the summer shall be sure of money. But from November till May they have nothing wherewith to make money: for within this country of Pembroke, whereof I chiefly use this present speech, and in the parts of Carmarthen and Cardigan shires next adjoining, to the same have no use of selling cattle in any market which use a great part of this buying at days, so that whatsoever you sell, they will have day of payment till summer, or else they will not deal with you. Likewise for their iron, salt, oil, linen-cloth, pitch, tar, spice and suchlike things that are to be had out of towns, the townsman sells the same at days also; and of all these things that he buys he seldom or never buys the value of 40 shillings of any one man. In this sort one man will be indebted £10 to ten several men or more, and to one man, especially to the Mercer you shall find 300 debtors and not one sum amount to 40 shillings, and some very small sums, whereof if diverse do pay, yet more break day[240] and suffer themselves to be sued, so that, as I said before, I have been present at a Hundred Court where has been 160 actions called and after they are once attached and the action entered, every man makes what shift he may for money to pay, and some pay the first court when there is but 8 pence or 12 pence charges, some for want of ability suffer the action to be recovered with 3 or 4 shillings charges, and of these you have many a score recovered and paid in these Base Courts every year. And thus much for the order and trade of living used by the poorer sort of people in Wales, whereby this multitude of small actions arises; for there are none but the poorer sort of people that are sued in those Base Courts. And as touching their disposition and nature, there are here in Wales many busy people greatly given to quarrels and suits; yes, some of the poorest wretches that you meet on the way will be soon moved.

And also you perceive how most of the country is champion,[241] and without enclosures, so that they till in the open fields in many and several pieces and keep their cattle in summer by herds among the pieces and fields of corn, and therefore one neighbour shall trespass another much, and thereupon all the summer time rise many actions of Trespass[242] which are entered and sued in those Base Courts, and surely in some points those Base Courts are not unnecessary: for I know some, that if it were not for fear of those actions of Trespass, would utterly spoil their neighbours, by eating up their corn and meadow, which they more carefully forbear fearing to be sued.

And now to answer that which you said unto me at the beginning, that it were convenient that all those actions were brought before the Justices of Assize in the Great Sessions, where law and justice is to be had indifferently. Surely, in my opinion, it were not fit so to do for two causes. The one is, it were too long a delay for poor men to stay the trial there for every small matter, for then the plaintiff should stay a whole year most commonly, for that the Sessions are held but twice a year. But another cause there is which would spoil and rob the poor of the country, that is, the great charges that should be recovered in every action, for there are few recoveries there under 30 or 40 shillings costs, and I have seen in an action of Trespass commenced there more for malice than good cause as it fell out in proof where the plaintiff recovered half penny damages and the costs drew almost to £3, and if this order should be taken in a short time it would utterly beggar[243] the poorer sort of people and almost all the country; yes, there would be more fees in these small actions recovered every year than ten of the greatest subsidies Her Majesty has out of Wales. And therefore I think they were not well acquainted with the state of those matters that would wish all these small actions to be brought to the Great Sessions, or that would have these Base Courts utterly dissolved, but rather the inconveniences and abuses thereof reformed. Now judge you whether were it a greater inconvenience to allow of these Base Courts in Wales with some of their abuses, or utterly to dissolve them and to bring this multitude of small actions to the Great Sessions.

BARTHOL: For the enormities in these Hundred Courts you say and think it would be sufficiently redressed so that those Hundred Courts were reduced to the County Court. But how can you devise to redress the defaults of these Courts Baron?

DEMETUS: It is not very easy indeed: for the gentlemen that are owners of these Courts would think themselves wronged to be deprived of their inheritance by suppressing them. But the injuries of these Courts Baron are nothing to be spoken of in respect of that which is done in the Hundred Courts: for there are new officers yearly elected, both the Deputy Sheriff and Bailiff and oftentimes the Clerk, and they are such most commonly as never before knew what office, law or justice meant, but whatsoever they think fit that they use for law, much like young practitioners in physic who, to practise their skill, murder many of their patients. Whereas the Stewards, Clerks and Bailiffs of these Courts Baron do still continue without removing, and are somewhat better skilled and practised in their rooms than those that never were acquainted therewith before. Yet might there far better order be taken with these Courts Baron than there is presently. But those Courts Baron do daily increase in number and spring up where none were before, and those that in ancient time never held plea, do now, by the example of other courts likewise hold plea. And who so would enter into the ancient and first erecting of these manors in Wales should soon discern that but few of them ought to hold Cognizance of Plea:[244] for there are many lordships and manors in Wales held of and under other lordships and manors higher than they, and are then Lords paramount,[245] which lordships paramount only for the most part have cognizance of Plea belonging to them throughout their precincts, and in such case the mean manors, although they have a Court Baron to call their tenants together to enquire for the lord's profit and casualities, yet had they never any authority to hold plea, but that is encroached of late years, and yet daily do as I said by the example of other courts: and if such search and view of diverse ancient records yet extant to be seen in the Tower of London[246] and in the Exchequer were duly had and those petty courts reformed accordingly, I think in some shires of Wales where there are now forty courts kept scarce fewer would be admitted to hold plea as aforesaid, and then these few might be provided of honest and discreet gentlemen to be stewards there, that would see justice administered indifferently.

Also Her Majesty might easily reform the disorders in Her Highness's courts by uniting diverse of these manors together, and thereof to make a court as concerning holding of pleas and determining of those kind of actions and for the same to appoint some one discreet gentleman to be Judge thereof that would and could sufficiently discharge the same. The like might diverse gentlemen do that have diverse small manors near adjoining the one to the other unite them and make one manor of diverse.

And as overseers of all these courts, if Her Majesty's Justices of Assize had some special authority committed unto them in their circuits to hear the complaints of the oppressed and to reform the disorders in those Base Courts from time to time according as they should find the inconveniences spring up, and if need were to associate some fit gentleman adjoining to sit with the steward in court to see justice ministered indifferently, and to lay down order and prescribe rules both for the fees and for the proceeding in all matters there, and for the punishing of the wilful Juries that obstinately and wilfully will pass against all evidence, and of the maintainers and barrators that haunt and follow these courts. And that the said Stewards (being reduced to a few by the means aforesaid) in doubtful matters might resort unto the said Justices for their directions. And to the end that none should be admitted to be Steward or deputy Steward but such as were of sufficiency, I could wish that the said Justices of Assize in their circuits should first have the examining of their skill therein and to be allowed by the said Justices before he should exercise the office, and the like for the sufficiency of the Clerks of those courts. For doubtless the ignorance and negligence of these Clerks already is and in time will be the cause of much trouble and disinheriting as well of her Majesty and other lords of manors and also of the tenants of those manors, and will be the cause of much trouble hereafter, if these faults of ignorant Clerks be not with speed looked into. And these or the like cares and reformations being had, doubtless those courts would, in a short time, come to good order, and would breed much good and great ease in the country, for it is necessary to have some convenient number of those Base Courts for the determining of small actions at home near the poor people that cannot travel far to seek law for so small causes, nor into courts of great expenses. And as Henry the Eighth (as it appears in the statute for the Ordinance of Wales anno 34)[247] did intend to send forth commissioners to enquire of the multitude or corporate towns in Wales, which of them were fit to be dissolved and which necessary to be retained, and where it were fit to erect new, so I could wish there were the like order taken for commission to be granted to enquire touching these Base Courts to reform the disorders thereof, to limit the number, to annex and unite them as were most fit as I have said before, and to allow some three or four in a shire, so that the poor suitors might travel and return home in a day, and not be driven to far journeys, nor yet to live in a country without law.

There are over and besides those Base Courts before recited diverse other courts in corporate towns which are accounted Courts of Record[248] for personal actions: for there they hold plea of debt, trespass, detinue,[249] trespass on the case and other personal actions, of what sum soever, were it £1,000 or more. And there are for the most part very unfit Judges to hear and determine matters of such great sums as oftentimes are depending before them. For they are mostly commonly removed yearly, and chosen by the commons of such corporations, sometimes very simple men, such as their simple corporations yield, I mean not of the good towns in Wales, but of diverse villages and hamlets in sight which, in old time, were incorporated by the Lords Marchers of those manors and still continue boroughs. Which King Henry the Eighth, as it appears by his statute made as aforesaid, had a purpose to grant out a commission under the Great Seal to enquire of, and upon certificate thereof[250] to dissolve those that were unnecessary, and retain them fit to be retained, and to erect others that should be fit. But if any such commission went forth, as I think there went none, sure I am there was nothing done. For there are in Wales yet a multitude of very mean villages scarce having six houses or cottages, and yet are allowed for corporations and boroughs, and in many of these they hold plea of great sums unfit for such Judges as are commonly in those places. I would wish the like order to be taken for these, as I have said for the Courts Baron in diverse points.

And now, to end I will show you of two manner of courts, which are in effect but Base Courts. Yet have I heard that the law of this land accounts them Courts of Records, and these are the Leets and the Sheriff's Turns, but in these courts the injuries done there are not very great, for that they are not courts that hold plea of matters between parties, but only are courts of inquiries for the smallest misdemeanours, as for affrays, assaults, rescues, bloodsheddings, pound breaches,[251] stopping highways, false weights and measures, and diverse other annoyances in the commonwealth. And those that are found guilty there are amerced[252] according to their offences, and therefore of those courts you shall hear but few complain.

These courts are many in number; for you have but few manors but have two Leets which are held every year before the steward of the manor and a Jury sworn to inquire of matters there, and in every hundred there is a Turn held twice every year before the Sheriff or his deputy, and these courts are great courts for assembly of people but little to do there, for all the inhabitants either do or should appear there then. And these be very ancient courts in England (but for the most part newly erected in Wales);[253] and in diverse parts of the realm called by diverse names.

And now Mr Barthol, I have as well as my memory and skill will serve, declared unto you the whole government of Wales as it is at this present, with the ordinary courts we have for our government from the chiefest to the meanest, and the proceedings in each of them, with such defects as I did judge in my conceit fit to be reformed, wherein I desire you so to think of everything that I have said, as of one man's opinion. For in conferring with others perchance you shall find them of other opinions *Quia quot capita tot sensus*,[254] every man as he likes best and, as you pass through the rest of Wales, you may briefly remember such things as you heard of me, and inquire the opinions of other men and hear their reason and censure. And thereof, as out of a well-furnished garden, with many flowers, gather the chiefest to make one sweet-smelling nosegay.[255]

BARTHOL: I thank you good Mr Demetus for your great kindness and pains herein showed to me being a stranger craving pardon for my boldness with you.

DEMETUS: There needs no pardon herein, for it as much pleased me to inform you hereof, as you to be thus by me rudely instructed, for I hope ere you depart hence (for I mean to entreat to be your host for two or three days) to learn of you matters to my great contentment, where also you shall see other matters that I hope will breed in you some contentment.

BARTHOL: The courtesy I find in you is such, that if I might any way pleasure you I should think myself very happy and bound to do it with a willing mind, but by your patience a little more of our former matters.

I perceive by that you have said that Wales, by the hard usage thereof in old time and by the evil magistrates and intolerable laws, grew to be disobedient to laws and uncivil among themselves. For seeing the Princes had no care of their good government but sent Judges and officers to spoil and oppress them, and ordained laws not to govern with civility, but to oppress with cruelty, the people grew disobedient to those laws and undutiful to those Princes, and after long oppressions grew desperate of themselves, choosing rather to die in defence of their ancient laws and liberties, than to live under such unnatural and unreasonable laws as were ordained for their government until that Henry the Eighth took care of the same, so that Wales at this day is a commonwealth newly reformed and not as yet settled in perfect estate. And now being governed by these good laws, since the 27th Henry the Eighth some defects[256] in that new settled government do appear, which with more ease might be redressed, then at the first the same was erected, and in time by little and little the same will grow to a perfect well-governed commonwealth. But I much marvel how upon the first alteration of the government of Wales (when King Henry the Eighth utterly abolished the Welsh laws and brought in the English laws)[257] the country received the same quietly and without great grudging and some rebellion, for new government and alteration of ancient laws is not easily received into any commonwealth without tumults, and innovation in government is accounted very dangerous in a commonwealth. And yet I hear not of you that Wales repined at altering their laws or inducing a new government.

DEMETUS: So it is dangerous to alter anything in a well-governed commonwealth, such as Wales then was not. But to such as live in bondage and slavery, innovations and alterations from cruelty to justice are sweet and pleasant; and then we, the poor Welshmen, that were cruelly oppressed by our governors,[258] I mean the strangers that were Stewards, Justices, Sheriffs and others, who had law to judge as pleased them, and not to justify as we deserved, were very glad of those new laws, and embraced the same with joyful hearts. And this caused those laws to be received so quietly whereas in times past many a bloody battle was fought before they received the cruel English laws and lawgivers wherewith they were oppressed.

BARTHOL: Surely these laws have brought Wales to a great civility from that evil government that was here in old time: for it is as safe travelling for a stranger here in Wales as in any part of Christendom, whereas in old time it is said robberies and murders were very common, (But since my coming into Pembrokeshire I have thought myself in the middle of England; I find the country to be so agreeable to the name of Little England as I have heard it called: how came it first to be so called?)[259]

[And yet (without offence unto you be it spoken) I was put in great fear how I should pass the upper part of Cardiganshire for it was told me that I must pass a place called Cwmystwyth where many thieves that lived as outlaws and some not outlawed indeed made their abode, and that they lived by open robbing,[260] but God be thanked I escaped their hands and they said that that place and thereabouts is

DEMETUS: never free from such persons. I pray you sir is it true and what should be the cause thereof? All the rest of Wales being so void of such as I hear and perceive it is.
Truly I am not acquainted with the place nor the persons.[261] Once or twice I have travelled that way; the place itself is very wild and desolate full of great and wild mountains and few inhabitants and thereabouts joins the three shires of Cardigan, Montgomery and Radnor together, being three shires in three several circuits ruled by three several Justices of Assize, which you cannot find in all Wales beside. And there such ill people, if they be pursued by one good Sheriff of one of these three shires they hope to be favoured of another. These two causes, as I think, makes them to draw together into that place above the rest of Wales.[262] But the fault indeed is in the gentlemen that are in authority thereabouts, the Sheriffs and Justices of the Peace, that they with more diligence and industry will not follow such bad people and their harbourers, and truly Sir, I am sorry to speak, I have heard that diverse of these gentlemen do not lose by those kind of spoilers and that it is very common that those thieves and outlaws do yearly compound and agree with those Sheriffs as soon as they come into office and reward them largely that they should not prosecute them eagerly for that year, and in this sort they live in companies, and will oftentimes come to the church and to fairs and markets and nothing said unto them. Those live upon the spoil of the poor and honest labouring people. And if they be thus supported and winked at by the Sheriffs and other gentlemen let those Sheriffs remember the saying of the Prophet: *Si videbas furem currebas cum eo* etc.[263] I would these things were diligently inquired of and some reformation provided, for doubtless, if the gentlemen adjoining would together endeavour themselves with all their forces and goodwills to suppress those, the kind of people there would not one be left in a short space. I have heard it reported for truth, and I partly believe it that any true man that has lost any cattle may come and talk with them at a place appointed in those mountains with a certain competent number of his friends and people with him so that the number be not such as shall be able to master the thieves, and there they will parley with him, and if any of the company of thieves have the man's cattle

unsold or spent they will deal honestly with him and take a reasonable sum of money of him to redeem his cattle and shall have a good pennyworth of his own.²⁶⁴ But if he chance to stay so long that the cattle be either sold or killed the thieves will tell him so plainly and wish him to spend no more labour in vain in seeking of the same. Thus they will give public meetings with any man that is desirous to speak with them, a thing that might seem strange in any other part of Wales, this only excepted.

BARTHOL: I am very sorry to hear this, and am heartily glad that I have escaped the danger and come into this quiet and civil country here of Pembrokeshire. Surely, it is a very quiet country, you promised at the beginning of our speeches that you would show some particular blessings of God bestowed by him more upon this country than upon the rest of Wales.

DEMETUS: The Lord be thanked for his blessings; truly we dwell and live here very quiet in a poor country and yet not void of God's blessings bestowed upon us, and we are of other countries about-noted to be and we ourselves must confess the same, that we are happy in three things, especially above other parts of Wales. The one is that ever since Wales was reduced to shireground we have been most happy for good, godly and grave Judges or Justices of Assize, diverse of them most singular and famous men as, namely first JUSTICE BROOKE,²⁶⁵ who afterwards was created Lord Chief Baron, a man greatly commended for his justice while he supplied the Rome of Justice in this country. After whom succeeded [JOHN] WALSHE,²⁶⁶ a man likewise well-spoken of, for these were all before my time. This man likewise was preferred to [blank line].

Then JUSTICE WYE,²⁶⁷ after whom succeeded MR RASTALL,²⁶⁸ a learned and just man and one well-acquainted with the people and affairs of the country for he dwelled here among us in the country. After him succeeded a worthy and learned gentleman MR GEORGE FETI-PLACE,²⁶⁹ who continued Justice till untimely death bereft us of him, his death being, as we take it, a plague to us unthankful; and unworthy people of such a worthy Judge, we thought ourselves so unhappy that we might never expect for the like worthy man to succeed him. And we thus with drooping heads and heavy hearts sorrowing the death of our worthy Judge and Senator. The Lord, by his mercy, moved our most dread sovereign Lady in the nineteenth year of her gracious reign to double our former happiness by sending unto us the most worthiest Judge that ever we or yet any other country had or ever we do expect to have. The Right Honourable SIR JOHN PUCKERINGE, KNIGHT,[270] now Lord Keeper of the Great Seal of England, who succeeding the said Mr Phetiplace, continued our Judge for the space of fifteen years to our great joy and comfort, who shortly after his coming to that place was worthily called to be Sergeant of the Law, and then of all the rest of the Sergeants of England by Her Highness was selected to be Her Majesty's sole Serjeant of the Law,[271] and so still continuing our Justice here until the 34th year of Her Majesty's most happy reign, that it pleased her most excellent Majesty worthily to call him to that highest type of honour in this land where we his poor beadsmen[272] of this his late circuit wish in heart and pray to that gracious God that has so blessed us by placing of him in that honourable place.[273] That our children's children out of this country may taste the sweetness that we do now by his honourable favour and countenance bestowed upon us daily, his lordship by his travel so many painful journeys into this our country, is grown so acquainted with the estate thereof as that of himself is able to discern the good man from the bad and can sever the sheep from the goats. Oh great happiness that has fallen upon this poor country by the first coming of this honourable man into the same.

And unto this honourable man was associated that worthy, wise and learned man MR RICHARD ATKINS,[274] who now you see our Chief Justice, a man for wisdom, learning and justice inferior to few before spoken of. A man that fears God, beloved for his virtue of the good and feared of the evil for his justice. He was the first associate that ever was in our country.[275] When the said Justice Atkins was preferred to be our Chief Justice, then was the other gentleman that you saw on the bench MR WILLIAM OLDSWORTH, ESQUIRE,[276] made the associate, who diverse years before had been as Deputy unto the said Lord Keeper in the place of Chief Justice, a man likewise both wise and learned and careful for the good of our country, which two Justices we so heartily affect and reverently obey and embrace their censures and decrees that you shall not in all their circuit once hear any man complain of any injustice or wrong done either voluntarily or negligently. The Lord preserve them long and long to rule among us here.

And here before I pass I will note unto you the hearty love and affection that the said Lord Keeper bears unto this poor country, which love he had in all his former government of the country showed in all his proceedings in so much that there passed no year but to his great pains he travelled in person to this country. And in the end, after his preferment to the honourable place he now supplies when his lordship saw he might no longer remain our Justice, yet to show his entire affection towards us and to grace this our poor country at the last instant would not yield up the office of Chief Justice until first his Lordship of himself had appointed the Great Sessions and made the writs for summoning thereof under his own *teste*, which writs are yet to be seen and do remain for ever of record among the records of *Sessione Quadragesima anno regni reginae ELIZABETHAE XXXIIIIth*.[277] Where you shall find *Teste Johanne Puckering Milite Domino Custode magni sigilli Angliae Justiciario ibidem*.[278] And this is a thing that we poor men here do greatly rejoice and not a little glory at saying that among all the records in England the like President is not to be seen. With this gentle *ultimum vale*[279] did this honourable man bid this poor country *adieu* and resign his office of Chief Justiceship there.

The second happiness noted to be in this our country of Pembrokeshire is the quietness and love that is among the gentlemen of this country, that hardly they are found asunder if they be in one town. But always together at meals and meetings in such loving sort that it is joyful to behold. So gentle in speeches, so courteous in behaviour each to other, striving to exceed in courtesy and kindness the one to the other, no one faction side or quarrel among them. So that it is a rare and seldom thing to hear of an affray or quarrel among the gentlemen of the chiefest sort, a most happy blessing in a country. With this is God pleased, the Prince well and carefully served, her laws obeyed and justice duly ministered.[280]

The third happiness and blessing which presently our country here enjoys is the store of good and godly preachers and ministers of God's Word that this our shire has in comparison of other parts of Wales, which is not so well furnished. There is within this shire eight or ten godly and learned ministers and preachers of the gospel which travel and labour in the Lord's vineyard, especially some above the rest that take their continual pains.[281] Although the rest now of late begin to be more slothful (yet not altogether idle) than they were before they obtained livings here in the country I number none here, but those that continually reside in the country upon their livings and travel among their neighbours, diverse other learned men we have beneficed in the country which, at times, visit their charge. Beside diverse good scholars and graduates that have livings in the country and yet not public preachers, this I reckon for a happiness for this poor shire of Pembroke thereby to put ourselves in remembrance how God has and daily from time to time does bless us above other parts of Wales with these and diverse other his benefits to the end that we might remember his blessings and be thankful unto Him therefore, and to frame our lives according to His Word that He may continue the same among us.

This last happiness also I have spoken to confound a shameless man that of late years to the slander of all Wales has not sticked[282] to put forth in print that all Wales had not so many preachers of God's Word as I have reckoned to be found in this poor and little country of Pembrokeshire, and yet was there at such time as he wrote his slanderous pamphlet diverse others besides beneficed in this country which since are departed, removed or deceased.[283]

This much of the happiness of our country have I spoken of in private unto you Mr Barthol which I would all our country people would consider of and with one heart and voice continually give God thanks therefore, left our unthankfulness, and being careless to consider from whom those his benefits do proceed he in his justice will deprive us from some or all of them. The loss of the least of which would make us wary of our livings,[284] life and country for what greater happiness can be to any country than first to have God's gospel preached sincerely, justice ministered uprightly and unity among the people. The Lord of his mercy continue it among us Amen.

BARTHOL: You truly said very well and recited three great benefits of God bestowed upon your country which, if the people of your country do not consider of, they are totally negligent of their own good. And doubtless God will deal with them no better than with His own chosen people the ISRAELITES, when they became careless and negligent of his laws by the plenty that grew among them by the like benefits as you now enjoy.[285] Then did he take away their good and godly Princes and sent them tyrants. Then he deprived them, then of their good and rightful Judges and sent them unjust and corrupt rulers and Judges that spoiled the people, robbed the fatherless and the widow. He took likewise from them his Prophets and diverse times sent them false Prophets, and in the end raised mighty enemies against them that utterly destroyed them and their country and delivered them captives to the cruel enemy. This was foretold them by the Prophets what should fall upon them; and why, which Prophets are daily read in your churches unto you and may be a warning unto you now of Pembrokeshire as it should have been to the Israelites for the selfsame God is still and not changeable.]

DEMETUS: Surely,[286] as I guess because the English tongue is generally and wholly spoken in the same, and in the lower part thereof no Welsh at all, so that they wonder when they hear any Welsh spoken, and will wonder and say, yonder is a Welshman. This country has been mere English since Henry the First's time, at which time Gilbert Strongbow, then earl of Strigoil or Chepstow, came hither with Normans and Englishmen and won most part of this country of Pembrokeshire together with Llanstephan, Oysterlow, Llanddowror and other parts which afterwards were taken away from Pembroke and added to Carmarthenshire, from Gruffudd, the son of Rhys ap Tewdwr, Prince of Wales,[287] and expelling the ancient inhabitants of the country inhabited the same with Normans and Saxons, whose posterity to this day continue in the country and still use only the old English tongue; which Normans and Saxons built the towns of Haverfordwest, Pembroke, Tenby and diverse others now decayed, built castles, villages and houses throughout the country and called the same after their own names, razing out the ancient names with the ancient inhabitants, and so by reason that this part of Wales continued English ever since, I judge that therefore this was called little England beyond Wales.

Another reason I will add for my fancy, which peradventure will please you to hear and methinks it makes for the name, which is this. The country of Wales being as our land of England, terms it a kingdom by itself and no part of the realm of England; when by conquest of the Princes thereof it was brought in subjection to the King of England, yet still did the laws of England hold it as a strange country and distinct from the realm of England, and therefore the King's courts of his laws viz the King's Bench and Common Pleas, would not make or send any process into any part of Wales, insomuch that it grew to be a maxim in our law *Quod breve Domini Regis non currit in Walliam*,[288] and yet it is apparent by diverse records to be seen that the King's Bench and Common Pleas at Westminster did direct the King's writ in the time of Henry the Sixth hither to the sheriff of Pembrokeshire for the trial of lands and offices within the county of Pembroke, and therefore I would infer that in old time the law of England, holding itself strange from Wales, yet would vouchsafe to acquaint itself and write to Little England beyond Wales, and this have I gathered to be another reason why it was called little England.[289]

BARTHOL: Truly, your reasons please me well, and surely it well deserves the name bestowed upon it. And for the three towns you have named, Pembroke, Haverford and Tenby, I have not found in Wales the like towns for entertainment and civil behaviour full of courtesy and kindness and served most plentifully of all things in their markets, whereby I judge your shire to be a big and large shire, otherwise the towns could not be so well served as I find them to be.

DEMETUS: Surely Mr Barthol it is not so, but it is one of the least shires of Wales, far less than it is accounted, and this opinion of yours has bred this poor country much wrong, for so I may well call it, for that of all the shires of Wales it only has been robbed and the chiefest members thereof stolen from it.

BARTHOL: Robbed? What mean you by that? I understand you not.

The Dialogue of the Government of Wales (1594)

DEMETUS: My eyes are full of tears to think of it, and my heart sorrowful that I am not of ability to be one of the least means to redress it, or at the least to acquaint some of the chief of the land how injuriously this poor country has been oppressed, hoping the motion of their good and honourable dispositions would make them not only to pity but also to relieve the same.

And to declare the means how this first came to pass, I must make known unto you, that by the Act of Parliament of 27 Henry the Eighth the King and his Council long before, by the advice of the best expert men of all Wales, consulted and considered how and into how many shires Wales should be divided, and what lordships were fit to be in every shire; and so in that Parliament it was concluded that Laugharne, Llanstephan, Llanddowror and diverse other members that are now held as part of Carmarthenshire, should be part and parcel of Pembrokeshire,[290] and so was it near of equal quantity, with some of the shires adjoining, and so it continued for the space of seven years viz until the 34 of Henry the Eighth at which time the gentlemen of Pembrokeshire, in courtesy and kindness to pleasure a stranger, made choice of a gentleman of worship of Carmarthenshire, but then dwelling in Pembrokeshire, to be Knight of that Parliament for Pembrokeshire, which gentleman, being thus chosen Knight for Pembrokeshire, imagined with himself how to work his native country of Carmarthen some good, being that countryman born and where his living wholly was, and to be in Pembrokeshire but for a time, and seeing in the Parliament there were diverse parcels of some shires taken and translated to be part of other shires, the said gentleman, finding this opportunity, procured the Knight of Carmarthenshire to move in Parliament to have the said lordships taken from Pembrokeshire and added to Carmarthenshire, upon which motion when the knight for Pembrokeshire (who should have withstood the same) yielded;[291] they were lost before any Pembrokeshire man knew thereof; and by this indirect means were these members lost and taken away from Pembroke and added to Carmarthenshire, being before far bigger and larger than the other, and so ever since has it continued. And not being so contented to defraud us as aforesaid, they under colour hereof, have also ever since withheld from us the lordships of Llanddowror, Llan-dawg and the Three Tranes,[292] and the same hitherto enjoyed as part of Carmarthenshire, although there be no mention made of them in that Act of 34 Henry the Eighth, whereof many inconveniences are like to ensue hereafter.

Which lordships so taken away and withheld are more in quantity than the fourth part of Pembrokeshire, so that this country is much lessened to Carmarthenshire grown well near twice as great as Pembrokeshire, and yet is Pembrokeshire, in all or most impositions, levies of men and other services always kept at as high a rate as Carmarthenshire, as though these members so taken away were still part and parcel of the same, and many times higher rated than Carmarthenshire, which makes the poor country to groan and grieve.

BARTHOL: Stay there, let me interrupt you while it is in my memory. I remember now one thing which you seem to deny, to prove that Pembrokeshire is as large or larger than Carmarthenshire, and therefore the Parliament might then upon good consideration take these parcels that you name from Pembroke to make Carmarthen of equal bigness with it, and this is so apparent as you cannot impugn it. Have you any skill in Cosmography or Geography?

DEMETUS: Yes Sir, I have some small skill in those things. I often overlook the maps of countries to see the situation of them, and to know the towns and other places of note with distances of them, wherein I take much delight.

BARTHOL: Have you seen the maps of the shires of Wales done by Mr Saxton in the year 1578?[293]

DEMETUS: I have seen them, and have them, and have often perused them.

BARTHOL: By those maps at the first sight it is so apparent and evident that Pembrokeshire is much longer than Carmarthenshire, and so shall you find it if you measure the length and breadth of both shires by a compass or thread, and therefore seeing his scale is true, as I trust you will confess, for the map makes proof thereof, and of itself cannot be denied but that Pembrokeshire must needs be larger than Carmarthenshire, how can you answer that objection?

DEMETUS: I perceive your error, and truly now since you spoke it, I think this might be one cause to induce the Lords of the Council to lay too great and unequal charge upon this country in setting forth men for Her Majesty's services into foreign parts: for diverse times Pembrokeshire has been charged to set out 150 men, when Carmarthenshire has set forth but 100,[294] and therefore I am glad you have moved this matter that I may open the fallacy therein, which is able to deceive any man by inspection and measuring of both maps, and therefore I pray you give me the hearing and I will discover a secret in art that will make plain that Pembrokeshire is far less than Carmarthenshire, although the map of Pembroke be larger in length and breadth than that of Carmarthen.[295]

BARTHOL: If you can do so, you shall make me marvel much: for if you admit that both the maps of these two shires be made by art in true symmetry, as geographers term it, it is, having the places laid down in true distance and right ells,[296] each to other as they stand on the earth, and allow that the one map be larger than the other, I think it must needs follow that the same country or shire must be larger than the other of the lesser map.

DEMETUS: So it seems to any man, yes to them of good skill in that art, but yet you may be deceived in that rule except you take great heed to the scales of both the maps; and therefore mark what I shall say unto you touching these two maps of Pembrokeshire and Carmarthenshire which, in this case, I will use for an example or demonstration to make you understand my sayings the better. True it is that the map of Pembrokeshire by measure is made longer than that of Carmarthen, by eight miles and a half by Carmarthen scale, and broader by five miles; but then you must mark the difference of the scales of both maps, and there you shall find the scale of Pembrokeshire to be of a larger size than that of Carmarthen by one fourth part and more. So that three miles in Carmarthen map contains more ground than four miles in the map of Pembrokeshire; for the scales of the maps of both shires are pricked[297] of ten miles apiece, and yet does the scale of ten miles of Carmarthen map make but six and a quarter of the other, so that in every ten miles there is three miles and three quarters difference. And this he was forced to do for that in one sheet of paper he did throng and compact together four whole shires, viz Carmarthen, Cardigan, Brecknock and Radnorshire besides such parts of Glamorgan, Hereford,

Monmouth, Shropshire, Montgomery, Merioneth and Pembrokeshire as fell within the square of that paper; and by thrusting so many shires into so little paper, he was forced to join the places nearer together to bring them all into true symmetry within so little a room, whereby his scale of force[298] must be very short and near together, and therefore in the map of Carmarthenshire, where an inch contains three miles and a half, in the map of Pembrokeshire an inch is but two miles. But when he came to Pembrokeshire, being the farthest and last shire of Wales that he described, he had no shire left to join with it in the whole sheet of paper, and therefore he opened the points of his compass and gave it a larger room than before; and therefore he placed every parish and town further asunder than he did in Carmarthenshire as may appear by sight of the maps; for in the map of Pembrokeshire it should seem that that country is not so well stored of towns and parishes, which Mr Saxton chiefly notes in his maps, and yet it is well known that it is as well inhabited for the quantity of most parts of Carmarthenshire. And this is the cause that the map of Pembrokeshire seems bigger than that of Carmarthen, because it contains as much paper as the other four shires, and this deceives any man upon the bare view of both maps. Do you understand my speeches or shall I make them plain unto you by some demonstration?

BARTHOL: I do well perceive your meaning, and if the scales of both shires do differ, as you say, then may it be as you have declared: but how may this be done by demonstration of maps that the truth may appear?

DEMETUS: It may be easily and truly done by amplifying the lesser map by squares (a thing usual and easy to be done of any mere Geographer) and reduced to the scale of the greater map, or contrary by lessening of the greater map to that of the lesser, and so to bring both maps to one self scale, and then the true quantity of each of them will appear to the view. Behold here I have the map of both the said shires reduced to one scale, and look, here is Pembrokeshire coloured over with red colour, and this is Carmarthenshire coloured with yellow as it was first limited before the adding of that part of Pembrokeshire to it, and this which is white in the middle between both is that part that was so taken away from

The Dialogue of the Government of Wales (1594)

	Pembrokeshire, and now do both shires appear in their true bigness, whereby you may perceive that Carmarthenshire was much larger than Pembrokeshire before the taking away of that part of ancient Pembrokeshire.[299]
BARTHOL:	This being true there were great reason it should be again restored, except there be some other cause, as that these lordships were part of Carmarthenshire before the same was limited to be parcel of Pembrokeshire by the 27th of Henry the Eighth, for I perceive Carmarthen and Pembroke were two of the eight ancient shires of Wales before the said statute of shireground;[300] for I remember that this was the reason of the restoring of the lordships of Hope[301] and St Asaph[302] back again to Flintshire whereof it had been parcel in ancient time, and by that statute of 27 Henry the Eighth the same was appointed to be parcel of Denbighshire which was found to be inconvenient,[303] and therefore by the statute of 33 Henry the Eighth, cap. 13 the said lordships were restored back again for the inconveniences found thereby.[304]
DEMETUS:	No, these lordships were no parcel of Carmarthenshire, but were ever since Strongbow's time parcel of the ancient county of Pembroke, for I have seen, which yet is forthcoming, a fair ancient deed made by Isabel, daughter to William Marshal,[305] sometimes earl of Pembroke, wherein she gives her lands of Oysterlow to Sir William Peverall, Knight,[306] to be held of the earldom of Pembroke,[307] which Oysterlow is that part that is furthest of this part taken away from Pembrokeshire, and parcel of Llanstephan. This deed was before the statute of *Quia Emptores terrarum*,[308] which proves that it was then parcel of Pembrokeshire, and so did it continue till the 34th of Henry the Eighth, and so were the rest of the lordships as Llanddowror, which is to this day held of the castle of Pembroke, as appears by the ancient and later Inquisitions thereof, which makes manifest that it was parcel of the ancient county of Pembroke before the said statute of 27 Henry the Eighth.
BARTHOL:	That makes also with you,[309] but what say you for the convenience of the inhabitants of this part, to which of both shires is this convenient for the ease and service of the inhabitants?
DEMETUS:	It is more convenient for the inhabitants to serve the Queen in all affairs with Pembrokeshire, for that they dwell generally

with more convenience to all the towns of resort in Pembrokeshire, as Haverfordwest, Pembroke and Tenby than to any town of Carmarthenshire, where usually assemblies are kept saving Carmarthen itself: for I have seen freeholders of Carmarthenshire dwelling within seven miles at the most of these towns of Pembrokeshire be forced to ride 36 miles to a Quarter Sessions of Carmarthenshire held at Llandovery. Also the inhabitants of Laugharne, Llan-dawg, Llansadyrnin, Pendine, Marros and other parts of that was taken away must pass a dangerous ford or venture over filthy passage to travel to Carmarthen, which is both troublesome and perilous without, whereas they have no such danger or trouble to any of the towns of Pembrokeshire; and for this and for many other causes it is more convenient for the inhabitants that they were reduced to be part of Pembrokeshire as they and their ancestors were from the beginning.

BARTHOL: You have answered all that I can object against you, and have very well satisfied me, that there are great reasons, and very requisite the same should be restored back again to your shire. I would you could as well satisfy the great estates of the land in whose power it lies to do you good.

DEMETUS: I will not leave you so, for besides that I have spoken, I have yet many reasons to persuade that it is fitter for the Queen's services, the state of the realm and more commodious both for Carmarthen and Pembrokeshires, that the same were restored and annexed to Pembrokeshire, which reasons I beseech you to hear, because I am desirous to acquaint you therewith. And first my reasons, that it is convenient for Her Majesty's services and the state of the realm it were so, are these.

Milford Haven stands in Pembrokeshire, whereby the country is subject to great peril of invasion, and therefore fitter that that country should be rather enlarged and strengthened than diminished and weakened that it might be the stronger to defend itself against any sudden invasion, and although these people dwell nearer Milford Haven, within the county of Carmarthen, than those of diverse parts of Pembrokeshire do, yet will they not be in that readiness of defence of the country as if they were part of the shire, for that they are under the commands and government of the Lieutenants and Magistrates of Carmarthenshire, and must stay till the rest of the inhabitants of Carmarthenshire be made ready to come together, which is a great delay and may hinder the service.

Pembrokeshire, by reason that Milford Haven runs up through the middle thereof, is divided and separated into two parts, so that if any enemies should land on the one side or part thereof, the other cannot speedily or conveniently come to the aid or rescue of the other by reason of the separation that is made by Milford; but this ancient part of Pembrokeshire is so seated that it is ready and indifferent to come to the aid and relief of either side of Milford, and therefore fittest to be annexed to Pembrokeshire as that parcel that is most ready and fittest to yield aid and relief against any enemy that should offer to invade the country.

Also, by the taking away of the said lordships from Pembrokeshire, the number of freeholders in Pembrokeshire is greatly diminished, for that now there are scarce 400 freeholders in the whole shire to serve at the Great Sessions, Quarter Sessions and all the other trials and services, whereas there are within Carmarthenshire above 1,500 freeholders to do service, so that by this means suits are much hindered and delayed in Pembrokeshire by reason of challenges[310] and the small number of freeholders, who also are overmuch burdened in those services to their great trouble and charge.[311]

Then that it were good for Carmarthenshire that it were restored to Pembrokeshire is manifest, by reason that the taking of these lordships from the one, and adding them to the other, Carmarthenshire is grown so great that the Justices of Assize there are much pestered with multitude of business in their Sessions as well of the gaol as of private suits[312] so that they are many times enforced to sit till nine or ten o'clock by candlelight, and yet often leave many matters undetermined, to the great trouble and hindrance of the inhabitants of the shire, whereas in Pembrokeshire they have not so much business as they have time to spare, but sometimes they arise from the bench having spent scarce an hour in a sitting.

Also, by taking away of these lordships from Pembrokeshire, there are diverse parish churches and part of the parish remaining still in Pembrokeshire, and the other part drawn to Carmarthenshire, so that the Constables and

Churchwardens of some parish, whose church is in Pembrokeshire, are sometimes dwelling out of the shire whereby Her Majesty's service and other affairs of both the shires are oftentimes hereby greatly hindered, especially touching the relief of maimed soldiers and the poor, whereby great contention has and daily does arise, and as yet cannot be decided, so that many of the inhabitants pay nothing towards these contributions in any of both shires, and some forced to pay in both shires.

Also Pembrokeshire, though it be not an island, yet has it as much land bordering upon the sea coast and both sides of Milford Haven and more than if it were an island by reason of Milford Haven that comes through the middle thereof sixteen miles up into the land; and therefore most of the inhabitants are mariners and seafaring men, so that the country yields but small store of land soldiers to serve in foreign services or defence of the country,[313] yet the same has always forced to set forth as many men for land services as any other shire in Wales, to the ever great burden and charge thereof, and therefore it were more reason it should have the ancient members thereof restored to itself again.

Also because they are so subject to peril of invasion, they have in these late years of trouble been enforced to train greater numbers of men than any two shires in Wales, and to arm themselves to the uttermost of their abilities, which other shires do not and thereby have greatly impaired themselves in wealth so that of late years Her Majesty's subsidy in that shire is decayed half in half and more of that it was heretofore. Also, by reason of Milford Haven and other good harbours on the sea coast, there happen many extraordinary events that put the country to great charges as of late the coming in of 300 soldiers for Ireland for Her Majesty's service anno 1597, and were wind-driven into Milford, and wanting victuals the country was forced to relieve them for the space of [blank] while they stayed for wind.[314]

Also in anno 1597, the coming thither of 75 Spanish captives which were relieved by the country for the space of eighteen weeks to their intolerable charge.[315]

Also, all or most of the maimed soldiers that come from Ireland do land in some port there, and by the statute the

Treasurers of that shire are forced to bestow money on them to conduct them to their shires,[316] and such as are impotent, sick or dangerously maimed remain oftentimes very long before they be able to depart the shire, and having nothing, the shire is forced to relieve them with meat, money and apparel, which has and still will be very chargeable to the shire, and therefore forced to bear and levy the greater sum yearly towards the relief of maimed soldiers then if these occasions were not.[317]

And oftentimes, by reason of the said haven and harbours, there are many pirates apprehended there and committed to the gaol of the shire, which stay long before commission come for their trial; and during their imprisonment the contrary is forced to find them, which often grows very chargeable and burdensome to so poor and small a shire, and therefore great reason that this country that is thus subject to these extraordinary charges, more than all the other shires of Wales, should have that part or portion of itself restored home again, to make it the more able to endure these burdens that other shires are not so subject unto.

Also Haverfordwest, the chief and principal town of the shire is exempted and made a county of itself at the selfsame Parliament, and by means of the said Sir Thomas Jones, Knight,[318] of the Parliament for favour he bore, being a near neighbour to the town, so that it does not contribute with it in any charge whereas all shires of Wales have all their chief towns to aid them in all charges and burdens of service.[319] There is no reason alleged in the Statute for the taking away of these lordships from Pembrokeshire, as there is for diverse other lordships mentioned in the same statute, the cause was for that there was no reason to be alleged, but all reasons were and are against it. But it was yielded and consented it should be so by the Knight of Pembrokeshire, who was the only motioner and procurer of the same as is before declared.

Also the form of Pembrokeshire, as now it is, is least to contain of any other form; for the same now is triangle or three-cornered, which form, as those know that are but meanly skilled in Geometry, contains least of all other forms or plots. Also, that part which adjoins to Carmarthenshire is concave as geometricians term it; that is, bowing in

	Pembrokeshire, like as the moon is in the last quarter: for Carmarthen there thrusts itself into Pembrokeshire. The like does the sea in diverse parts thereof, especially in Brides Bay,[320] between Milford Haven and St David's Head. And lastly, it wants so much ground out of the very middle thereof as Milford Haven is in breadth and length which is two miles in breadth and 16 in length besides diverse great creeks thereof spreading on both sides into the land, and that in the middle and best soil of the shire, whereby Pembrokeshire cannot be so populous nor contain so much land for people to inhabit as an inland shire of the like bigness to the view.)[321]
BARTHOL:	You have spoken of many things here within your country of Wales, which methinks are very necessary to be reformed, many of which, as you say, cannot be done but by Parliament. And therefore I would think it very fit, that these were collected together, and the inconveniences of each of them laid down with reasons to persuade the reforming of them, and at some Parliament the Knights and Burgesses of the Parliament that should be for Wales were all made acquainted therewith and to join together to seek reformation thereof no better time than now that you are so happy to have such a Lord Keeper that is so well-acquainted with the state and government of Wales as his honour is.
DEMETUS:	Yes, and these two right honourable earls of Pembroke and Worcester,[322] chief patrons and careful conservators and protectors of this poor country of Wales, being both descended out of this country, and that withal so heartily love and affect the same that doubtless, considering their entire affection to their country, their authority and places they now possess, might and must greatly further the proceedings; so that now presently this present time and age seems to show and offer forth itself as most fit for the purpose, the way open, the means and instruments apparent, the causes and occasions ripe and ready as the fruit in Autumn. God, of his goodness stir up the mind of some well-affected man to be forward herein for the good of his country.
BARTHOL:	Amen. And now if you will give me leave and (the hour approaching that for this time we must break of our speeches) let me try my memory how I can recount and recapitulate these defects and wants which you have before recited in this

your government of Wales, and that you think fit to be reformed in your commonwealth and country, wherein, as I remember, you spoke of some imperfections and disorders which might well be reformed by the chief Judges and rulers of those courts wherein they were and are used, being rather defects in the orderly and good proceedings than imperfections and wants in the late established law of your country so to be reformed in the High Court of Parliament; and some others that of necessity must be reformed by Parliament and not otherwise. Wherefore, for the help of my memory and method's sake I will first recite those of the first, and then those matters that you think fit to be reformed by Parliament.

DEMETUS: With a good will good Sir, and I will aid you therein as far as my memory shall be able if need be.

BARTHOL: As my memory serves me, the first thing that you find grief by and think fit to be reformed was the smallness of charges accorded to the injured party at the Council of the Marches which, as you say, is the cause of many troublesome suits and much wrong.

The second was the multitude of small suits and frivolous which is brought into that Court to the great trouble of the Judges there and of the poor commons of the country.

The third was the long and many unnecessary processes against defendants used in this court more than in any other, which is a great delay of justice to the plaintiff and a mean to the defendants to delay the cause from judgement for a long time: all which three defects lie in the power and authority of the Lord President and Council there, to reform at their will and pleasure. But this last inconvenience you thought would hardly be reformed for the hindrance of the fees of the Secretary in that Court.

Then next you spoke of a negligence that the examinations of all prisoners were not more carefully perused in the Great Sessions, whereby you say many felonies are compounded and many transgressors escape punishment, which defect may also be easily reformed and prevented by the careful diligence of the Justices of Assize and other officers.

Fifthly, you touched the defect of Justices in their negligent examining touching robberies and burglaries, and of the witnesses touching the value of the thing stolen which also lies in themselves with careful need to reform, and the rather when they are admonished and warned of the same.

Next you spoke of the inconvenience in keeping the Great Sessions and one Term at the Council of the Marches yearly in Lent which you say is a hindrance to the thrift of the country, and as I remember, you said that poor husbandmen do most complain of this, whose complaint for the most part is heard last of all others.

The seventh matter which you wished to be reformed was the disorderly proceeding of the Attorneys in the Chancery Court before the Justices of Assize, and want of more fitting days for the hearing of causes depending there, which things also the Justices there reform at their pleasure.

Then you noted very well the wilful and bad abuse used by Justices of the Peace in lingering of pleas upon recognizances forfeited and in traverses entered upon indictments of Trespass, and such like before them in their Quarter Sessions, whereby the Queen is greatly hindered, for that all those matters are passed over with frivolous pleas and demurrers until a general pardon come.

Ninthly, you noted another abuse of the said Justices of the Peace in keeping their Quarter Sessions out of the due time, wherein you seemed that they were touched with breech of their oath. Thus, as far as I remember are the nine points or defects which you wish were redressed, and which I find may be reformed by the Judges and rulers of the courts, wherein they are committed or omitted.

And now I will see how I can remember those things which are of greater moment and which must be moved in Parliament before redress may be obtained, in which the first, as I remember, was the inconvenience that Sheriffs and Escheators here in Wales are not sworn at home in their own shires as they are in England, but are forced to travel far out of the country, whereof as you have alleged, arises inconvenience both to Her Majesty and to the parties themselves, which defect as you say cannot be helped without altering the words of the statute in that behalf.

The second of these inconveniences is that Justices of Peace and Sheriffs of Wales are not limited to be of some reasonable living, seeing that Wales yields now men sufficient of living in every shire to supply those rooms, and which were not to be found when these laws were made for Wales by King Henry the Eighth.

The third of these inconveniences is that whereas it pleases the Queen's Majesty to receive the accounts of all her officers of Wales here at Her Majesty's Audit in the country, yet, notwithstanding, the Collectors of the Subsidies in Wales are forced to go to the Exchequer at Westminster to pay and pass their accounts there, which things, as you said, might at ease by the Knights and Burgesses at every Parliament at the granting of those subsidies be well motioned[323] and happily brought to pass.

Fourthly, you remembered diverse inconveniences now used in Base Courts and Hundred Courts, and among other things the great multitude of those Base Courts, which disorders are here too long and tedious to be repeated, and which you think fit to be reformed by Parliament if otherwise it could not be brought to pass.

And lastly, methought by your speeches that the disorders of the Sheriffs' Bailiffs are fit to be questioned and redressed among the disorders of those Base Courts.

And now that I have thus recounted in brief the effect of these matters, I mean as soon as I can obtain convenient time and place, to write down the effect of all your speeches, least I shall hereafter forget the same and so lose the fruit of this our conference, which being done shall only serve me for my own private use: for so I commonly use to do in many matters of like effect.

DEMETUS: And unto these former matters, which you have very well remembered, I will add one thing which comes to my mind very fit to be reformed by act of Parliament, that is, whereas the chief records which concern all men's lives, lands, livings and substance in England, do remain in the Courts of Chancery, Exchequer, King's Bench, Common Pleas, or the Treasury at Westminster, which records are things so precious unto the Prince and subject that the stealing of any party thereof out of these courts or places is made felony by act of parliament anno 8 Henry the Sixth.[324] And seeing that the records of the Great Sessions in Wales are of no less force or value to the subjects of that country, methinks that it were very convenient the wilful stealing or embezzling of any of these records should likewise be made felony as well as embezzling of the records of the said courts at Westminster. And now Mr Barthol I perceive a messenger comes to call us to dinner; we will here break of our speech and walk in and take such things as God sends, and defer our further speeches till after dinner.

Notes

[1] CCL, Phillipps MS 2,105 has the following title; 'A Dialogue of the Present Gouernment of Wales Anno Domini 1594 whereine aswell the ordinary proceedinges of Justice in most of the Coortes theare is breefely handled, what mattere ech Coorte determineth as also some deffectes not provided for when Wales was first brought to Sheere grownde and nowe fitte to be redressed by Parliament.

Together with some Inconveniences that may be reformed by the Judges and ministers of those Coortes.' The first four lines of the title-page are illuminated in gold and colours, with rubrication in text, and the MS is bound in limp vellum.

[2] Cf. 'afterward, when King Edward had brought the countrie to his subiection, he placed English officers to keepe them vnder, to whome most commonlie he gaue the forfaits and possessions of such Welshmen as disobeied his lawes, and refused to be ruled by the said officers: the like did the other Kings that came after him. The said officers were thought oftentimes to be ouer-seuere and rigorous for their owne profit & commoditie'; D. Powel, *The historie of Cambria, now called Wales* (1584), 'To the reader' [pp. ix–x]. 'In what brickle and unstable estate men stood in those days! For the roads, incursions and slaughters between countries are not forgotten of such as now live; and, in elder time, the treaties of the princes of Wales are a sufficient witness. Hereof it came to pass that the Kings of England, at sundry times, with great armies, invaded Wales to the great disquietness of the realm of England, and small gain to Wales'. Rice Merrick, *Morganiae Archaiographia: A Book of the Antiquities of Glamorganshire*, ed. B. Ll. James (Barry, 1983), p. 67.

[3] Owen's major theme in the *Dialogue* is his praise of the Tudor legislation (1536–43), but, at the same time, he casts a critical eye on the legal and administrative structure which it established. Powel and Merrick, together with other contemporary chroniclers typical of their generation, echo similar sentiments. Both refer to the 'alteration' in 'the estate' of government which ushered in a new age in Wales as part of the body politic of the English Protestant state.

[4] The dialogue was a unique literary genre, Greek in origin; see, for example, Mimes of Sophron of Syracuse (50 BC), the dialogues of Plutarch and Lucien (second century AD), Plato's dialogues and, in Roman literature, Cicero's trea-

tise, Tacitus's *Dialogues de Oratoribus* and Seneca's dialogues. Sixteenth-century English works of this kind were published, such as Sir Thomas More, *Dialogue concerning Heresies* (1529), Thomas Elyot, *Pasquyll the Playne* (1540), and Sir Thomas Smith, *A Discourse of the Commonweal of this Realm of England* (1549). See also William Thomas, *Pilgrim, a Dialogue on the Life and Actions of King Henry the Eighth*, ed. J. A. Froude (London, 1861). The author was a native of Llanigon, Brecknockshire, and served as an informal royal tutor to Edward VI and later Clerk of the Privy Council (1550–3); *ODNB*, 54, pp. 381–4. Owen incorporates his opinions and comments as a dialogue between two persons knowledgeable in legal and administrative institutions, their structures and workings. One is a Pembrokeshire country gentleman (Demetus, representing Owen himself, who was educated at Barnard's Inn, London (1574)), and the other is Barthol, an imaginary German lawyer from Frankfurt, who practises civil law at Antwerp. The *Dialogue* is structured using the Socratic method, which had gained favour after the publication of Erasmus's *Coloquia*. *DP*, II, p. 3 (no. 3). As noted above, see also Sir Thomas More, *Dialogue concerning Heresies*, Thomas Elyot, *Pasquyll the Playne*, and Sir Thomas Smith, *A Discourse of the Commonweal of this Realm of England*.

[5] The 'present happy estate' refers to the condition of society in Wales in the years after the 'Acts of Union' (1536–43). Cf. 'And the most mightie Prince, Kynge Henry the eighth ... deliuered them wholly from all seruitude and made them in all poyncts equale to the Englishmen. Wherby it commeth to passe that laying aside their old manners, they, who before were wonte to lieu most sparingly are now enritched and do imitate the Englishmen'. Humphrey Lhuyd, *The Breuiary of Britayne*, trans. T. Twyne (London, 1573), fo. 60a.

[6] This is a reference to 'A Treatise of Lordshipps Marchers in Wales' by George Owen, which again reveals his immense knowledge of the historical topography of Wales. *DP*, III, pp. 127–286.

[7] This brief summary reveals the breadth of Owen's knowledge and understanding of the legal and administrative structure of post-1536 Wales. For a broad survey of the legal background to Owen's age, from the Acts of Union to the early seventeenth century, see T. G. Watkin, *The Legal History of Wales* (Cardiff, 2007), pp. 124–48.

[8] The Council in the Marches of Wales, established in July 1471 on the granting of the Principality, the Duchy of Cornwall and the County Palatine of Chester to Edward, Prince of Wales, heir apparent to Edward IV. This Council was increased to twenty-five members in February 1473. Originally its function was to administer the Prince's lands and revenues in Wales and the Marches, but eventually it became a principal organ of government to maintain law and order in those regions. Williams, *Council in the Marches of Wales*, pp. 3–11; C. A. J. Skeel, *The Court in the Marches of Wales: A Study in Local Government during the Sixteenth and Seventeenth Centuries* (London, 1904), pp. 24–30.

[9] In CCL, Phillipps MS 2,105 only.

[10] See Owen, 'Cruell Lawes against Welshmen', *DP*, III, pp. 120–6; *Statutes*,

pp. 31–6 (Sts 2 Henry IV cc.12–20; 4 Henry IV cc.26–34); H. T. Evans, *Wales and the Wars of the Roses* (Sutton, repr. 1998), ch. 2, pp. 11–16. CCL, MS 2, 105 includes the 'Cruell Lawes' at the end of the treatise, entitled 'Cruell lawes against Welshmen' ([fo. [37a]–[38b]]). See *DP*, III, pp. 120–6.

[11] A reference to the Tudor legislation 1536–43. The command was that he should care for his people in Wales: 'that he should have a special care for the benefit of his own nation and countrymen the Welshmen'. This cannot be substantiated.

[12] The Courts of Great Sessions were created by St. 34–5 Henry VIII c.26 (1543), cls 5–14. *Statutes*, pp. 102–4; W. R. Williams, *The History of the Great Sessions in Wales 1542–1830, together with the Lives of the Welsh Judges* (Brecknock, 1899), pp. 12–17; G. Parry (ed.), *A Guide to the Records of Great Sessions in Wales* (Aberystwyth, 1995), pp. iv–vii. The courts enjoyed the same authority as the Courts of King's Bench and Common Pleas in England, exercising commissions of assize, gaol delivery and *oyer et terminer*. Like the Court of Common Pleas, these regional courts heard pleas of the Crown and pleas and actions real, personal and mixed.

[13] One member for each shire in Wales, except the new shire of Monmouth, which obtained two, and one member for each shire-town, except Merioneth, which was not represented because of its poor economic resources. St. 27 Henry VIII c.26, cls 28–9; *Statutes*, pp. 89–90.

[14] Originally one Justice of Assize (i.e. a Justice who held periodic legal sessions in each shire for the administration of civil and criminal justice) was appointed in each circuit, but in St. 18 Elizabeth I c.8 (1576) it was deemed necessary to appoint an extra Justice for each circuit because Wales, according to the statute, had been 'reduced to great obedience to Her Majesty's laws, and the same greatly inhabited, manured and peopled'. *Statutes*, pp. 152–3 (p. 153 here).

[15] Justices of the Peace were appointed, mainly from among the gentry, in the eight existing shires of Wales in 1536; St. 27 Henry VIII c.5; *Statutes*, pp. 67–9; *Cal.CQSR*, intro., pp. xxvii–lix; T. H. Lewis, 'The Justice of the Peace in Wales', 120–32; Jones, *Law, Order and Government in Caernarfonshire, 1558–1640*, ch. 2, pp. 30–72.

[16] Hywel ap Cadell, King of Deheubarth (900–*c*.950), grandson of Rhodri Mawr of Gwynedd (*c*.878 AD). He was the famous lawgiver who reorganised the laws and customs of Wales in his latter years, and is described as 'King of all Wales' ('O rat Duw ... brenhin Kymry oll'). J. E. Lloyd, *A History of Wales from the Earliest Times to the Edwardian Conquest* (2nd edn, London, 1911), I, pp. 337–8; 'tywyssawc Kymry oll', S. J. Williams and J. E. Powell (eds), *Cyfreithiau Hywel Dda yn ôl Llyfr Blegywryd* (Cardiff, 1942), p. 1.

[17] St. 34–5 Henry VIII c.44. 'There shall be four Prenotaries for the making of all judicial process and for the Entring of all Pleas, Process, and Matters of Record'. The Protonotary was the clerk of the Great Sessions. One was appointed to each circuit. Williams, *Great Sessions in Wales*, p. 14; *Cal.CQSR*, pp. xxi–xxiii, xlv; *Statutes*, p. 110.

[18] Sessions of the Peace were held quarterly by the Justices of the Peace in each shire. St. 2 Henry V c.4 (1414) provided that they should be held in England in the weeks following the Epiphany, the close of Easter and the Feasts of the Translation of St Thomas the Martyr and St Michael the Archangel; *SR*, II, *1377–1504*, p. 177. St. 34–5 Henry VIII c.26 is more specific than St. 27 Henry VIII c.5 in relation to Welsh appointments. See *Statutes*, pp. 67–8, 113–14, and Sts Edward III c.12 (1362) and 12 Richard II c.10 (1388); *SR*, I, *1101–1377*, p. 374, and II, *1377–1504*, p. 58; *Cal.CQSR*, pp. lxxxvi–lxxxvii.

[19] A bond by which a person undertakes before a court or a magistrate to observe a legal condition, or the sum pledged as surety for that bond.

[20] A court, introduced into the Principality in 1284, and presided over by the county sheriff. It dealt with pleas under forty shillings. It was regarded by Owen as the best and most efficient of the Base Courts in Wales, and described as 'the judicial and administrative organ of the shire'. St. 34–5 Henry VIII c.26 cl. 73; *Statutes*, p. 117; *Cal.CQSR*, pp. xlviii–xlix; W. H. Waters, *The Edwardian Settlement of North Wales in its Administrative and Legal Aspects, 1284–1343* (Cardiff, 1935), p. 99.

[21] The chief royal representative in the shire with fiscal and administrative duties. In 1543 it was legislated that sheriffs should be appointed yearly, but could be reappointed. *Statutes*, pp. 114–15 (cls 61–4); J. Hurstfield, 'County government 1530–1660', in R. B. Pugh and E. Crittall (eds), *The Victoria History of the Counties of England: A History of Wiltshire*, V (Oxford, 1957), pp. 105–6.

[22] The sheriff was responsible for supervising royal revenues in the shire, escheated goods and forfeited lands. Escheators were appointed in 1543, one in each shire, with a property qualification of £5 freehold land. St. 34–5 Henry VIII c.67; *Statutes*, p. 116.

[23] Loose and unclaimed animals wandering in the manors.

[24] A tax on income from wages, rents and moveables, first imposed by Henry VIII. Commissioners were normally appointed by the Crown, but payments were assessed in local committees. St. 3 Henry VIII c.22; *SR*, III, *1509–1545*, pp. 43–4.

[25] A royal or seigniorial official employed to collect or receive money due to the Crown or private lord.

[26] In CCL, Phillipps MS 2,105 only.

[27] The much maligned Hundred Court, normally held on a three-weekly basis. On the change from commote to hundred regional delimitations Edward I used Hundred Courts in place of the old Commotal Courts, the suitors being freeholders who were summoned by traditional officials known as *rhaglaw* (lieutenant) or *rhingyll* (sergeant). St. 34–5 Henry VIII c.26 cl.73; *Statutes*, p. 117.

[28] In CCL, Phillipps MS 2,105 only (p. 10).

[29] This section in round brackets is in BL, Harleian MS 141 only.

[30] A Court of private jurisdiction which defended the lord's rights within his landed possessions. It administered the customary law of the manor or lordship

and had been a valuable source of income. It was presided over by stewards and was held every fifteen days, dealing with actions below forty shillings. St. 34–5 Henry VIII c.26; *Statutes*, p. 117 (cl. 74).

31 The Court Leet was a lordship court exercising the lord's jurisdiction. Males (between the ages of 12 and 60) were required to attend and, in Pembrokeshire, it was held between May and Michaelmas. It was a Court of Record dispensing royal justice. In it Constables were normally elected and local by-laws formulated. For Courts Baron and Courts Leet see Richard Price of Brecon, son of Sir John Price, 'Letter to Lord Burghley upon the abuse of the *Cymmortha* and the general state of Wales', in Ellis, *Original Letters Illustrative of English History*, III, pp. 44–5.

32 Often untrustworthy officers employed by the sheriff to maintain law and order and attend to the running of the courts. This section in italics differs in CCL, Phillipps MS 2,105 (pp. 10–11) from the text in BL, Harleian MS 141.

33 A legal devise by Edward I to introduce English criminal law. It was a Court of Record meeting twice a year, after Easter and Michaelmas, in each commote. Freeholders and other landowners attended and it dealt with offences against the peace and encroachment on royal rights. Waters, *Edwardian Settlement*, p. 114; *Statutes*, pp. 5–6. '… the sheriff by the oath of twelve freeholders of the most discreet and lawful, or more at his discretion, shall diligently make inquiry upon the articles touching the Crown and dignity of our Lord the King' (Statute of Wales, 1284).

34 A reference to Sir John Puckering, Lord Keeper of the Great Seal, who was appointed sole Justice of Assize of the Carmarthen circuit (1577–92). He was appointed Lord Keeper in 1592. Williams, *Great Sessions in Wales*, pp. 163–4.

35 Oysterlow > Esterlwyf (Ysterlwyf) > Ystlwyf, a commote in Cantref Gwarthaf. *DP*, I, pp. 45–6 (no. 2), 213–14; G. M. Richards, *Welsh Administrative and Territorial Units, Medieval and Modern* (Cardiff, 1969), p. 226. It was sometimes known as the lordship of Llanddowror.

36 Proceeds with BL, Harleian MS 141 only.

37 A customary saying to distinguish south Pembrokeshire, heavily Normanised, from the native Welsh northern region of the shire. *Desc. Pembs.*, pp. 14, 36–7, 166, 200. 'The said county of Pembrokeshire is usually called Little England beyond Wales and that not unworthily … Mr Camden calls it *Anglia Transwallia* … for that the most part of the county speaks English, and in it no use of the Welsh … a stranger travelling from England … shall hear nothing but English, and … would think that Wales were environed with England, and would imagine he had travelled through Wales and come into England again.' (p. 36). See also William Camden's *Britannia* 1695 edition (repr. 1971), p. 631.

38 *Quod breve Domini Regis non currit in Walliam*, meaning that royal power, as represented in the writ (*breve*) was not enforceable in the Marches. He was very knowledgeable in the history and structure of the marcher lordships. See 'A description of the dominion of Wales'; also *A Treatise of Lordshipps Marchers in Wales*, BL, Harleian MS 141, fos 1–27; *DP*, III, pp. 127–286.

[39] The famous English surveyor and cartographer, born at Sowood, West Riding of Yorkshire; *ODNB*, 49, pp. 153–5. He was commissioned by Elizabeth I to produce a survey of all the counties in England and Wales. He also published a wall-map of both countries in 1583 and is regarded as the 'father of English cartography'. He published his *Atlas of England and Wales* (1579), containing the earliest maps of the Welsh shires. Pembrokeshire, Glamorgan and Monmouthshire were printed on separate sheets so that Pembrokeshire appeared to be larger than other counties. Owen feared that this might be disadvantageous to the shire with regard to taxation levels.

[40] Both MSS continue at this point.

[41] *Desc. Pembs.*, pp. xxviii–xxxix: 'a sloven wallowing' means a negligent person wallowing on the grass. In view of his varied activities and decisive action to safeguard his own landed interests, Owen himself was far from fitting that description of himself.

[42] This 'pamphlet', referred to again in *Dialogue*, pp. 74, 81 [110, 117] is probably a figment of Owen's imagination, designed probably to impress Barthol with his literary skills and legal knowledge.

[43] An imaginary name derived from 'Bartolus de Saxoferrato', the Italian lawyer, who died in 1357. He was one of the most important Continental jurists in the Middle Ages. Civil lawyers who were taught by this Bartolus were highly regarded, and that may explain why this name was adoped by Owen.

[44] A reference to the mutinous sacking of Antwerp in 1576 and the atrocities committed by Spanish troops following the death of Luis Requesens (3 March 1576), the governor of the Netherlands after the duke of Alva. The city surrendered to the Spanish in September of that year. Following the horrific attacks in that year its inhabitants were tortured and women were raped and put to death. This was described as the 'three-day orgy of the "Spanish Fury"', when 8,000 of the city's inhabitants were killed and part of it was razed to the ground. M. Rady, *The Netherlands: Revolt and Independence, 1550–1650* (London, 1987), pp. 34–5, 58; P. Geyl, *The Revolt of the Netherlands, 1555–1609* (2nd edn, London, 1958), pp. 149–50; J. Israel, *The Dutch Republic: Its Rise, Greatness and Fall 1477–1806* (Oxford, 1995), p. 185.

[45] Demetia (Dyfed), land of the Demetae tribe in west Wales, a branch of the Brythonic inhabitants in early Britain. Lloyd, *History of Wales*, I, pp. 74–5, 261.

[46] Famous universities were established at Vienna (1365), Heidelberg (1386), Leipzig (1409), Tübingen (1477) and Wittenberg (1502).

[47] See n. 44.

[48] Ovid, the Roman poet (43 BC–AD 17). *Tristia* (Sad Things), elegiac poems in five books, written in AD 8–12 during his exile from Rome at Tomis, on the island of Miletus, on the west coast of the Black Sea.

[49] A study of the general features of the earth and the universe. Owen was interested in this science and in the earth's geological formation, and was regarded,

The Dialogue of the Government of Wales (1594)

on one occasion, as the 'father of English geology'. W. H. Fitton, 'The Silurian System', *The Edinburgh Review*, 73, April 1841, 3; cited in *Desc. Pembs.*, p. xxxvii.

50 The content of this section by Barthol is typical of the Renaissance spirit, the broadening of knowledge and human experience in the known world.

51 In this opening remark Barthol, in fact, expresses Owen's own view of the state of Wales in the 1590s. Owen is so eager to impress on his visitor how well-ordered the country was under the Tudors that he allows Barthol to make a premature statement before he has had the opportunity to question Demetus and to draw lengthy conclusions himself from his observations.

52 This statement raises the issue of whether or not Barthol, being ignorant of the Welsh language, was prejudiced. Although he admires the politeness which he had experienced in different parts of Wales on his journey, he does not praise the Welsh people for preserving their ancient language and culture, as would be expected of a Renaissance figure. In fact, he shows indifference towards the use of Welsh in Wales as the spoken language of the vast majority of the Welsh people.

53 *Obiter dictum*, 'incidental remark'.

54 A memorial of military victory.

55 Units of military government.

56 That is, Upper and Lower.

57 *Nisi prius*, 'unless before'. A writ directing that a case be brought before the King's Bench at Westminster, 'unless before' the circuit Justice had heard it at his Assizes.

58 Although Demetus gives Barthol the opportunity to praise Pembrokeshire, he refrains from explaining the essential differences between England and Wales.

59 A sister-language of Welsh, spoken until the eighteenth century, mainly by then in the western parts. The language died, so it is believed, in the 1770s, on the death of Dolly Pentreath, fishwife and fortune-teller of Mousehole on Mounts Bay, Cornwall.

60 'Foot-cloth' refers to the cloth which hanged down on either side of a horse used to protect the rider's feet. Berwick-on-Tweed is a fortified town situated in Northumbria on the Anglo-Scottish borders.

61 *Anglia transwalina*, 'England across Wales'. See n. 37.

62 Meteing> 'measuring' limits and boundaries. Barthol's wide travels in Europe, particularly France and his native Germany, gave him ample opportunity to compare Continental legal structures with those in England and Wales. In this section it is Owen himself who reveals his knowledge, which he obtained, presumably, during his stay at Barnard's Inn. Barthol's knowledge of all parts of Wales is sparse. He has very little to say in this treatise about Gwynedd, Powys and south-east Wales and the border areas. Although Owen had good knowledge of the Welsh administrative system and its geographical features, this may reflect his own inexperience, since he had not visited other areas of Wales.

[63] This comment reveals George Owen's own intention to give Demetus priority in these matters. Very little attention is given to the gentry of north Wales in this section. Doubtless, men of the social status of Sir Thomas Mostyn of Flintshire, John Salusbury of Llewenni, Sir John Wynn of Gwydir, Sir William Thomas of Caernarfon and Sir Richard Bulkeley III of Baron Hill would have offered him hospitality and informed him of Wales's administration in north Wales. Moreover, Barthol says nothing about Conwy or Caernarfon castles, which is surprising, in view of his reputed antiquarian interests, and there is no indication of where he was shown hospitality during his journey in north and south Wales. Imaginary though Owen's text is, it still reflects his concentration almost exclusively on himself as Demetus and his native Pembrokeshire.

[64] The earliest Lord Presidents were appointed from among English bishops, and later ones from high-ranking nobility with Welsh connections. The six bishops who were first appointed held English sees. They were John Alcock, bishop of Rochester (1473–1501), William Smyth, bishop of Coventry and Lichfield (1501–12), Geoffrey Blythe, bishop of Coventry and Lichfield (1512–25), John Veysey, bishop of Exeter (1525–34), Rowland Lee, bishop of Coventry and Lichfield (1534–43) and Richard Sampson, also of that diocese (1543–8). The most notable and certainly most notorious among them was Rowland Lee, appointed two years before the first Act of Union. Among his lay successors were John Dudley, earl of Warwick (1548–50), William Herbert, 1st earl of Pembroke (1550–3) and, in Owen's own time, Henry Herbert, 2nd earl of Pembroke (1587–1601).Williams, *Great Sessions in Wales*, pp. 8–9; Williams, *Council in the Marches of Wales*, pp. xiv, 1, 37–8 et seq. The most prestigious and longest serving were Sir Henry Sidney (1560–87) and, among the Vice-Presidents, Sir William Gerard, who became Lord Chancellor of Ireland, and John Whitgift, bishop of Worcester and subsequently Archbishop of Canterbury; ibid., pp. 348, 360.

[65] At Westminster Hall the Court of Chancery dealt with cases in equity, supplementing Common Law, administering justice according to the 'king's conscience', to which the oppressed could appeal. It was often concerned with punishing royal debtors and recovering lands, goods and chattels belonging to the Crown. It possessed common-law and equity jurisdiction.

[66] *Cymorthas* was regarded as a legal form of communal aid or 'free benevolence', on the occasion of a marriage or other social event, but had become abused as enforced exactions on tenants by powerful lords or gentry, chiefly in the Marches of Wales, although it was practised in the Principality as well. The custom was abolished officially in 1534 (St. 26 Henry VIII c.6); *Statutes*, p. 57; W. Rees, *South Wales and the March 1284–1415: A Social and Agrarian Study* (Oxford, 1924), pp. 229–34. 'Bidale' and 'Tenants' Ale' were also customs which brought financial profit to landowners. Note the second earl of Pembroke's plea to the deputy-lieutenants of Caernarfonshire on 27 March 1596: 'You have ever bene forwarde in *comorthas* for your owne privat gaynes, wherefore I conceive you wilbe mutch more forwarde in this *comortha*

for the publick good of the whole State.' T. Jones Pierce (ed.), *Clenennau Letters and Papers in the Brogyntyn Collection*, p. 31. See also Richard Price's letter to Lord Burghley deploring such high-handed activity when, despite the statute, private licences were granted by the Council in the Marches to unscrupulous gentry. Ellis, *Letters Illustrative of English History*, III, pp. 42–4.

67 The high-profile *Camera Stellata*. The Privy Council, together with the Chief Justices of the King's Bench and Common Pleas, sat as a court of equity dealing mainly with serious offences committed by the nobility. This institution served as a court of justice holding public sittings twice a week during legal terms. It acted as the judicial section of the Privy Council and possessed civil as well as criminal jurisdiction. Its business increased and jurisdiction widened in the middle years of the Tudor century, especially after August 1540. Its origins are traced to the jurisdiction of the King's Council in the fifteenth century. Under Wolsey its procedure was formalised, its jurisdiction defined and its powers extended. By 1540 it formed one of two bodies, the other being the Privy Council. Although it has gained a notorious reputation for its ruthless punishment of criminals, it was a highly respected body and regarded as a central cog in the Tudor legal machinery. P. Williams, 'The Star Chamber and the Council in the Marches of Wales, 1558–1603', *BBCS*, XVI, pt. iv (1956), 287–97; I. ab O. Edwards (ed.), *A Catalogue of Star Chamber Proceedings Relating to Wales* (Cardiff, 1929), intro., pp. iii–vi. For a detailed study of Privy Council and Star Chamber relations with Wales see M. K. Lloyd, 'The Privy Council, Star Chamber and Wales, 1540–1572' (unpublished Ph.D. dissertation University of Wales, 1987), esp. chs 4–7, pp. 45–394.

68 *Ad perpetuam rei memoriam*, 'to the undying memory of the matter'.

69 The Feast of Epiphany, twelve days after Christmas.

70 Trinity Sunday was the next after Whit Sunday.

71 1 November.

72 The Council in the Marches, despite its weaknesses, was essential to secure law and order in Wales, and its value in maintaining government became evident during the tense last quarter of the sixteenth century, when Catholic forces at home and abroad threatened the realm. Owen concurred with the view that it continued to operate effectively as a vital link with the organs of the central government. Williams, *Council in the Marches of Wales*, pp. 323–5.

73 A legal appointee to represent clients in legal proceedings.

74 A gold coin, first minted by Edward III, and originally valued at 6*s.* 9*d.*, but worth 10*s.* in Owen's day.

75 *Sub poena*, 'under penalty'. A writ issued by a court summoning a person to appear.

76 *Non est inventus*, 'he is not found'. A return by a sheriff declaring that a person outside his jurisdiction to be arrested could not be found.

77 This short section is not in CCL, Phillipps MS 2,105 and is scored out in BL, Harleian MS 141.

[78] A system of jurisprudence which supplements the Common Law and provides a remedy where none exists at law.

[79] Ecclesiastical courts (*curiae Christianitatis*). These courts held jurisdiction in ecclesiastical matters, including the Court of Arches of Canterbury, Chancery Court of York and Consistory Courts of dioceses among others, some by now obsolete.

[80] The Lord President at the time was Henry Herbert, second earl of Pembroke, closely attached to the Leicester faction at Court. His seat was at Wilton, near Salisbury, and he owned several estates in Glamorgan. Williams, *Council in the Marches of Wales*, p. 276; *ODNB*, 26, pp. 688–9.

[81] Owen has given the Council his recommendation. He, like others of his social *milieu*, feared that disorder might again occur if it were to be abolished. Cf. the lawyer Dr David Lewis's comments referring to the dangers which arose from inefficiency: 'That the counsaile may imploye them selves to se the country well ordered and guyded in good obedyence rather then to here pleas for lande & other things which might receve ende by the course of the comein lawes with more spede & lesse charge then there.' *CSPDom, 1547–1580*, CVII, 4 (i), p. 514; D. Ll. Thomas, 'Further notes on the Court of the Marches', *Y Cymmrodor*, XIII (1900), 130–3; D. Mathew, 'Some Elizabethan documents', *BBCS*, VI, pt. i (1931), 77.

[82] The oldest court dealing with civil disputes, dating from the twelfth century.

[83] The Exchequer was responsible for receiving royal revenues: Barthol described it as 'the Prince's treasury'. The name is derived from *scaccarium* (chessboard), i.e. a chequered tablecloth designed to keep accounts using counters. It was originally a court of revenue and a section of the *Curia Regis*. It had a separate existence after 1312 and became a Common Law Court and Court of Equity dealing with all actions (excepting actions real), especially financial litigation.

[84] A court of civil jurisdiction dealing with property, contract, trusts, wills etc. It practised equity jurisdiction (appeals and petitions) to supplement the Common Law. It was a more flexible court than the other Common Law courts and was presided over as judge by the Chancellor, and the first among a number of eminent Chancellors was Sir Thomas More. When the Chancellor was absent the Master of the Rolls presided. The court's jurisdiction was maintained until 1873–5, when, by law, it was replaced by a division of the High Court of England and Wales.

[85] Tribunals for recovery of small debts between 40s. and £5. Summary jurisdiction was practised and orders were made by oaths of parties 'consonant to equity and good conscience'.

[86] *Magister Rotulorum*, Keeper of the Records and Lord Chancellor's assistant. In Edward I's reign judicial authority was given to this officer within the jurisdiction of the Court of Chancery.

[87] Annually elected magistrates performing duties of consul, such as bodyguards of a Roman General or Emperor.

The Dialogue of the Government of Wales (1594)

88 Common Law Court superior in status to other central Courts of Common Pleas and Exchequer. Its judge was the Lord Chief Justice.
89 See n. 67.
90 An antiquated word meaning 'deception', 'beguilement' and 'trickery'.
91 Lord Keeper of the Great Seal, also known as Lord Chancellor. In St. 5 Elizabeth I c.18 (1562) it was made the same office.
92 That is, individually.
93 The Duchy of Lancaster Court. Dealing with equity cases relating to lands held of the Crown and matters of revenue in the duchy.
94 The Court of Wards and Liveries was created in 1503 for enforcing the feudal rights of the Crown. It was formally regarded as such in 1540 and inquired into lands held in chief of the Crown (St. 32 Henry VIII c.46). The chief officer was the Master of King's and Queen's Wards and a Surveyor of Liveries was added to it in 1542, thus it was designated Court of Wards and Liveries. This court helped to control the aristocracy and increase royal revenue.
95 The Court of Requests or Court of Poor Men's Cases was a Court of Equity created in the fourteenth century hearing civil complaints. It eventually became a committee of the Privy Council, over which the Lord Keeper presided.
96 Evidence again to show that it is Owen, not Barthol, who is knowledgeable in these judicial institutions, revealing his legal education.
97 The anti-Welsh laws of 1401–2. Sts 2 Henry IV c.12, 16–20, and 4 Henry IV c.26–34; *Statutes*, pp. 33–6.
98 R. R. Davies, *The Revolt of Owain Glyn Dŵr* (Oxford, 1995), pp. 77–83; R. R. Davies, 'Richard II and the Principality of Chester, 1397–99', in F. R. H. Du Boulay and C. M. Barron (eds), *The Reign of Richard II: Essays in Honour of May McKisack* (London, 1971), pp. 256–79.
99 This paragraph reveals Owen's cautious admiration for Owain Glyndŵr and his contempt for Henry IV. It is surprising that Reginald de Grey, lord of Ruthin, is not even mentioned at this point, in view of his central role at the outset of revolt.
100 Again, an indication of Owen's sympathy for Glyndŵr. Although his argument is flawed, his sentiments are clearly expressed. He does not wish to appear disloyal to the Crown, but utterly deplores the outcome of the dynastic wars between Yorkists and Lancastrians.
101 Possibly Adam of Usk in *Chronicon Adae de Usk*, who described his ferocity: 'Velut alter Assur, furoris Dei virga, inauditam tyrannidem ferre et flamma miserime vibravit.' ('like a second Assyrian, the rod of God's anger, he did deeds of unheard-of cruelty with fire and sword'). E. Maunde Thompson (ed.), *Chronicon Adae de Usk* (London, 1904), pp. 78, 247.
102 Cf. Sir Dafydd Trefor's elegaic ode in honour of Henry VII: 'Duw a'i roes yn lle Moesen, / Gwae ni o'i ddwyn, Gwynedd wen'. NLW, Llanstephan MS 120,248 ['God gave him to us in place of Moses, / Woe to us his departure, radiant Gwynedd']. Note also Huw Machno's ecstatic eulogy of Henry in an

ode to Sir John Lloyd, Sergeant-at-Arms: 'Yn rhwydd o hyn i'n rhyddhau, / Yn frenin iownfawr rannau; / Iesu erom roes Harri, / Seithfed yn nodded i ni' ['Easily from this, to liberate us / Jesus gave us Henry the Seventh as a resplendent King and patron']. NLW, Cwrtmawr MS 27,55.

[103] Owen exaggerates at this point. Individual Welshmen did receive education during the fifteenth century, although it was in the following century that the student population grew. Glanmor Williams, 'Education and culture down to the sixteenth century', in J. L. Williams and G. Rees Hughes (eds), *The History of Education in Wales*, I (Swansea, 1978), pp. 23–7. The anti-Welsh laws were not as severely executed as some historians believe. They were legislated primarily to meet the emergencies of the times, although they remained on the statute book for many years after the revolt (abolished by St. 21 James I c.28, *SR*, IV, pt. ii, *1586–1624*, pp. 1239.) When the revolt began to subside, less pressure was placed on the native population. Some economic recovery occurred, especially in the Marches and less inhospitable areas of the Principality. Not all Welsh privileges were withdrawn in many commotes and royal pardons were purchased, albeit for heavy fines. R. A. Griffiths, 'Wales and the Marches', in S. B. Chrimes, D. Ross and R. A. Griffiths (eds), *Fifteenth-Century England 1399–1509: Studies in Politics and Society*, pp. 148–50.

[104] Solomon, son of King David, was known for his wisdom: 'God gave Solomon deep wisdom and insight, and understanding as wide as the sand on the seashore, so that Solomon's wisdom surpassed that of all men of the east and of all Egypt. For he was wiser than any man.' 1 Kings 4: 29–31.

[105] Cf. William Morgan's comment in his epistle dedicatory of the Welsh Bible to Elizabeth I: 'For ... what an affectionate care your Majesty has for your British subjects ... I plead with the most earnest prayers that you will graciously favour my efforts ... such as I trust will prove not only an abiding monument of your zeal for the truth and regard for your British subjects, but also a token of their most devoted affection for your Majesty.' W. Hughes, *Life and Times of Bishop William Morgan* (London, 1891), p. 126. The 'affection' felt by the Welsh people for the Queen was evidently manifested in several sources by littérateurs. It is questionable, however, whether the lower orders, often seriously affected by dire poverty and economic stringency, felt the same way towards a dynasty whose legislation was unduly harsh. Cf. *Desc. Pembs*. p. 202: 'Of the body of this Pembrokeshire prince has sprung and budded out such joys as make the hearts of all good subjects to leap for joy, as first in extinguishing our home and domestic sedition as also in thinking upon the happy issue out of his loins ... our late and most gracious Sovereign Lady Queen Elizabeth, whose long and peaceful government was, and may be a mirror, or rather an admiration, to all princes.'

[106] Born Owain ap Maredudd ap Tudur of Penmynydd, Anglesey, a member of the prominent 'Tudor' family descended from Ednyfed Fychan, seneschal of Llywelyn ap Iorwerth (the Great). Owain served in Henry V's court, became

known as Owen Tudor, and married Catherine de Valois, daughter of Charles VI of France, the King's widow, in 1429. Although not regarded favourably, the marriage was not considered to be illegal at the time. S. B. Chrimes, *Henry VII* (London, 1972), pp. 5–8; T. Artemus Jones, 'Owen Tudor's marriage: a missing statute', in T. Artemus Jones, *Without My Wig* (Liverpool, 1945 edn), pp. 21–32. George Owen followed Welsh tradition by stating that the Welsh Tudors descended from Cadwaladr ('the Blessed'), son of Cadwallon ap Cadfan of Gwynedd (d. AD 664). In legend this Cadwaladr is regarded as a military figure who, it was believed, would return to lead the Britons triumphantly to victory over the Saxons, thereby regaining the ascendancy over Britain (the 'British inheritance'). This tradition is incorporated in the obscure prophetic poetry of the fourteenth century and forms part of the Galfridian version of the early history of Britain. Glanmor Williams, 'Prophecy, poetry and politics in medieval and Tudor Wales', in Glanmor Williams, *Religion, Language and Nationality in Wales: Historical Essays* (Cardiff, 1979), pp. 73, 82, 84. '681: In that year Cadwaladr ap Cadwallon, the last King who reigned over the Britons, went to Rome; and there he died ... And thenceforth the Britons lost the crown of kingship, and the Saxons obtained it'. Thomas Jones (ed.), *Brut y Tywysogion or The Chronicle of the Princes [Peniarth MS, 20 Version]* (Cardiff, 1952), p. 1. 'The voice ordered ... that he should do penance and he would be numbered among the blessed ... the voice added that, as a reward for his faithfulness, the British people would occupy the island again at some time in the future, once the appointed moment should come.' Geoffrey of Monmouth, *The History of the Kings of Britain*, trans. Lewis Thorpe (Penguin Books, Harmondsworth, 1966), p. 283. Henry Tudor flew the banner of Cadwaladr on the field of battle at Bosworth, depicting the Red Dragon, purported to be associated with Cadwaladr. It was one of three standards displayed by Henry at St Paul's in 1485.

[107] Henry's father, Edmund Tudor, eldest son of Owen Tudor, was created earl of Richmond in 1452. He married Margaret, heiress of John Beaufort III, duke of Somerset. Edmund died on 3 November 1456, possibly at Carmarthen castle, and was buried at the Greyfriars there. His son, Henry, was born posthumously on 28 January 1457 at Pembroke castle, the residence of his uncle Jasper Tudor, created earl of Pembroke in 1452. Chrimes, *Henry VII*, pp. 12–14. See Roberts, 'Wyrion Eden: the Anglesey descendants of Ednyfed Fychan in the fourteenth century', in Roberts, *Aspects of Welsh History*, pp. 178–214.

[108] For further discussion of the exact location where Henry Tudor landed see S. B. Chrimes, 'The landing place of Henry of Richmond, 1485', *WHR*, 2, 22 (1964), 173–80; E. W. Jones, *Bosworth Field and its Preliminaries: A Welsh Retrospect, 1485–1985* (Liverpool, 1984); H. T. Evans, *Wales and the Wars of the Roses* (repr. Stroud, 1998), pp. 129, 166.

[109] Henry Tudor landed with his motley army at Dale, adjacent to Angle on the south Pembrokeshire coast, on 7 August 1485. For a Welsh viewpoint of the

battle of Bosworth see E. W. Jones, *Bosworth Field ... A Welsh Retrospect, 1485–1985*.

[110] An ecclesiastical metropolis, generally equivalent to an archbishopric. It is interesting to note that Owain Glyndŵr, in his Pennal Policy (1406), planned to have St David's restored as a metropolitan. Edmund Tudor's remains were moved to St David's cathedral in 1536, before the surrender of Carmarthen priory to the Crown on 30 March 1538 during the dissolution. Davies, *Revolt of Owain Glyn Dŵr*, p. 172; Gerald of Wales, *The Journey Through Wales and the Description of Wales*, ed. Lewis Thorpe (Penguin Books, Harmondsworth, 1980 edn), pp. 159–60, 163–4; *Owain Glyn Dŵr 1400–2000* (Aberystwyth, 2000), [3]. According to Lewys Glyn Cothi, the celebrated fifteenth-century professional poet, it appears that his marble tomb was made at St David's: 'Ei fedd a wnaethpwyd yn fur / Ym Mynyw o faen mynor' ['His tomb was made of marble stone on a wall at St David's']. D. R. Johnston (ed.), *Gwaith Lewys Glyn Cothi* (Cardiff, 1995), no. 10, p. 32; For a second elegy see T. Roberts and I. Williams (eds), *The Poetical Works of Dafydd Nanmor* (Cardiff/London, 1923), pp. xv, 41–3.

[111] Genesis 50: 25; Exodus 13: 19; Joshua 24: 32.

[112] A reference to the Roman Catholic Church in the Middle Ages, regarded by Protestant leaders as a long period of spiritual destitution. Cf. Nicholas Robinson, bishop of Bangor, who in his letter to Sir William Cecil on 7 October 1567 stated of his diocese: 'I finde by my small experience among them here, yt ignorance contineweth many in the dregges of superstition, which did grow chefely upon ye blyndnes of the clergie'; Mathew, 'Some Elizabethan documents', 78; *CSPDom. 1547–1580*, XLIV, 27, p. 301.

[113] Owen may have based this sentiment on the preamble to the 'Act of Union' (1536): 'His Highness therefore, of a singular Zeal Love and Favour that he beareth towards his subjects of his said Dominion of Wales ... hath ... ordained enacted and established', *Statutes*, p. 76.

[114] A reference to the administrative structure of Wales subsequent to the 1536–43 legislation, whereby the Courts of Great Sessions, with their attendant Chanceries and Exchequers, served the whole of Wales.

[115] Judicially, the new shire was placed in the Oxford assize circuit, thus being directly subject to the central courts at Westminster. Socially and culturally, however, most regions of Monmouthshire were thoroughly Welsh. G. J. Williams, *The Welsh Tradition of Gwent* (Cardiff, 1968); D. J. Davies and N. Davies, *Is Monmouthshire in Wales? The Legal and Historical Answer* (Griffithstown, 1943); A. Roderick, 'A history of the Welsh language in Gwent', *Gwent Local History*, no. 50 (Spring, 1981), 13–39; J. G. Jones, 'The gentry of Gwent and the Welsh language after the Acts of Union', *The Monmouthshire Antiquary*, XVIII (2002), 65–84.

[116] *Statutes*, pp. 102–3. The office was based on that of Justice in the northern and southern Principalities of Wales from 1284 to 1543. The marcher system in

each lordship provided its own chief judicial official. St. 27 Henry VIII c.26; *Statutes*, pp. 81–2; St. 34–35 Henry VIII c.26; *Statutes*, pp. 102–3.

[117] St. 34–35 Henry VIII c.26, cls 6–13; *Statutes*, pp. 102–4. 'the said Justices ... shall hold all manner of Pleas of the Crown ... and also to hold Pleas of Assises, and all other Pleas and Actions real, personal and mixt'.

[118] The attempt to influence a jury or jurors corruptly.

[119] The legal process whereby possession of, or right to, property or compensation is gained or regained.

[120] St. 27 Henry VIII c.26; *Statutes*, pp. 89–90. Representation was broadly half of that given to English constituencies. Poor economic conditions were largely responsible for this arrangement.

[121] A plea whereby action is delayed until a matter of dispute was resolved in a court of law.

[122] St. 18 Elizabeth I c.8; *Statutes*, pp. 152–6; Williams, *Great Sessions in Wales*, pp. 16–17.

[123] Sheriffs were usually appointed for life as from 1284, which led to abuse of office in many instances. Three were usually nominated yearly for each shire by the Council in the Marches to the Privy Council on the morrow of All Souls (*crastino animarum*).

[124] Sheriffs in the Principality were often appointed from among the English nobility, who were usually absentee and farmed their offices. St. 4 Henry IV c.32 (1402); *Statutes*, p. 36. Some influential Welshmen were appointed early after 1284, such as Gruffudd ap Rhys, Gruffudd ap Owen, Madog Llwyd, Einion ap Ieuan, Ieuan ap Hywel, Gruffudd ap Dafydd and Cynwric ap Gruffudd. Waters, *Edwardian Settlement*, pp. 171–3.

[125] Royal or seigniorial officer who was responsible for reverting lapsed property to the Crown or lord if the owner died intestate without heirs.

[126] The Keeper of Crown Pleas. The Coroner inquired into sudden death and treasure trove, occasionally assisted by a jury. This officer, elected in the County Court, was created in 1194 and his duties were formulated in *Statute De Officio Coronatores* (1276). Normally two Coroners were appointed in each shire, and were originally appointed in the Principality in 1284. St. 34–35 Henry VIII c.26; *Statutes*, pp. 116–17.

[127] Owen revelled in the Tudor policy of granting local offices of trust to Welshmen: 'King Henry the Eighth came to redress those enormities ... and to give the Magistrates of their own nation'; Glanmor Williams, 'Prophecy, poetry and politics in medieval and Tudor Wales', in Glanmor Williams, *Religion, Language and Nationality in Wales: Historical Essays*, pp. 85–6.

[128] A writ issued in the Court of Chancery which was the basis of real actions at Common Law.

[129] Judges in the Court of Chancery.

[130] St. 34–35 Henry VIII c.26, cls 5–21; *Statutes*, pp. 102–5.

[131] *Teste*, 'witness'.

[132] Originally a barrier between the judgement seat and the court, subsequently used to describe the court itself.

133 *Quia bonum ... omnibus uti*, 'because it is good to know all but not to use all'.
134 The guilty party.
135 A bond by which a person undertakes to observe the peace, pay a debt or appear when summoned, and the sum pledged as surety for such an agreement.
136 *Pro forma*, 'as a matter of form'.
137 The Great Inquest was the Grand Jury composed of usually twelve freeholders returned by the sheriff to sessions of the peace. They received indictments and inquired on oath whether there was sufficient evidence to send an accused party to court.
138 Bolt, 'sift', 'investigate'.
139 Clapped, 'placed quickly'.
140 Reaching a compromise or settlement.
141 Incite to action, urge, instigate.
142 Barabbas, the thief released by Pilate on the demand of the Jews during Christ's trial. *Matthew*, 27: 16. 'There was then in custody a man of some notoriety, called Jesus Bar-Abbas.'
143 An Attorney General was appointed for each of the four circuits in Wales. In St. 34–35 Henry VIII c.26 the King's Attorney and Solicitor were to be appointed *ex officio* Justices of the Peace in each shire, together with the Lord President of the Council in the Marches, members of the Council and Justices of Assize; *Statutes*, p. 43.
144 'Composition, 'compromise', 'agreement'.
145 Articles of trade.
146 *Commoditas omnis sua fert incommode secum*, 'Every convenience brings its own drawbacks'.
147 See n.16 where references are made to studies of Hywel ap Cadell's legal accomplishment at Whitland.
148 There has been some discussion of whether the Courts of Great Sessions in fact practised their equity jurisdiction in a Chancery Court from their inception. Evidence indicates that this was the case. See G. Parry (ed.), *A Guide to the Records of Great Sessions in Wales* (Aberystwyth, 1995), pp. vii–ix.
149 Officers managing causes in court and professional pleaders in a Court of Justice respectively.
150 St. 18 Elizabeth c.8; *Statutes*, pp. 152–6.
151 This court was introduced into Wales by St. 27 Henry VIII c.5. This statute was passed in the last session of the Reformation Parliament, which opened on 4 February 1536, a statute generally regarded as being more significant than the 'Act of Union' itself. *Statutes*, pp. 67–9; *Cal.CQSR*, pp. xxxiii–xxxv, lxxxvi–lxxxviii; Jones, *Law, Order and Government in Caernarfonshire, 1558–1640*, ch. 2, pp. 30–72. For the broader picture of the county magistracy see J. H. Gleason, *The Justices of the Peace in England 1558 to 1640: A Later Eirenarcha* (Oxford, 1969); W. O. Williams, 'The county records', *Transactions of the Caernarfonshire Historical Society*, X (1949), 79ff.
152 Their residences were mainly substantial farmhouses rather than mansions, which enabled them to set themselves apart from their social inferiors. E. W.

Wiliam, '"Let use be preferred to uniformity": domestic architecture', in J. G. Jones (ed.), *Class, Community and Culture in Tudor Wales* (Cardiff, 1989), pp. 171–5.

[153] This is an error, for the verse occurs in Exodus 18: 21. Jethro was Moses' father-in-law: 'But you should search for capable, god-fearing men among all the people, honest and incorruptible men, and appoint them over the people as officers over units of a thousand, of a hundred, of fifty, or of ten.'

[154] St. 1 Edward III c.16 (1326–7); *SR*, I, *1101–1377*, p. 257. 'For the better keeping and maintenance of the peace, the King wills, that in every county good men and lawful which be ... in the country shall be assigned to keep the peace.'

[155] St. 18 Edward III c.2 (no. 2); *SR*, I, *1101–1377*, p. 301. '... shall be assigned Keepers of the Peace ... and ... with other wise and learned in the Law, shall be assigned by the King's Commission to hear and determine Felonies and Trespasses done against the Peace'.

[156] St. 34 Edward III c.2, cl. 2 (1344); *SR*, I, *1101–1377*, p. 301. 'That two or three of the best of reputation in the counties shall be assigned Keepers of the Peace by the King's commission; and at what time need shall be, the same, with other wise and learned in the law, shall be assigned by the King's commission to hear and determine Felonies and Trespasses done against the Peace in the same counties and to inflict Punishment reasonably according to [law and reason, and] the manner of the Deed.'

[157] Exodus 18: 21.

[158] St. 34–35 Henry VIII c.26, cl. 56; *Statutes*, p. 113. See also St. 34 Edward III c.1 (1360–1); *SR*, I, *1101–1377*, p. 364. The £20 qualification imposed in England was waived in Wales for economic reasons. Rowland Lee's letter to Thomas Cromwell in 1534 makes plain his view of this exemption: 'And also, for Justices of the Peace and of Gaol Delivery to be in Wales, I think it not much expedient ... there are very few Welsh in Wales above Brecknock who have 10 li land, and their discretion is less than their land.' *CSPDom.*, X (1536), 453, p. 182.

[159] St. 18 Henry VI c.11 (1439); *SR*, II, *1377–1504*, p. 309. '... whereof some be of small substance by whom the people will not be governed nor ruled, and some for their necessity do great Extortion and Oppression upon the people, whereof great inconveniences be likely to rise daily if the King thereof do not provide Remedy.'

[160] *Quia necessitas cognit turpia*, 'because necessity forces vile deeds'.

[161] In this section Owen refers to a weakness in the social structure. Barthol appears to be unaware that the Welsh gentry were not materially qualified for office. The inference, however, that they were 'blind and ignorant', which Demetus ascribes to Barthol, is exaggerated and misguided. There were many skilful lawyers and administrators, members of the landed gentry, who had served the Crown and marcher lordships well before 1536, even before 1400. For further examination of the landed means of Gwynedd gentry in the mid-

sixteenth century see R. Stephens, *Gwynedd, 1528–1547: Economy and Society in Tudor Wales* (Ann Arbor, 1975), ch. 3, pp. 39–82.

162 Owen's comment that Welsh 'magistrates' were commissioned to the bench after the Act of Union is an important pointer to the prophetic tradition stemming from Geoffrey of Monmouth's writings. See Williams, 'Prophecy, poetry, and politics in medieval and Tudor Wales', in *Religion, Language and Nationality on Wales*, pp. 85–6.

163 Owen post-dates progressive developments in Welsh society at this stage, placing far too much emphasis on the accession of Henry Tudor and the Welsh legislation of Henry VIII. Socio-economic developments concomitant with political affairs showed signs of progress well before the Tudor accession. See G. Roberts, 'Wales and England, antipathy and sympathy 1282–1485', in *Aspects of Welsh History* (Cardiff, 1969), pp. 295–318 (esp. pp. 304–10); W. R. B. Robinson, 'The Tudor revolution in Welsh government, 1536–43: its effects on gentry participation', *English Historical Review*, CIII (1988), 1–20. On educational progress see Glanmor Williams, *Renewal and Reformation: Wales, c.1415–1642* (Oxford, 1993), pp. 419–35; W. P. Griffith, *Learning, Law and Religion: Higher Education and Welsh Society, c.1540–1640* (Cardiff, 1996).

164 The Welsh Bible was translated by William Morgan, vicar of Llanrhaeadr-ym-Mochnant in the diocese of St Asaph, in 1588. The New Testament and Book of Common Prayer were translated in 1567 by William Salesbury, Richard Davies and Thomas Huet (Book of Revelation). Glanmor Williams, 'Bishop William Morgan and the first Welsh Bible', in Glanmor Williams, *The Welsh and their Religion: Historical Essays*, pp. 173–229. For further comment on illiteracy see Morgan's dedication of the Bible to Elizabeth I in E. Gwynn Matthews, 'William Morgan in his own words ; the preface to the 1588 Welsh Bible', *Transactions of the Denbighshire Historical Society*, 53 (2004), 90–104. John Penry also referred to the need of the Welsh people to 'be freed from that destroieing grosse darkenesse of ignorance'. J. Penry, *Three Treatises Concerning Wales*, ed. D. Williams (Cardiff, 1960), p. 12. See also the poet Siôn Tudur's lines in an eulogy to Morgan: 'Niwl fu dros Gymru a'i gwŷr ... Dwyn gras i bob dyn a gred / Dwyn geiriau Duw'n agored.' ['Mist befell Wales and its people ... all believers obtained grace and God's words were revealed.']. R. G. Gruffydd, *The Translating of the Bible into the Welsh Tongue by William Morgan in 1588*, pp. 38–9.

165 This section is a splendid, if somewhat contrived, eulogy, rhetorical in style and typical of the response of littérateurs to Tudor policy in Wales. It is characteristically hyperbolic, especially when referring to the material means of the gentry, but forcefully indicative of the advancement of landowning families in the post 1536–43 period. Note the cleric Humphrey Prichard's similar general comment in his preface to Dr John Davies's (or Siôn Dafydd Rhys's) *Cambrobrytannicae Cymraecave Linguae Institutiones* (London, 1592): 'We all live on the same island, we are citizens of the same state; the same law is

available for the one and the other of us, and the same very famous Queen: business matters, friendships, co-assemblies, marriages, legal and religious matters – are common among us and the English.' Ceri Davies (ed.), *Rhagymadroddion a Chyflwyniadau Lladin, 1551–1632* (Cardiff, 1980), p. 91 (translation from a Welsh version of the original Latin).

166 Note that it is Henry VIII who is at this point called the 'Moses of Wales'.
167 Prosecuting party.
168 In a letter to Sir Francis Walsingham, the Queen's Secretary of State, Dr David Lewis heavily criticised the actions of Justices of the Peace and other officers, which draws attention to the 'dysorders in Wales' of the mid-Elizabethan era. Among them he states that Justices and others in office will not 'apprehende or take any suche persons as hathe any frende of any accompte, although their faltes be neuer so grevous & apparent … but will playe bo pype, seest me, & seest me not, and this haue grown by impunytye whereof do procede all maner of disorders'. Mathew, 'Some Elizabethan documents', 76. Severe though Lewis's comments are, they do restore some balance to contemporary views of the efficiency of Tudor governments in Wales, as reflected in Owen's narrative here.
169 *Dialogue*, pp. 44–8 [86–90].
170 Device, expedient, stratagem.
171 A reference to 'benefit of clergy', which allowed clergy to avoid trial in secular courts. It was extended to those among them who could read the first verse of Psalm 51 (in black print) in the Psalter ('God, be gracious to me in your faithful love; in the fullness of your mercy blot out my misdeeds'). This privilege was abolished in St. 7–8 George IV c.28.
172 The act of equipping and supporting private armies to defend a lord's interests.
173 This statement is surprising because Owen served for many years (1584–1609) as Justice of the Peace for his shire. He was also Sheriff in 1587 and 1602, Deputy Vice-Admiral of Pembrokeshire and Cardiganshire, and Deputy Lieutenant of Pembrokeshire. *DWB*, p. 661; *ODNB*, 42, pp. 199–202. His shrewd observations in the *Dialogue* reveal his detailed knowledge of the structure and function of the Court of Quarter Sessions. Phillips, *Justices of the Peace in Wales and Monmouthshire*, pp. 207–11.
174 A bond by which an individual undertakes legally in court to observe some condition, such as keeping the peace, paying a debt, etc. A sum of money (known as consideration) is pledged as surety for this undertaking.
175 *Scire facias*, 'You shall inform'.
176 The Clerk of the Quarter Sessions court was chiefly responsible for preparing records and seeing that the routine business agenda of the court was run efficiently. In 1545 St. 37 Henry VIII c.1 restored the right of the Custos Rotulorum to appoint to the clerkship. *SR*, III, *1509–1545*, p. 985.
177 *Particeps criminis*, 'accomplice in crime/the deed'.
178 St. 2 Henry V c.4; *SR*, II, *1377–1504*, p. 177.
179 See *Cal.CQSR*, lxxxvi; St. 2 Henry V c.4; *SR*, II, *1377–1504*, p. 177.

180 This short insert does not appear in CCL, Phillipps MS 2,105.
181 See n. 20 for further detail of the County Court.
182 The recovery of goods unlawfully taken subject to establishing the validity of recovery in a court of law.
183 This Court was not a Court of Record but was described as 'merely a larger Court Baron'.
184 Mary, 'Holy Mary' or 'By Saint Mary'.
185 Open letter from the Crown conferring this right upon him. The Writ of Aid commanded subjects of the Crown to assist him in performing his duties.
186 *Dedimus Potestatem*, 'we have given the power'. The delegation of royal power to other officials in local government.
187 A person or persons who goes security for another; one who is usually financially legally bound for another.
188 Examiner of accounts and expenditure.
189 Bond, 'binding agreement or engagement'.
190 Chief Council of State and a prerogative court, exercising the Crown's supreme power in specific cases nominated by the Crown and dependent on the royal will. Modern historians argue that changes in its structure had already taken place in Thomas Wolsey's time and that Thomas Cromwell, who succeeded him as Chief Minister of the Crown, did not, as Elton argued, initially design to recreate it as part of a 'Tudor revolution in government'. Despite Cromwell's own contribution, Wolsey was also responsible for establishing the institutional independence of the Courts of Request and Star Chamber. See J. A. Guy, 'The Privy Council: revolution or evolution?', in C. Coleman and D. Starkey (eds), *Revolution Reassessed: Revisions in the History of Tudor Government and Administration* (Oxford, 1986), pp. 8–9, 59–85; G. R. Elton, *The Tudor Revolution in Government* (Cambridge, 1953), ch. 5, pp. 317–69; G. R. Elton, 'Tudor government: the points of contact: II The Council', *Transactions of the Royal Historical Society*, 5th ser., 25 (1975), 195–6.
191 '… the said sheriffs shall have their Patents and Commissions under the Great Seal of England, as Sheriffs of England have, and shall make and take Oaths and Knowledges of recognizances before the President and Justices … by Virtue of the King's Writ of *Dedimus Potestatem* … for the due Execution of their Offices, and for their just and true Accounts before the King's Auditor or Auditors assigned for Wales.' *Statutes*, p. 115.
192 Modern research shows that the view held by A. H. Dodd and others that Welsh MPs voted en bloc on all issues relating to Wales is by now unacceptable. Lloyd Bowen, *The Politics of the Principality: Wales c.1603–1642* (Cardiff, 2007), p. 81; *Dialogue*, pp. 66, 69, 114–19; A. H. Dodd, 'Pattern of politics', 70; A. H. Dodd, 'Wales under the early Stuarts', in A. J. Roderick (ed.), *Wales Through the Ages*, II (2nd impr., Llandybïe, 1965), p. 56.
193 A Writ of Error issued from Chancery required records of an indictment to be sent from courts, such as Quarter Sessions, to a superior court, such as Great

Sessions, for review. It was a means by which appeals were heard in the Court of Common Pleas.
194 The Grand Inquest, up to twenty-three in numbers, presented criminals for trial. The Second Inquest, or Petty Jury of twelve members, investigated the truth of the presentment.
195 The true copy of, or extract from, a court record, usually financial.
196 'Amerciaments' were arbitrary fines imposed by lower courts such as Courts Leet; 'Waifs' is a stolen article disposed of by a thief in flight and forfeited to the Crown or Lord. 'Stray' means 'abandoned goods'.
197 Barons of the Exchequer. Chief officers of the Exchequer, usually appointed from local noble or gentry familes, who functioned regionally and centrally.
198 Receivers of customs.
199 Financial tax or aid, usually to the Crown. Before 1536 the Principality did not pay subsidies and contribute to expenses of coastal defence, but the situation changed after 1536. *Cal.CQSR*, p. xxxii.
200 This short insert does not appear in CCL, Phillipps MS 2,105.
201 In this context the sovereign state based on royal power, as established by Henry VIII. In the 1547 *Book of Homilies* it is stated that: 'Every degree of people ... hath appointed to them their duty and order so that in all things is to be lauded and praised the goodly order of God: without the which no house, no city, no commonwealth can continue and endure.' (from *An Exhortation concerning good order and obedience to rulers and magistrates*). J. Griffiths (ed.), *The Two Books of Homilies appointed to be read in Churches* (Oxford, 1859), p. 105.
202 To enter or encroach unlawfully upon another's land or property, an offence which, together with debt, caused the most court actions.
203 Malicious stirrers of discord and ill-feeling, causing an offence punishable by Common Law.
204 A person who unlawfully supports a suit in which he or she is not concerned, or the perpetrator of an action of aiding a party in litigation without lawful cause. It also came to mean 'bearing' or extending patronage, that is, giving unlawful aid, countenance or support to criminals, again punishable at Common Law.
205 *Capias ad satisfaciendum*, 'Take as much as will satisfy you'. A writ to take the debtor's body until satisfaction be made in a civil action.
206 A writ to stay process of law in a legal action.
207 This is a reference to St. 34–35 Henry VIII c.26; *Statutes*, pp. 127–8: '... no execution of any judgement given or to be given in any Base Court be stayed or deferred by reason of any Writ of False Judgement, but that execution shall and may be had and made at all times before the reversal of the said judgement, the pursuit of the said writ notwithstanding'.
208 *Statutes*, p. 127.
209 A writ bringing appeals to the High Court from lower courts, not of record, according to Common Law.
210 i.e. a Writ of Error in the English Court of Chancery.

211 Posting, 'to travel at speed or in haste'.
212 See n. 66.
213 This sentence occurs in CCL, Phillipps MS 2,105 only (fo. 25a), and ends Demetus's contribution at this point. What follows in round brackets is to be found in BL, Harleian MS 141 only.
214 Glanmor Williams (ed.), *Glamorgan County History*, IV (Cardiff, 1974), pp. 153–4.
215 This reference to St. 26 Henry VIII c.26 regards Monmouthshire as a Welsh shire, although its judicial structure tied it to England. St. 4 Henry IV c.27; *Statutes*, p. 34.
216 St. 34–35 Henry VIII c.26, cls 61–4, 73. *Statutes*, pp. 114–17. The 'Sheriff's Turn' was a tour of a county made twice yearly by the sheriff who presided at the Hundred Court, and on these occasions a 'Court of Record' was also held, where proceedings were recorded.
217 The Statute of Wales (*Statutum Walliae*) 1284, also known as the 'Statute of Rhuddlan'. *Statutes*, pp. 2–7. For the significance of the statute see Llinos Beverley Smith, 'The Statute of Wales, 1284', *WHR*, X, 2 (1980), 127–54.
218 An early Welsh medieval administrative unit, two commotes usually forming one cantref.
219 *Statutes*, p. 117.
220 Turns were held after Easter and Michaelmas. *Statutes*, p. 118. A Court of Record which fined or imprisoned and where the proceedings were permanently recorded. By charter, the lord had the right to hold the Court once or twice a year.
221 St. 27 Henry VIII c.26 cl.26; *Statutes*, p. 89.
222 St. 34–35 Henry VIII c.26, cl. 3; *Statutes*, p. 102.
223 St. 27 Henry VIII c.26 cls 22–4; *Statutes*, pp. 87–8; St. 34–35 Henry VIII c.26, cls 61–5; *Statutes*, pp. 114–16.
224 'Colour' in this context means 'the image projected' by a person or persons or by a court or any other organisation. Cf. Dr David Lewis's recommendation in his letter to Sir Francis Walsingham, referring to bailiffs and other offending royal officials in the shires: 'yf they shalbe fownde to haue wyncked & not to haue don theire offices carefully and syncerelye, are to be kepte in prison untill those persons [criminals] be apprehended and brought in, to be ponished accordinge to theire defectes'. Mathew, 'Some Elizabethan documents', 76.
225 *Quo Warranto*, 'By what warrant?', that is, by what authority/authorisation? A writ to determine by what authority a person claimed an office, franchise or privilege.
226 Perpetual rent obtained from lands held in fee simple payable by the freeholder.
227 Stick, 'to hesitate'.
228 St. 27 Henry VIII c.26, cls 3–4. *Statutes*, pp. 77–8.
229 From the Anglo-Saxon *gildan*, a payment or contribution, which meant that

Monmouthshire dues and taxes were to be paid subject to the direction of Westminster.
[230] Ewyas Harold was annexed to the hundred of Webtree in Herefordshire.
[231] St. 27 Henry VIII c.26, cls 11–13; *Statutes*, pp. 82–5.
[232] Pillaging as a method of demanding excessive taxation, and causing ruin by depredations or extortions. See Dr David Lewis's comments on county officials in his letter to Sir Francis Walsingham (1575): 'Men of no substance nor of credyte made sheriffs and justices of the peace which most lyve by pillage and pyllynge.' Mathew, 'Some Elizabethan documents', 76.
[233] The section begun on p.100, containing the BL, Harleian MS 141 text only, ends at this point.
[234] Unidentified manuscript. A marginal note in CCL, Phillipps MS, in a later hand has, as a title 'Dialogue of Reformation in Wales'. It is probably a product of Owen's imagination. Other surveys and critical comments survive, such as Sir William Gerard's discourse, entitled 'Information of ye disorders of wales, 1575', but that work does not appear to have been the source. See D. Ll. Thomas, 'Further notes on the court of the Marches', *Y Cymmrodor*, XXII (1900), 130–58 (Appendix E); Second Discourse, 159–63 (Appendix F). See also D. Lewis, 'The Court of the President and Council of Wales and the Marches from 1474–1575', *Y Cymmrodor*, XII (1897); Price's letter to Lord Burghley, in Ellis, *Original Letters Illustrative of English History*, III, pp. 41–8.
[235] A bondsman or rustic servant.
[236] See D. Powel, *The historie of Cambria, now called Wales*, pp. 340–2. Between 21 and 31 October 1282 'gravamina' were presented to John Pecham, Archbishop of Canterbury. Royal officials, Llywelyn stated, had despoiled the Welsh people as if they were Saracens and Jews, and he had gained no redress for his complaints: 'For he and all the Welsh were oppressed, despoiled and reduced to servitude by royal justices and bailiffs, contrary to the peace agreement and all justice, even more than if they were Saracens or Jews ... Nor has he had any amends but always more ferocious and crueller justices and bailiffs were sent; and when these were sated by their unjust exactions, others were sent anew to despoil the people, to such an extent that the people preferred to die than to live.' H. Pryce (ed.), *The Acts of Welsh Rulers, 1120–1283* (Cardiff, 2005), pp. 618, 620; J. Beverley Smith, *Llywelyn ap Gruffudd, Prince of Wales* (Cardiff, 1998), p. 454.
[237] In CCL, Phillipps MS 2,105 only (fo. 26a).
[238] Normally, judgement in these courts was given by suitors to the court and not the lord's steward. *Glamorgan County History*, IV, p. 161.
[239] See Owen's own survey of Pembrokeshire commodities, *Desc. Pembs.*, ch. 7, pp. 57–61; B. Howells, 'The economy, 1536–1642', in E. Davies and B. Howells (eds), *Pembrokeshire County History*, III, *Early Modern Pembrokeshire, 1536–1642* (Haverfordwest, 1987), pp. 66–75.

[240] Break day, 'interruption of continuity'.
[241] Champion, 'champaign', open country. From Old French 'champagne'.
[242] This action has several meanings, for example, trespass with violence, but it usually refers to entry without right on another's property.
[243] Beggar, 'reduce to poverty'.
[244] Cognizance (or *conusance*) of Plea, a privilege granted by the Crown to a town or other place to hold pleas of all contracts.
[245] Lords paramount, 'supreme lords'.
[246] L. Fox, *English Historical Scholarship in the Sixteenth and Seventeenth Centuries* (Oxford, 1956), pp. 12–13. Note Sir John Wynn of Gwydir's comment on the difficulty in obtaining sources to enable him to compile his family history: 'from the reign of Henry the fourth to Edward the first there is no certainty or very little of things done other than what is to be found in the Prince's records which now, by tossing the same from the Exchequer at Caernarfon to the Tower and to the offices in the Exchequer at London, as also by ill-keeping and ordering of late days, are become a chaos and confusion for any man to find things', Wynn, *History of the Gwydir Family and Memoirs*, p. 24. For background see V. H. Galbraith, 'The Tower as an Exchequer Record Office in the reign of Edward II', in A. G. Little and F. M., Powicke (eds), *Essays in Medieval History Presented to Thomas Frederick Tout* (Manchester, 1925), pp. 231–47.
[247] St. 34–35 Henry VIII c.27; *Statutes*, pp. 106–7.
[248] Courts of Record are courts whose proceedings are formally enrolled and considered valid as evidence of fact with the authority to fine or imprison.
[249] Wrongful detention of personal chattels.
[250] St. 34–35 Henry VIII c.27. *Statutes*, pp.106–7.
[251] Pound breaches, i.e. purpresture, the illegal enclosure of land or encroachment on the land or property of another.
[252] Usually a fine.
[253] In BL, Harleian MS 141 only.
[254] *Quia quot capita tot sensus*, 'because there are as many opinions as heads'.
[255] A bouquet or posy of sweet-scented flowers. See Wynn, *History of the Gwydir Family and Memoirs*, p. 35: Maredudd ap Ieuan's instruction to Robin Achwr in a gymnastics assembly at Gwydir was to 'deliver this nosegay to the best gentleman you see in the company upon the credit of your skill'.
[256] CCL, Phillipps MS 2, 105 adds here: 'since the Seven and twentieth of King Henry the Eighth which is now about 57 years, some defects'.
[257] St. 27 Henry VIII c.26, cl. 2: 'and that the Laws Ordinances and Statutes of the Realm of England, for ever, and none other Laws Ordinances and Statutes, from and after the said Feast of All Saints [1 November] next coming, shall be had used practised and executed in the said Country or Dominion of Wales ... in like Manner Form and Order as they be and shall be had ... in this Realm'. *Statutes*, p. 76. Note, however, that the final decision on partible inheritance was not reached until 34–35 Henry VIII c.26, cls 26, 91–3; *Statutes*, pp. 122–3.

[258] Note the words of Rice Merrick: 'This alteration of government is worthy of remembrance as well for the singular commodity the inhabitants of Wales receive thereby as the commonwealth universally ... Now, since Wales was thus, by gracious King Henry VIII, enabled with the Laws of England ... they are exempted from the dangers before remembered ... What was then justifiable by might, although not by right, is now to receive condign punishment by law ... This unity engendered friendship, amity, love, alliance ... assistance, wealth and quietness. God preserve and increase it.' *Morganiae Archaiographia*, pp. 67–8.

[259] From this point (*Dialogue* pp. 92–100) BL, Harleian MS 141 is unclear and excludes more relevant material contained in CCL, Phillipps MS 2,105, which is followed from this point onwards to p. 100 where BL, Harleian MS 141 is resumed. [See pp. 126–32].

[260] An isolated region notorious for harbouring thieves and outlaws. Owing to the flexible conditions which existed between the Principality, the Marches and border English shires in the late Middle Ages ample opportunities were given to lawbreakers to move between lordships, governed by different jurisdictions, to avoid punishment and to form their own bands of brigands, often in liaison with unscrupulous marcher lords and gentry. Lawlessness was endemic in those days, and the notable centres for such activity were the upper reaches of Nanconwy, Y Graig Lwyd (Llanymynaich), Cefn Digoll (near Welshpool), Gwern-y-gof (Ceri), Cwmystwyth and Mawddwy. E. Roberts, *Dafydd Llwyd o Fathafarn* (Darlith Flynyddol Eisteddfod Genedlaethol Cymru Maldwyn a'i Chyffiniau 1981), pp. 8–11. Such groups were not necessarily *banditti* but rather freeholders and lower gentry dissatisfied with government and administration. 'Plant Mat' were, by reputation, notorious brigands in the Cwmystwyth, Devil's Bridge area. See George Borrow, *Wild Wales: The People, Language and Scenery* (Fontana/Collins, 1982 impr.), p. 402; J. Williams, 'History of Radnorshire', *AC*, IV (3rd ser., 1858), 558; S. R. Meyricke, *The History and Antiquities of the County of Cardigan* (Brecon, 1907), p. 240; J. G. Jones, 'Lewis Owen, sheriff of Merioneth, and the "Gwylliaid Cochion" of Mawddwy in 1554–55', *Journal of the Merioneth Historical and Record Society*, XII, no. 3 (1996), 221–40; E. A. Rees, *Welsh Outlaws and Bandits: Political Rebellion and Lawlessness in Wales, 1400–1603* (King's Norton, 2001), ch. 14, pp. 208–21. When describing the desolation in the Nanconwy/Hiraethog regions during the dynastic wars of the mid-fifteenth century, Sir John Wynn, in his *History of the Gwydir Family*, refers to the connections between brigands and fugitives in areas on the north-eastern March: 'they had to their backstay friends and receptors, all the county of Merioneth and Powysland. These ... kept most part of that country all waste and without inhabitant.' *History of the Gwydir Family and Memoirs*, p. 52; R. M. Jones, 'Y Ddraig Lwyd', in J. E. Caerwyn Williams (ed.), *Ysgrifau Beirniadol*, XVIII (Denbigh, 1992), pp. 180–8.

[261] However, he was knowledgeable in the social, economic and geographical details of counties in north-east wales. *DP*, IV, 'The Description of Wales', pp. 503–56, 558–85, 585–716. On Montgomeryshire he states: 'much theafte and other vnrulynesse with troubles amonge themselves' (p. 691), on Radnorshire: 'vnruly, spotted with oppressions, idle life, and excesse in gameing, government & good order, neglected, much theafte, & little thrifte' (p. 479) and on Cardiganshire: 'abounding in theaft' (p. 479). Thomas Pennant's comments on this theme are restricted to eastern Merioneth and the Gwylliaid Cochion Mawddwy: 'After the wars of the houses of *York* and *Lancaster* multitudes of felons and outlaws inhabited this country; and established in these parts, for a great length of time, from those unhappy days, a race of profligates, who continued to rot, burn, and murder, in large bands, in defiance of the civil power; and would steal and drive whole herds of cattle, in mid-day, from one county to another, with the utmost impunity.' T. Pennant, *A Tour in Wales* (London, 1784), II, p. 93. For more information on the Merioneth brigands see Robert Vaughan's description of Lewis Owen's assassination in Lewys Dwnn, *Heraldic Visitations of Wales*, II (Llandovery, 1846), pp. 336–7; Jones, 'Lewis Owen ... and the "Gwylliaid Cochion"', 221–40. See also Sir John Wynn of Gwydir's comments on the menacing brigands of Nanconwy and the Hospice of the Knights of St John of Jerusalem at Ysbyty Ifan. *History of the Gwydir Family and Memoirs*, pp. 51–2. For another aspect of extortionate practices perpetrated by one of higher status in mid-Tudor Montgomeryshire see Peter R. Roberts, 'A petition concerning Sir Richard Herbert', *BBCS*, XX, pt. I (1981), 45–9.

[262] This reference follows what Dr David Lewis states concerning negligence among local government officials: 'Men of no substance nor of credyte made sheriffes and justices of the peace which most lyve by pollinge and pyllynge. The auctoritye of the counsaile there is not regarded as it hathe ben for neither she[r]iffe, Justice of the peace ... will so carefully apprehende or take any suche persons as hathe any frende of any accompte, althoughe their faltes be neuer so grevous & apparent', Mathew, 'Some Elizabethan documents', 76.

[263] 'If you meet a thief, you choose him as your friend.' (*Book of Psalms*, 50: 18). Cf. Dr David Lewis's comment on this kind of behaviour in an endorsement to a letter sent to Sir Francis Walsingham: 'yf they [i.e. Sheriffs, Justices etc.] shalbe founde to haue wyncked & not to haue don theire offices carefully and syncerelye, are to be kepte in prison'. Mathew, 'Some Elizabethan documents', 76.

[264] Note St. 27 Henry VIII c.7, where legislation forbids Foresters from demanding exorbitant fines for the return of stray Cattle to their owners: 'that then the same Cattle to be redelivered to the Owner ... the said Owner ... reasonably paying for the keeping of such cattle after the Rate of the Time that such Cattle shall have been in the Custody and keeping of any such Foresters'; *Statutes*, p. 72.

[265] Sir David Brooke. The first to hold the office of Justice of Great Sessions for the Carmarthen, Cardigan and Pembroke circuit (1542–51). Williams, *Great Sessions in Wales*, pp. 161–2.
[266] John Walshe, Justice of Common Pleas and Justice of the Carmarthen circuit (1551–60). Williams, *Great Sessions in Wales*, p. 162.
[267] Richard Wye, Justice of the Carmarthen circuit (1560–70). Williams, *Great Sessions in Wales*, p. 162.
[268] John Rastall, Justice of the Carmarthen circuit (1570–4). Williams, *Great Sesssions in Wales*, pp. 162–3. Served as Deputy-Justice of the Brecknock circuit in 1556 and 1560. Ibid., pp. 126–7.
[269] George Fetiplace, Justice of the Carmarthen circuit (1574–7). Williams, *Great Sessions in Wales*, p. 163.
[270] Sir John Puckering, Justice of the Carmarthen circuit (1577–8) and its first Chief Justice (1577–92); member of the Council in the Marches (1586) and the first Welsh judge who sat in Parliament for a constituency within his judicial circuit, namely Carmarthen boroughs (19 November) and Bedford in 1584, but soon after chose Bedford, which he represented until September 1585. Williams, *Great Sessions in Wales*, pp. 163–4; W. R. Williams, *The Parliamentary History of the Principality of Wales, 1541–1895* (Brecknock, 1895), pp. 51–2.
[271] Sergeant-at-Law, a barrister of the highest rank.
[272] One, acting as a pensioner or almsman, who prays for the soul of a benefactor.
[273] He was appointed Lord Keeper of the Great Seal on 28 April 1592. As Queen's Sergeant he conducted the impeachment of Sir John Perrot, Lord Deputy of Ireland, for high treason. *Welsh Judges*, pp. 163–4; R. Turvey (ed.), *The Treason and Trial of Sir John Perrot* (Cardiff, 2005), pp. 70–1.
[274] Richard Atkins, Justice Associate of the Carmarthen circuit (1578–92), Member of the Council in the Marches (1594), and Chief Justice (1592–1610). Williams, *Great Sessions in Wales*, pp. 164–5.
[275] St. 18 Elizabeth I c.8, in which another Justice is added to serve in each Court of Great Sessions. *Statutes*, p. 154.
[276] William Oldesworth, Deputy to Puckering on the Carmarthen circuit (1589–91), second Justice (1592–1603). Member of the Council in the Marches (1602). Williams, *Great Sessions in Wales*, p. 165.
[277] 'In the Lent Session in the 34th year of the reign of Queen Elizabeth.'
[278] 'Witness Sir John Puckering, Lord Keeper [or Guardian] of the Great Seal of England and Justice of the same.'
[279] *Ultimum vale*, 'the final farewell'.
[280] Owen, pursuing his own agenda, is obviously deceiving Barthol at this stage into thinking that Pembrokeshire was governed in an exemplary manner. In fact, county families, such as the Perrots, Wyrriots and Stepneys, were continually at odds with each other over land and property: 'the distribution of *largesse*, the hospitality and the generous way of living praised by the bards concealed the fact that many squires of note kept bands of retainers and depen-

dants ... while the chronic insecurity of everyday life, heightened by family feuds, sometimes welled up into outbursts of disorder culminating in ... small-scale private warfare'. Howell, 'Studies in the social and agrarian history of ... Pembrokeshire', pp. 169–70.

[281] Owen is clearly praising the clergy in his native shire, but his evidence is weak. His attitude is different from that shown by John Penry in 1587, whose views on the condition of the Church were disparaging. Owen has nothing to say about the notorious Marmaduke Middleton, bishop of St David's, who died a year before the *Dialogue* was written. In 1593 Middleton described the people of his diocese as being 'greatly infected with atheism and wonderfully given over to vicious life.' *CSPDom., 1581–1590*, CLXII, no. 29, p. 119. In 1593 the Privy Council ordered an inquiry into religious practices in Pembrokeshire, where it was stated that 'idolatrous and superstitious monuments' were prominent icons in religious ritual among the people. D. Walker, 'Religious change 1536–1642', in *Early Modern Pembrokeshire*, III, pp. 112–13.

[282] Stick, 'to hold back, to hesitate'.

[283] This is a reference to John Penry of Cefn-brith, near Llangamarch in Brecknockshire, and presumably to *An Aequity of a Humble Supplication* (1587): 'we have not teaching Ministers among vs, & that some order may be taken by your Maiesty and the estate, whereby wee may bee freed from that destroieing grosse darcknesse of ignorance, wherein we nowe are bewrapped to the woe of our soules for euer'. J. Penry, *Three Treatises concerning Wales*, p. 12. Since he lived for most of his short life outside Wales, the exact sources used by Penry to argue his case are not known, but it is assumed that his evidence derived from the diocese of St David's and from what local contacts he may have had. However, it is difficult to corroborate Owen's evidence because sources for St David's in the period 1583–1603 are scanty, but it appears that the quality of the clergy in the diocese left much to be desired in Pembrokeshire by the close of the sixteenth century. *CSPDom., 1547–1580*, LXVI, 26, p. 362. Cf. Nicholas Robinson, bishop of Bangor, complained in a letter to Sir William Cecil in 1567 about the 'ye blyndnes of the clergie', and in 1583 about the 'great want of preachers' in his diocese. Mathew, 'Some Elizabethan documents', 78 ; *CSPDom., 1581–1590*, CLXV, 1, 3, p. 143 (1583); Glanmor Williams, *Wales and the Reformation* (Cardiff, 1997), pp. 301–2, 305–8; J. G. Jones, 'John Penry: government, order and the "perishing souls" of Wales', *Trans. Cymmr.* (1993), 60–77; *idem*, 'John Penry: the early Brecknockshire Puritan firebrand', *Brycheiniog*, XXXVII (2005), 27–38.

[284] In this context meaning sustenance and material means of living.

[285] '... the county of Pembroke ... being subdued by Gilbert Strongbow, being a mighty and valiant gentlemen of no small power or prowess, who first subdued a great part of Monmouthshire called Strigoil and Chepstow ... and from thence enterprised the conquering of the county of Dyfed, now called

Pembrokeshire, which he accomplished in the time of Henry I ...', *Desc. Pembs.*, p. 178. Richard Strongbow (d.1176), earl of Pembroke and Strigoil, was the son of Gilbert fitz Gilbert of Clare, earl of Pembroke.

286 BL, Harleian MS 141 is resumed here, and continues from where it was replaced by a clearer Phillipps MS text. See p. 126 where the BL text ends with the words 'how came it first to be so called?' At this point the Phillipps text is added in an appendix as a parallel version and only approximates the BL text from here to the point from where both texts are identical to the end. See Appendix (pp. 179–80) for the Phillipps MS text (fo. 33a–34a).

287 For Oysterlow see n. 35.

288 St. 27 Henry VIII c.26. *Statutes*, pp. 79–87. See also c.17, p. 86.

289 See J. Dodderidge, *The History of the Ancient and Modern Estate of the Principality of Wales, Duchy of Cornwall and Earldom of Chester* (London, 1630), p. 24: 'for a great part of west Wales was comprehended within the Shire of Pembrooke, which is a very ancient Shire of Wales, and the Territory thereof conquered by the English, in the time of William Rufus ... This Earledome of Pembrooke had in ancient time palatine iurisdiction, and therefore in some records is called *regalis comitatus Pembrochie.*'

290 St. 27 Henry VIII c.26; *Statutes*, p. 86.

291 St. 34–35 Henry VIII c.26; *Statutes*, p. 128. Sir Thomas Johns/Jones of Haroldston, eldest son of John ap Thomas, younger brother of the celebrated Sir Rhys ap Thomas of Abermarlais, Carmarthenshire. Sir Thomas married Mary, widow of Sir Thomas Perrot, and represented Pembrokeshire (1541–4 and 1547–52) and Caernarfonshire (1558) in Parliament. On his marriage, he became lessee of the lordship and manor of Haverfordwest, and of the castle, lordship and manor of Laugharne. S. T. Bindoff (ed.), *The History of Parliament: The House of Commons, 1509–1558*, II (London, 1982), pp. 453–4; W. R. Williams, *Parliamentary History of the Principality of Wales*, p. 154. For a concise description of the boundary changes see *Desc. Pembs.*, xxxix.

292 Trane Clinton, Trane March and Trane Morgan, all parts of the barony of St Clears. *Royal Commission on Land in Wales and Monmouthshire* (London, 1896); D. Ll. Thomas, *Memorandum relating to Agriculture and Land Tenure ... in Wales*, Appendix M, p. 443. These areas comprised lands in Llanfihangel Abercywyn, Llangynin, Llanfallteg, Llanboidy, Llanglydwen, Llan-gan, Llandysilio, Henllan, St Clears and Laugharne.

293 Richard Saxton, whose cartographical work was well known to George Owen, practised as an estate surveyor, and published an *Atlas of England and Wales* (1579). Three of the Welsh shires were produced on separate sheets, namely Monmouthshire, Glamorgan and Pembrokeshire. Humphrey Llwyd's map of Wales had appeared earlier (1575), but Saxton undertook the task of producing maps of the Welsh shires. D. Huw Owen, *Early Printed Maps of Wales* (NLW, 1996), [5], [7].

294 Military service abroad, particularly in Ireland and on the Continent, was constantly an issue in relations between the Privy Council and the Council in

the Marches and the Welsh localities, particularly in maritime areas. Pembrokeshire was in a vulnerable position, and although it was smaller in size than Carmarthenshire, Owen states that it was commissioned to supply 150 soldiers for foreign service, compared to Carmarthenshire, which was to provide only 100 soldiers, a strategy which Owen considered to be grossly unfair. The war with Spain, which broke out in 1585, continued even after the victory over the Spanish Armada (1588), and the danger from Catholic Ireland and the Spanish land and naval forces caused considerable anxiety in all maritime areas of Wales. J. G. Jones, 'The defence of the realm: regional dimensions c.1559–1604', in J. G. Jones, *Conflict, Continuity and Change in Wales c.1500–1604: Essays and Studies* (Aberystwyth, 1999), pp. 132–5; Glanmor Williams, *Renewal and Reformation: Wales c.1415–1642* (Oxford, 1993), pp. 363–72.

[295] George Owen produced his map of Pembrokeshire in 1602, which was used by William Camden in *Britannia* (1607 edn). See *Desc. Pembs.*, xli.

[296] Ells, 'distances, directions'.

[297] Pricked, 'marked off'.

[298] Of force, 'of necessity'.

[299] A facsimile of an early copy of Owen's map of Pembrokeshire and Carmarthenshire based on Saxton's map *Cambriae* (1579) is printed in Thomas Dineley, *The Account of the Official Progress of his Grace Henry the First Duke of Beaufort Through Wales in 1684* (London, 1888), p. 256 (CC1). It is entitled 'Pembrook and Carmarthen sheres reduced to one true scale of miles whereby the true quantity of ech sheere may be discerned & how much land hath ben taken from Pembrok & added to Ca[r]marthen sheere by the statute of 34 H 8'. Since this section is not included in Phillipps MS 2, 105 it appears that it was added after 1594. Charles, *George Owen*, pp. 151–2.

[300] *Desc. Pembs.*, pp. 5–7.

[301] Hopesdale, with its castle at Caergwrle, coincides with the parish of Hope, having replaced the Welsh commote of Yr Hôb.

[302] A parish in the commote of Is Dulas and the cantref of Rhos.

[303] St. 27 Henry VIII c.26, cl. 8; *Statutes*, p. 80.

[304] St. 33 Henry VIII c.13, cls 3–4 (1541); *Statutes*, pp. 98–9.

[305] The third daughter of William Marshal, fourth earl of Pembroke, known as 'the Marshal' (c.1146–1219), soldier and administrator. *ODNB*, 36, pp. 815–22.

[306] Sir William Peverel, baron of Nottingham (c.1090–1155). *ODNB*, 43, pp. 968–9.

[307] Isabel Marshal was the wife of Maredudd ap Rhys Grug. Maredudd obtained Oysterlow from Gilbert Marshal, earl of Pembroke, for a payment of 700 marks, and he did service at Pembroke, not Carmarthen. R. F. Walker, 'The Earls of Pembroke, 1138 to 1389', in R. F. Walker (ed.), *Pembrokeshire County History*, II, *Medieval Pembrokeshire* (Haverfordwest, 2002), p. 64.

[308] *Quia Emptores terrarum*, 'for as much as purchasers of lands ...'. St. 18 Edward I c.1 (1289). A statute which restricted sub-infeudation and enabled

new manors to be created. *SR*, I, *1101–1377* (London, repr. 1963), p. 106. It is also called the Statute of Westminster III, which stated that every freeman was to be allowed to sell his lands, but the purchaser was to hold those lands of the chief lord when taking the place of the seller or vendor.

309 The meaning here possibly is: 'That is a fact with which you also agree.'

310 The act of challenging or objecting to juries on count of summoning them or to defects in individual jurors.

311 Challenges to juries, either the whole panel or individuals, chiefly on grounds of inefficiency or prejudice.

312 Criminal and civil business.

313 Owen was well informed about defence matters, for he was appointed Deputy-Lieutenant of Pembrokeshire, with Thomas Perrot (1587), Deputy Vice-Admiral of Pembrokeshire and Cardiganshire (1598) and Sheriff of his shire (1587, 1602). *ODNB*, 42, p. 200. 'I find ... Pembrokeshire to be worst manred [trained military recruits in the event of war] and hardest to find personable and serviceable men, so that the Lieutenants and Commissioners for Musters are more toiled in seeking thirty or forty personable men than their neighbour shires are to find a hundred ... the county, especially of late years, is fallen much to trade to sea and a great part of the county's people are seamen and mariners which may not be taken up for land services, and many of them continually abroad at sea and seldom to be found at home, which is a special matter which should be regarded in laying of numbers of men for foreign service upon this shire.' *Desc. Pembs.*, pp. 45, 46–7. Cf. correspondence regarding foreign service in T. Jones Pierce (ed.), *Clenennau Letters and Papers*, p. 39, nos 133–4 (1597).

314 Milford Haven was vulnerable to Spanish attack during the war 1585–1604. B. Howells, 'Government and politics, 1536–1642', in *Early Modern Pembrokeshire*, III, pp. 142–6; *CSPDom. 1595–1597*, CCLXV, 101, p. 562; J. G. Jones, 'The Defence of the Realm', in *Conflict, Continuity and Change in Wales*, pp. 123–45; B. Howells, 'Government and politics, 1536–1642', pp. 142–3. This section was added to the text, which was completed in 1594.

315 It is clear that passages in the BL text were introduced into the *Dialogue* after 1594, when the original work was compiled. This is one example, namely the capture of Spanish prisoners in 1597. For the background see B. Howells, 'Government and politics, 1536–1642', pp. 142–7; B. Howells, 'The Elizabethan squirearchy of Pembrokeshire', *The Pembrokeshire Historian*, I (1959), 29; *Acts of the Privy Council*, XXXVIII (1597–8), pp. 119–20; HMC, *Calendar of the Marquis of Salisbury Manuscripts* (Hatfield House MSS), XIV (London, 1923), pp. 88–9.

316 The tax originated in a statute of 1592 (St. 35 Elizabeth I c.4). Justices of the Peace appointed a Treasurer in each county and Petty Constables levied quarterly rates in each parish, and three monthly accounts were submitted to the High Constables. The monies were then transferred to the Treasurer. J. G. Jones, *Law, Order and Government in Caernarfonshire, 1558–1640*, p. 138.

317 The unpopular 'Maimed soldiers' mize' or tax. It originated in a statute passed in 1592 (St. 35 Elizabeth I c.4). Justices of the Peace selected individual recipients of the pension and a Treasurer was appointed to administer the mize in each shire. *SR*, IV (Pt.ii), pp. 847–9.

318 Sir Thomas Johns/Jones of Haroldston, son and heir of John ap Thomas of Abermarlais, Carmarthenshire. Haverfordwest was the largest town in Wales at the time. It was unique in that it possessed its own lord-lieutenant. Its prosperity was established on the trade of its port on the Cleddau river.

319 St. 34–35 Henry VIII c.26, cl. 124; *Statutes*, pp. 130–1.

320 St Brides Bay, south-west Pembrokeshire, between Skomer and Ramsey islands.

321 Both sources are identical in content from this point to the end of the *Dialogue* (CCL, Phillipps MS 2,105, fo. 34a). See note 213.

322 Henry Herbert, second earl of Pembroke, of Wilton in Wiltshire, President of the Council in the Marches (1586–1601). He was the eldest son of Sir William Herbert, first earl of Pembroke. *Council in the Marches of Wales*, pp. 241–2, 276–96. He was a querulous and impulsive person. *ODNB*, 26, pp. 688–9. Edward Somerset, fourth earl of Worcester, was appointed to the Council in 1590. Ibid., 51, pp. 575–7. He was the only son of Sir William Somerset, third earl of Worcester. He became a Protestant, but was reputed to have some Catholic leanings.

323 Motioned, 'proposed'.

324 St. 8 Henry VI c.12, cl. 3 (1430). By this statute the embezzling of a record, whereby the court judgement is reversed, is declared a felony. *SR*, II, *1377–1504*, p. 249; *Cal.CQSR*, xxi–xxii; *DP*, III, pp. 118–19 (n. 4); Wynn, *History of the Gwydir Family and Memoirs*, pp. 24, 121. Wynn went a step further than Owen, by deploring the dire condition in which the Principality records in north Wales were kept in London: '... ill-keeping and ordering of late days, are become a chaos and confusion for any man to find things in order as were needful for him to have who would be ascertained of the truth of things done from time to time'.

Appendix

Phillipps MS 2, 105, fo. 33a–34a (see p. 132)

And surely I must say again you are in a happy civil country for the people differ far in manners and behaviour from diverse parts of Wales.

Also your towns are not as the rest of the towns of Wales are; you are mere English like in all points to the English towns. When I came to the fine town of Tenby I wondered to see the people whom I found so full of courtesy and kindness towards me a stranger that it made me to admire. Rich and poor, young and old yielded me reverence, entertained me, invited me, accompanied me because I was a stranger. Truly it is one of the finest little towns and inhabited with best people that ever I came in. And your ancient shire town of Pembroke, though now greatly decayed, yet still does it carry the show of a good town, loving people and courteous, very civil and orderly the decay of that town being the head of your shire and which was in such estimation as it has been in your country in times past made my heart sorry and for your good town of Haverfordwest. I never came into a town of better entertainment nor where I was better used by very civil people. I could not imagine that I was then in Wales it seems that that town of Haverfordwest is a very thriving town. And many townsmen of good wealth which doubtless they well deserve. God continue his blessings among them. It seems that your country of Pembrokeshire is a bigger shire when these towns are so well maintained.

DEMETUS: No truly but a little shire not much above twenty miles the longest way that one can measure from one corner to another. And it cannot contain much ground therein for it is a triangle form being as those that are anything skilled in Geometry know that in that form it does contain least of all other. Also that part that adjoins to Carmarthenshire is concave as Geometricians term it, that is bowing inward like in form to the moon in the last quarter for Carmarthenshire thrusts itself in roundness into our shire and therefore it can contain but a little quantity of ground within it. And here I must tell you of a great wrong that our poor little shire of Pembroke has had in times past by taking away a great part thereof, for when Wales was first divided into shireground then were the lordships of Laugharne, Llanstephan and Oysterlow allotted by parliament to be part of Pembrokeshire. But afterwards we having chosen a worshipful gentleman of Carmarthenshire to be Knight of the Parliament for Pembrokeshire; he procured the said lordships of Laugharne, Llanstephan and Oysterlow to be taken away from Pembrokeshire and to be annexed to his own country of Carmarthenshire. Whereas the same shire of Carmarthen was far larger than Pembrokeshire before the same was so taken from it. By which Act Pembrokeshire was greatly dismembered so that those who dwell within seven miles of Haverfordwest, which is the middle of Pembrokeshire, are now in Carmarthenshire and have eighteen miles to travel to Carmarthen town and now Carmarthenshire is almost twice as big as Pembrokeshire and some parishes are by that means half in Pembrokeshire and half in Carmarthenshire which is a very unfit thing and breeds much inconvenience, so that now Pembrokeshire is not over in breadth from Nolton upon the seashore to Egremont in Carmarthenshire standing upon the river Cleddau but ten English miles wherein is to be noted and known to such as shall peruse the map of Pembrokeshire lately set forth, that Mr Christopher Saxton who took great pains in describing and parting of all the shires of Wales and England has been deceived by those that should have given him better instruction and information for he in his map of Pembrokeshire has laid down the parish and church of Egremont aforesaid standing close upon the river of Cleddau upon the east brink thereof to be within Pembrokeshire whereas the same is in truth in Carmarthenshire, and taken from Pembrokeshire by the means I have before declared, for in that place the river of Cleddau parts both shires.

Bibliography

Original sources

Cardiff Central Library
Phillipps MS 2, 105.

National Library of Wales
Brogyntyn MS 6, 56b.
Cwrtmawr MS 27, 55.
Llanstephan MS 38, I, 16, 20, 24, 29, 36, 41, 55, 176; MS 120, 248; MS 133, 756, 780, 781.
NLW MS 2377; 13, 687.

Printed original sources

Acts of the Privy Council of England, new ser., 1587–8, 1596–7, ed. J. R. Dasent (London, 1890–1964).
Ascham, Roger, *The Scholemaster* (London, 1570).
Ballinger, J. (ed.), *Calendar of Wynn (of Gwydir) Papers, 1515–1690* (Aberystwyth, 1926).
Bindoff, S. T. (ed.), *The History of Parliament: The House of Commons, 1509–1558*, II (London, 1982).
Bowen, I. (ed.), *The Statutes of Wales* (London, 1908).
Camden, William, *Britannia* (London, 1695 edn, repr. 1971).
Carew, Richard, *The Survey of Cornwall*, ed. F. E. Halliday (London, 1953).
Charles, B. G., 'The second book of George Owen's description of Pembrokeshire', *NLWJ*, V, iv (1948), 265–85.
Churchyard, Thomas, *The Worthiness of Wales* [1587] (London, 1776).
Davies, Ceri (ed.), *Rhagymadroddion a Chyflwyniadau Lladin, 1551–1632* (Cardiff, 1980).
Davies, John, *Cambrobrytannicae Cymraecaeve Linguae Institutiones* (London, 1592).
Doddridge, J., *The History of the Ancient and Modern Estate of the Principality of Wales, Duchy of Cornwall and Earldom of Chester* (London, 1630).
Dwnn, Lewys, *Heraldic Visitations of Wales*, 2 vols, ed. S. R. Meyrick, I and II (Llandovery, 1846).
Ellis, Henry (ed.), *Original Letters Illustrative of English History*, vols II and III (2nd ser., London, 1827).

Elyot, Sir Thomas, *The Book Named the Governor* [1531], ed. S. E. Lehmberg (London, 1975).

Erasmus, Desiderius, *The Colloquies of Erasmus*, ed. Craig R. Thompson (University of Chicago Press, 1965).

Flenley, Ralph (ed.), *A Calendar of the Register of the Queen's Majesty's Council in the Dominion and Principality of Wales and the Marches of the Same, 1569–1591* (Cymmrodorion Record Series, London, 1916).

Geoffrey of Monmouth, *The History of the Kings of Britain*, trans. Lewis Thorpe (Penguin Books, Harmondsworth, 1966).

Gerald of Wales, *The Journey Through Wales and The Description of Wales*, ed. Lewis Thorpe (Penguin Books, Harmondsworth, 1980).

Griffiths, J. (ed.), *The Two Books of Homilies appointed to be read in Churches* (Oxford, 1859).

Griffiths, R. A. (ed.), *Sir Rhys ap Thomas and his Family: A Study in the Wars of the Roses and Early Tudor Politics* (Cardiff, 1993).

Gruffydd, R. G., *The Translating of the Bible into the Welsh Tongue by William Morgan in 1588* (London, 1988).

HMC, *Calendar of the Marquis of Salisbury Manuscripts (Hatfield House MSS)*, XIV (London, 1923).

HMC, *Report on Manuscripts in the Welsh Language*, ed. J. Gwenogvryn Evans, vol. 1 (London, 1898).

HMSO, *Letters and Papers, Foreign and Domestic of the Reign of Henry VIII ...*, eds J. S. Brewer, J. Gairdner and R. H. Brodie (London, 1862–1932).

HMSO, *Calendar of State Papers Domestic, 1547–1610*, ed. R. Lemon and M. A. E. Green (London, 1856–71).

Humphrey, Lawrence, *The Nobles or of Nobilitye* (London, 1563).

Johnston, D. R. (ed.), *Gwaith Lewys Glyn Cothi* (Cardiff, 1995).

Jones, E. D., 'The Brogyntyn Welsh Manuscripts', *NLWJ*, VI, 1949–50, 223–48.

Jones, Thomas (ed.), *Brut y Tywysogion or The Chronicle of the Princes [Peniarth MS, 20 Version]* (Cardiff, 1952).

Knafla, Louis A. (ed.), *Kent at Law 1602: The County Jurisdiction: Assizes and Sessions of the Peace* (London HMSO, 1994).

Lambarde, William, *A Perambulation of Kent*, ed. R. Church (Bath, 1970).

Leland, John, *Itinerary in Wales, 1536–1539*, ed. L. Toulmin Smith (London, 1906).

Lewis, David, 'The Court of the President and Council of Wales and the Marches from 1478–1575', *Y Cymmrodor*, XII, i (1897), 1–64.

Llwyd, H., *The Breuiary of Britayne*, trans. T. Twyne (London, 1573).

Mathew, D., 'Some Elizabethan documents', *BBCS*, I (1931), 70–8.

Merrick, Rice, *Morganiae Archaiographia: A Book of Glamorganshire Antiquities*, ed. B. Ll. James (Barry, 1983).

Miles, Dillwyn (ed.), *The Sheriffs of the County of Pembroke, 1541–1976* (Haverfordwest, 1976).

Owen, D. Huw, *Early Printed Maps of Wales* (NLW, 1996).

Owen, George, *The Description of Pembrokeshire: George Owen of Henllys*, ed. Dillwyn Miles (Llandysul, 1994).
Owen, George, *The Description of Penbrokshire*, vol. 3, ed. Henry Owen (London, Cymmrodorion Record Series, 1906).
Owen, George, *The Taylors Cussion*, ed. E. M. Prichard (London, 1906).
Owen, Henry, 'The Vairdre Book', *Archaeologia Cambrensis*, IV, 6th ser. (1904), 143–5, 275–84.
Parry, G. (ed.), *A Guide to the Records of Great Sessions in Wales* (NLW, Aberystwyth, 1995).
Peacham, Henry, *The Compleat Gentleman* (London, 1622).
Pennant, Thomas, *A Tour in Wales*, 3 vols, II (London, 1784).
Penry, John, *Three Treatises Concerning Wales*, ed. D. Williams (Cardiff, 1960).
Phillips, J. R. S. (ed.), *The Justices of the Peace in Wales and Monmouthshire, 1541 to 1689* (Cardiff, 1975).
Pierce, T. Jones (ed.), *Clenennau Letters and Papers in the Brogyntyn Collection*, Pt. 1, *NLWJ Supplement* series IV, i (Aberystwyth, 1947).
Powel, David, *The Historie of Cambria, now called Wales* [1584] (Amsterdam/New York, 1969).
PRO *Lists and Indexes, no. IX: List of Sheriffs for England and Wales* (London, 1963 edn).
Pryce, H. (ed.), *The Acts of Welsh Rulers, 1120–1283* (Cardiff, 2005).
Pugh, T. B., 'The "Indenture for the Marches" between Henry VII and Edward Stafford (1477–1521), duke of Buckinghan', *English Historical Review*, LXXI (1956), 436–41.
Roberts, T. and I. Williams (eds), *The Poetical Works of Dafydd Nanmor* (Cardiff/London, 1923).
Royal Commission on Land in Wales and Monmouthshire (London, 1896): D. Ll. Thomas, *Memorandum relating to Agriculture and Land Tenure ... in Wales.*
Smith, Thomas, *A Discourse of the Commonweal of This Realm of England*, ed. M. Dewar (Charlottesville, Virginia, 1969).
Starkey, Thomas, *A Dialogue between Reginald Pole and Thomas Lupset, Lecturer in Rhetoric at Oxford*, ed. K. M. Burton (London, 1948).
Starkey, Thomas, 'A Dialogue between Cardinal Pole and Thomas Lupset', in J. M. Cowper (ed.), *England in the Reign of King Henry the Eighth*, extra ser. 12 [Early English Text Society] (London, 1871).
Thomas, D. Ll. (ed.), 'Gerard's Second or "abbreviated" Discourse', *Y Cymmrodor*, XIII (1900), 159–63.
Thomas, D. Ll., 'Further notes on the Court of the Marches', *Y Cymmrodor*, XIII (1900), 97–158.
Thompson, Craig R., 'Translations of Lucian', in *The Complete Works of St Thomas More*, vol. 3 (i) (Yale University Press, 1974).
Thompson, E. Maunde (ed.), *Chronicon Adae de Usk* (London, 1904).
Turvey, R. (ed.), *The Treason and Trial of Sir John Perrot* (Cardiff, 2005).

Williams, S. J. and J. E. Powell (eds), *Cyfreithiau Hywel Dda yn ôl Llyfr Blegywryd* (Cardiff, 1942).
Williams, W. Ogwen (ed.), *Calendar of the Caernarvonshire Quarter Sessions Records*, I, *1541–1558* (Caernarfon, 1956).
Williams, W. R. (ed.), *The History of the Great Sessions in Wales 1542–1830, together with the Lives of the Welsh Judges* (Brecknock, 1899).
Wynn, John, *History of the Gwydir Family and Memoirs*, ed. J. G. Jones (Llandysul, 1990).

Secondary sources: books

Borrow, George, *Wild Wales: Its People, Language and Scenery* (Fontana/Collins, 1982 impr.).
Bowen, Lloyd, *The Politics of the Principality: Wales, c.1603–1642* (Cardiff, 2007).
Bradshaw, B. and Peter Roberts (eds), *British Consciousness and Identity: The Making of Britain, 1533–1707* (Cambridge, 2003).
Brooks, F. W., *The Council of the North* (Historical Association, 1966).
Burke, P., *Culture and Society in Renaissance Italy, 1420–1540* (London, 1972).
Caspari, Fritz, *Humanism and the Social Order in Tudor England* (Chicago, 1954).
Charles, B. G., *George Owen of Henllys: A Welsh Elizabethan* (Aberystwyth, 1973).
Chrimes, S. B., *Henry VII* (London, 1972).
Chrimes, S. B., C. D. Ross and R. A. Griffiths (eds), *Fifteenth-Century England, 1399–1509* (Manchester, 1972).
Coleman, C. and D. Starkey (eds), *Revolution Reassessed: Revisions in the History of Tudor Government and Administration* (Oxford, 1986).
Crowson, P. S., *Tudor Foreign Policy* (London, 1973).
Davies, D. J. and N. Davies, *Is Monmouthshire in Wales? The Legal and Historical Answer* (Griffithstown, 1943).
Davies, E. and B. Howells (eds), *Pembrokeshire County History*, III *Early Modern Pembrokeshire, 1536–1642* (Haverfordwest, 1987).
Dodd, A. H., *Studies in Stuart Wales* (Cardiff, 1971 edn).
Du Boulay, F. R. H. and C. M. Barron (eds), *The Reign of Richard II: Essays in Honour of May McKisack* (London, 1971).
Elton, G. R., *The Tudor Revolution in Government* (Cambridge, 1953).
Evans, H. T., *Wales and the Wars of the Roses* (Sutton, repr. 1998).
Fox, L., *English Historical Scholarship in the Sixteenth and Seventeenth Centuries* (Oxford, 1956).
Geyl, P., *The Revolt of the Netherlands, 1555–1609* (London, 2nd edn, 1958).
Gleason, J. H., *The Justices of the Peace in England 1558 to 1640: A Later Eirenarcha* (Oxford, 1969).

Bibliography

Griffith, W. P., *Civility and Reputation: Ideas and Images of the 'Tudor Man' in Wales* (Bangor, 1995).

Griffith, W. P., *Learning, Law and Religion: Higher Education and Welsh Society, c.1540–1640* (Cardiff, 1996).

Griffiths, R. A., *Sir Rhys ap Thomas and his Family: A Study in the Wars of the Roses and Early Tudor Politics* (Cardiff, 1993).

Gruffydd, R. G. (ed.), *A Guide to Welsh Literature c.1530–1700* (Cardiff, 1997).

Guy, John, *Tudor England* (Oxford, 1990 edn).

Hales, J. R., *Renaissance Europe, 1480–1420* (London, 1971)

Heal, F. and C. Holmes, *The Gentry in England and Wales 1500–1700* (Macmillan, Basingstoke, 2002 edn).

Hearder, H. and H. R. Loyn (eds), *British Government and Administration: Studies Presented to S. B. Chrimes* (Cardiff, 1974).

Hughes, W., *Life and Times of Bishop William Morgan* (London, 1891).

Israel, J., *The Dutch Republic: Its Rise, Greatness and Fall 1477–1806* (Oxford, 1995).

Jenkins, G. H. (ed.), *A Social History of the Welsh Language: The Welsh Language Before the Industrial Revolution* (Cardiff, 1997).

Jones, E. W., *Bosworth Field and its Preliminaries: A Welsh Retrospect, 1485–1985* (Liverpool/Llanddewibrefi, 1984).

Jones, G. E., *The Gentry and the Elizabethan State* (Swansea, 1977).

Jones, J. G. (ed.), *Class, Community and Culture in Tudor Wales* (Cardiff, 1989).

Jones, J. G., *Gwylliaid Cochion Mawddwy* (Darlith Glyndŵr, Machynlleth, 1994).

Jones, J. G., *Law, Order and Government in Caernarfonshire, 1558–1640: Justices of the Peace and the Gentry* (Cardiff, 1996).

Jones, J. G., *The Welsh Gentry 1536–1640: Images of Status, Honour and Authority* (Cardiff, 1998).

Jones, J. G., *Conflict, Continuity and Change in Wales c.1500–1603: Essays and Studies* (Aberystwyth, 1999).

Jones, W. R. D., *The Tudor Commonwealth 1529–1559* (London, 1970).

Kelso, R., *The Doctrine of the English Gentleman in the Sixteenth Century* Massachusetts, 1964).

Kendrick, T. D., *British Antiquity* (London, 1970 edn).

Little, A. G. and F. M. Powicke (eds), *Essays in Medieval History Presented to Thomas Frederick Tout* (Manchester, 1925).

Lloyd, H. A., *The Gentry of South-West Wales 1540–1640* (Cardiff, 1968).

Lloyd, J. E., *A History of Wales from the Earliest Times to the Edwardian Conquest* (London, 2nd edn, 1911).

McKisack, M., *Medieval History in the Tudor Age* (Oxford, 1971).

Maltby, W. S., *The Black Legend in England: The Development of Anti-Spanish Sentiment 1558–1660* (Durham, N.C., Duke, 1971).

Meyricke, S. R., *The History and Antiquities of the County of Cardigan* (Brecon, 1907).

Owen, G. D., *Elizabethan Wales: The Social Scene* (Cardiff, 1962).

Oxford Dictionary of National Biography, ed. H. C. G. Matthews and Brian Harrison (Oxford, 2004).

Peter, J. and R. J. Pryse, *Enwogion y Ffydd*, I (London, 1878).

Rady, M., *The Netherlands: Revolt and Independence, 1550–1650* (London, 1987).

Rees, D. C., *Tregaron: Historical and Antiquarian* (Llandysul, 1936).

Rees, E. A., *Welsh Outlaws and Bandits: Political Rebellion and Lawlessness in Wales 1400–1603* (King's Norton, 2001).

Rees, W., *South Wales and the March 1284–1415: A Social and Agrarian Study* (Oxford, 1924).

Reid, R. R., *The King's Council in the North* (London, repr. 1975).

Richards, G. M., *Welsh Administrative and Territorial Units, Medieval and Modern* (Cardiff, 1969).

Roberts, Enid, *Dafydd Llwyd o Fathafarn* (Darlith Flynyddol Eisteddfod Genedlaethol Cymru Maldwyn a'i Chyffiniau 1981).

Roberts, Glyn, *Aspects of Welsh History*, ed. A. H. Dodd and J. G. Williams (Cardiff, 1969).

Roderick, A. J. (ed.), *Wales Through the Ages*, I (Llandybïe, 1960).

Skeel, C. A. J., *The Court in the Marches of Wales: A Study in Local Government during the Sixteenth and Seventeenth Centuries* (London, 1904).

Smith, J. Beverley, *Llywelyn ap Gruffudd, Prince of Wales* (Cardiff, 1998).

Stephens, R., *Gwynedd, 1528–1547: Economy and Society in Tudor Wales* (Ann Arbor, 1975).

Thomas, D. R., *The Life and Work of Bishop Davies and William Salesbury* (Oswestry, 1902).

Turvey, Roger, *Pembrokeshire: The Concise History* (Cardiff, 2007).

Waters, W. H., *The Edwardian Settlement of North Wales in its Administrative and Legal Aspects, 1284–1343* (Cardiff, 1935).

Watkin, T. G., *The Legal History of Wales* (Cardiff, 2007).

White, Eryn M., *The Welsh Bible* (Stroud, 2007).

Williams, G. J., *The Welsh Tradition of Gwent* (Cardiff, 1968).

Williams, Glanmor and R. O. Jones (eds), *The Celts and the Renaissance: Tradition and Innovation* (Cardiff, 1990).

Williams, Glanmor, *Reformation Views of Church History* (London, 1970).

Williams, Glanmor (ed.), *Glamorgan County History*, IV (Cardiff, 1974).

Williams, Glanmor, *Religion, Language and Nationality in Wales: Historical Essays* (Cardiff, 1979).

Williams, Glanmor, *The Welsh and their Religion: Historical Essays* (Cardiff, 1991).

Williams, Glanmor, *Wales and the Act of Union* (Bangor, 1992).

Williams, Glanmor, *Renewal and Reformation: Wales c.1415–1642* (Oxford, 1993).

Williams, Glanmor, *Harri Tudur a Chymru/Henry Tudor and Wales* (Cardiff, 1985).

Williams, Glanmor, *Wales and the Reformation* (Cardiff, 1999).
Williams, J. L. and G. Rees Hughes, *The History of Education in Wales*, I (Swansea, 1978).
Williams, Penry, *The Council in the Marches of Wales under Elizabeth I* (Cardiff, 1958).
Williams, Penry, *The Later Tudors: England 1547–1603* (Oxford, 1998).

Secondary sources: articles and chapters

Baker, J. H., 'The dark age of English legal history, 1500–1700', in D. Jenkins (ed.), *Legal History Studies 1972* (Cardiff, 1975), 1–27.
Bowen, D, J., 'Y cywyddwyr a'r dirywiad', *BBCS*, XXIX, III (1981), 453–96.
Bowen, D. J., 'Graddedigion Eisteddfodau Caerwys 1523 a 1567/8', *Llên Cymru*, II, i (1952), 129–34.
Bowen, I., 'Grand juries, justices of the peace and quarter sessions in Wales', *Trans. Cymmr.* (1936), 51–104.
Caspari, Fritz, 'Sir Thomas Elyot', in Fritz Caspari, *Humanism and the Social Order in Tudor England* (Chicago, 1954), 76–109.
Davies, C. S. L., 'A rose by another name: why we are wrong to talk about "the Tudors"', *The Times Literary Supplement*, 13 June (2008), 14–15.
Davies, J. Conway, 'Letters of admission to the rectory of Whitechurch', *NLWJ*, IV, i and ii (1945), 83–8.
Dodd, A. H., 'The pattern of politics in Stuart Wales', *Trans. Cymmr.*, 1948, 8–91.
Dodd, A. H., 'Wales under the early Stuarts', in A. J. Roderick (ed.), *Wales Through the Ages*, I (Llandybïe, 2nd impr. 1960), pp. 54–61.
Elton, G. R., 'Tudor government: the points of contact: II The Council', *Transactions of the Royal Historical Society*, 5th ser., 25 (1975), 195–211.
Elton, G. R., 'Reform and the Commonwealth's Men of Edward VI's reign', in *The English Commonwealth 1547–1640*, ed. P. Clark et al. (Leicester, 1979).
Evans, Euros Jones, 'Noddwyr y beirdd yn sir Benfro', *Trans. Cymmr.* (1972–3), 123–69.
Fitton, W. H., 'The Silurian System', *The Edinburgh Review*, 73, April 1841, 1–41.
Galbraith, V. H., 'The Tower as an Exchequer Record Office in the reign of Edward II', in A. G. Little and F. M. Powicke (eds), *Essays in Medieval History Presented to Thomas Frederick Tout* (Manchester, 1925), pp. 231–47.
Griffiths, Ralph A., 'Wales and the Marches', in S. B. Chrimes, C. D. Ross and R. A. Griffiths (eds), *Fifteenth-Century England, 1399–1509* (Manchester, 1972), pp. 145–72.
Guy, J. A., 'The Privy Council: revolution or evolution', in C. Coleman and D. Starkey (eds), *Revolution Reassessed: Revisions in the History of Tudor Government and Administration* (Oxford, 1986), pp. 59–85.
Gruffydd, R. G., 'The Renaissance and Welsh literature', in Glanmor Williams

and R. O. Jones (eds), *The Celts and the Renaissance: Tradition and Innovation* (Cardiff, 1990), pp. 17–40.

Herrup, Cynthia B., 'Law and morality in seventeenth-century England', *Past and Present*, 106 (1985), 102–23.

Howells, B. E., 'The Elizabethan squirearchy of Pembrokeshire', *The Pembrokeshire Historian*, I (1959), 17–40.

Howells, B. E., 'The economy, 1536–1642', in E. Davies and B. Howells (eds), *Pembrokeshire County History*, III, *Early Modern Pembrokeshire* (Haverfordwest, 1987), pp. 60–93.

Hurstfield, J., 'County government 1530–1660', in R. B. Pugh and E. Crittall (eds), *The Victoria County History of the Counties of England: A History of Wiltshire*, V (Oxford, 1957), pp. 80–110.

Jones, E. D., 'George Owen Harry', *The Pembrokeshire Historian*, 6 (1979), 58–75.

Jones, Francis, 'An approach to Welsh genealogy', *Trans. Cymmr.* (1948), 302–446.

Jones, Francis, 'Griffith of Penybenglog: a study in Pembrokeshire genealogy', *Trans. Cymmr.* (1938), 125–54.

Jones, J. G., 'Changing concepts of gentryhood: some reflections', *Brogliaccio I di Lettera*, XIII (1973), 25–37.

Jones, J. G., 'The Welsh poets and their patrons c.1550–1640', *WHR*, IX, 3 (1979), 245–77.

Jones, J. G., 'Concepts of order and gentility', in J. G. Jones (ed.), *Class, Community and Culture in Tudor Wales* (Cardiff, 1989), pp. 121–57.

Jones, J. G., 'John Penry: government, order and the "perishing souls" of Wales', *Trans. Cymmr.* (1993), 47–81.

Jones, J. G., 'Lewis Owen, sheriff of Merioneth, and the "Gwylliaid Cochion" of Mawddwy in 1554–55', *Journal of the Merioneth Historical and Record Society*, XII, no. iii (1996), 221–40.

Jones, J. G., 'Robert Holland a *Basilicon Doron* y Brenin Iago', in J. E. Caerwyn Williams (ed.), *Ysgrifau Beirniadol*, XXII (Denbigh, 1997), pp. 161–88.

Jones, J. G., 'The defence of the realm: regional dimensions c.1559–1604', in J. G. Jones, *Conflict, Continuity and Change in Wales c.1500–1603: Essays and Studies* (Aberystwyth, 1999), 113–53.

Jones, J. G., 'The world of poets and patrons: cultural affinities and conflicts', in J. G. Jones (ed.), *Conflict, Continuity and Change in Wales c.1500–1603: Essays and Studies* (Aberystwyth, 1999), pp. 198–245.

Jones, J. G., 'The Welsh gentry and the image of the "Cambro-Briton", c.1603–25', *WHR*, XX, 1 (2000), 615–55.

Jones, J. G., 'The gentry of Gwent and the Welsh language after the Acts of Union', *The Monmouthshire Antiquary*, XVIII (2002), 65–84.

Jones, J. G., 'John Penry: the early Brecknockshire Puritan firebrand', *Brycheiniog*, XXXVII (2005), 27–38.

Jones, Michael A., 'Cultural boundaries within the Tudor state: Bishop Rowland Lee and the Welsh settlement of 1536', *WHR*, XX, ii (2000), 227–53.

Jones, R. Gwyndaf, 'Sir Richard Clough of Denbigh *c*.1530–1570', Pt 2, *Transactions of the Denbighshire Historical Society*, 20 (1971), 57–101.

Jones, R. M., 'Y Ddraig Lwyd', in J. E. Caerwyn Williams (ed.), *Ysgrifau Beirniadol*, XVIII (Denbigh, 1992), pp. 164–88.

Jones, T. Artemus, 'Owen Tudor's marriage: a missing statute', in T. Artemus Jones, *Without My Wig* (Liverpool, 1945 edn), pp. 21–32.

Lewis, C. W., 'The decline of professional poetry', in R. G. Gruffydd (ed.), *A Guide to Welsh Literature c.1550–1700*, III (Cardiff, 1997), pp. 29–74.

Lewis, T. H., 'The Justice of the Peace in Wales', *Trans. Cymmr.* (1943–4), 120–32

Lloyd, Howell A., '"Famous in the field of number and measure": Robert Recorde, Renaissance mathematician', *WHR*, XX, ii (2000), 254–82.

Matthews, E. Gwynn, 'William Morgan in his own words: the preface to the 1588 Welsh Bible', in *Transactions of the Denbighshire Historical Society*, 53 (2004), 79–107.

Miles, Dillwyn, 'Pembrokeshire antiquarians', *Journal of the Pembrokeshire Historical Society*, 17 (2008), 21–7.

Penry, John, 'A Treatise Containing the Aequity of an Humble Supplication', in D. Williams (ed.), *Three Treatises Concerning Wales* (Cardiff, 1960), pp. 3–45.

Roberts, Glyn, '"Wyrion Eden": the Anglesey descendants of Ednyfed Fychan in the fourteenth century', in Glyn Roberts, *Aspects of Welsh History*, ed. A. H. Dodd and J. G. Williams (Cardiff, 1969), pp. 179–214.

Roberts, Glyn, 'Teulu Penmynydd', in Glyn Roberts, *Aspects of Welsh History*, ed. A. H. Dodd and J. G. Williams (Cardiff, 1969), pp. 240–74.

Roberts, Glyn, 'Wales and England: antipathy and sympathy, 1282–1485', in Glyn Roberts, *Aspects of Welsh History*, ed. A. H. Dodd and J. G. Williams (Cardiff, 1969), pp. 295–318.

Roberts, Peter R., 'A petition concerning Sir Richard Herbert', *BBCS*, XX, pt. 2 (1963), 45–9.

Roberts, Peter R., 'The "Act of Union" in Welsh history', *Trans. Cymmr.* (1972–3), 49–72.

Roberts, Peter R, 'Tudor legislation and the political status of "the British Tongue"', in G. H. Jenkins (ed.), *The Social History of the Welsh Language: The Welsh Language Before the Industrial Revolution* (Cardiff, 1997), pp. 123–52.

Roberts, Peter R, 'Tudor Wales, national identity and the British inheritance', in B. Bradshaw and Peter Roberts (eds), *British Consciousness and Identity: The Making of Britain, 1533–1707* (Cambridge, 2003 edn), pp. 8–42.

Robinson, W. R. B., 'The Tudor revolution in Welsh government, 1536–43: its effects on gentry participation', *English Historical Review*, CIII (1988), 1–20.

Roderick, A., 'A history of the Welsh language in Gwent', *Gwent Local History*, no. 50 (Spring, 1981), pp. 13–39.

Smith, J. Beverley, 'Crown and community in the Principality of north Wales in the reign of Henry Tudor', *WHR*, III, ii (1966), 145–72.

Smith, Llinos Beverley, 'The Statute of Wales', *WHR*, X, ii (1980), 127–54.

Thomson, G. Scott, 'The origin and growth of the office of Deputy-Lieutenant', *Transactions of the Royal Historical Society*, V, 4th ser. (1922), 150–66.

Walker, D., 'Religious change, 1536–1642', in E. Davies and B. Howells (eds), *Pembrokeshire County History*, III, *Early Modern Pembrokeshire* (Haverfordwest, 1987), pp. 94–125.

Wiliam, E. W., '"Let use be preferred to uniformity": domestic architecture', in J. G. Jones (ed.), *Class, Community and Culture in Tudor Wales* (Cardiff, 1989), pp. 159–96.

Williams, G. A., 'The bardic road to Bosworth: a Welsh view of Henry Tudor', *Trans. Cymmr.* (1986), 7–31.

Williams, Glanmor, 'Bishop William Morgan and the first Welsh Bible', in Glanmor Williams, *The Welsh and their Religion: Historical Essays* (Cardiff, 1991), pp. 173–229.

Williams, Glanmor, 'Prophecy, poetry and politics in medieval and Tudor Wales', in Glanmor Williams, *Religion, Language and Nationality in Wales: Historical Essays* (Cardiff, 1979), pp. 71–86.

Williams, Glanmor, 'Sir John Pryse of Brecon', *Brycheiniog*, XXXI (1998–9), 49–63.

Williams, Glanmor, 'The Renaissance', in Glanmor Williams and R. O. Jones (eds), *The Celts and the Renaissance: Tradition and Innovation* (Cardiff, 1990), pp. 1–16.

Williams, J., 'History of Radnorshire', *AC*, IV (3rd ser., 1858), 469–558.

Williams, Penry, 'The Star Chamber and the Council in the Marches of Wales, 1558–1603', *BBCS*, XVI, iv (1956), 287–97.

Williams, Penry, 'The attack on the Council in the Marches, 1603–1642', *Trans. Cymmr.* (1961), pt. i, 1–22.

Williams, W. O., 'The county records', *Transactions of the Caernarfonshire Historical Society*, X (1949), 79–103.

Williams, W. O., 'The social order in Tudor Wales', *Trans. Cymmr.* (1967), pt. ii, 167–78.

Unpublished dissertations

Howells, B. E., 'Studies in the social and agrarian history of medieval and early modern Pembrokeshire' (unpublished MA dissertation, University of Wales, 1956).

Lloyd, M. K., 'The Privy Council, Star Chamber and Wales, 1540–1572', (unpublished Ph.D. dissertation, University of Wales, 1987).

Index

Abermarlais 175, 178
Aberystwyth 67
Abraham 11
Acta Romanorum Pontificum (1558) 6
Alcock, John, bishop of Rochester 13, 154
All Saints, Feast of 69
Anglesey 3, 67, 111, 112, 113
Anglia transwalina 67, 153
Anglo-Spanish War (1585–1604) 11, 16, 47, 49, 79, 176, 177
Anjou 65
Antwerp 11, 46, 62, 148, 152
Aristotle 37
Arthur, King 13, 103
Ascham, Roger 5, 38, 42
Assize, Judge(s) of 25, 26, 29, 30, 34, 58, 61, 83, 84, 85, 86, 88, 91, 98, 99, 102, 103, 104, 110, 118, 120, 122, 127, 140, 144, 145, 149
Astrologians 64
Atkins, Richard 129, 173
attachment 73, 74
Attornies, royal 21, 25, 57, 71, 72, 76, 89, 92, 100, 108, 145
Auditor(s) 20, 85, 105
Auvergne 65

Bale, John 6
Barabbas 88, 162
Barnard's Inn 1, 38, 148, 153
base courts x, 26, 28, 59, 60, 61, 101, 102, 107, 109, 110, 113, 118, 120, 121, 122, 123, 146, 150, 167
Beaufort, Margaret 159
benefit of clergy 105
Berwick-on-Tweed 66, 153
bidale 154

Blythe, Geoffrey, bishop of Coventry and Lichfield (1503–31) 14, 154
Bohemia 85
Boke Named the Governour, The (1531) 5
bonheddig 37
borough charter 30
Bosworth Field (1485) 3, 159, 160
Brecknockshire 22, 27, 113, 115, 136
Brecon 20
Bride's Bay/St Brides Bay 143, 178
Bristol 13
Britannia (1586) 6
Brittany 65
Brooke, Sir David 128, 173
Bryto and Phylamatheus 117
Bulkeley, Sir Richard III (Baron Hill) 6, 154
Burgundy 65

Cadwaladr ap Cadwallon (the Blessed) 81, 159
Cadwallon ap Cadfan 159
Caergwrle 176
Caernarfon 20
Caernarfon castle 154
Caernarfonshire 48, 67, 112, 113
Caerwys *Eisteddfodau* (1523, 1567–8) 10
Cambridge 66
Camden, William 6, 7, 151
Canaan 82
Canterbury 66
Canterbury, archbishop of 78
capias ad satisfaciendum, writ of 109, 167
Cardiganshire 40, 67, 113, 119, 126, 127, 136
Carew, Richard 6, 7

Carlisle 66
Carmarthen 20, 30, 82, 139, 180
Carmarthenshire x, 30, 51, 61, 67, 113, 119, 132, 135, 136, 137, 138, 140, 143, 179
Cartography 8
Castiglione, Baldassare 5
Catherine de Valois 159
Cecil, Sir William (Lord Burghley) 48, 155, 160, 174
Cefn Digoll 171
Cemais, barony of 1, 2, 10, 38, 37, 39
Chamberlain 105
Charles VI 159
Charters of Enfranchisement (1505–8) 33
Chepstow 132
Cheshire 66
Chester 66
Churchwardens 31, 141
Churchyard, Thomas 14
Cicero 37, 38
Cilycyffaith 10
Cleddau 180
Clerk of the Peace 24, 25, 100, 105
Close of Easter 100
Clough, Sir Richard 46
cognizance of pleas 123, 124, 170
Collector of Subsidies 59, 106, 146, 167
College of Arms 4, 7
Committees of the Cause 76
Common law 69, 75, 92, 157
Commonwealth men 39
Commote(s) 112
Constables 140, 151
contempt 73
Conwy castle 154
Cornish language 12, 66
Cornwall 62
Cornwall, duchy of 13
Coroner(s) 20, 26, 84, 101, 104, 108, 161, 162
cosmography 62
Council in the Marches x, 10, 13, 14, 15, 17, 18, 19, 21, 25, 26, 28, 31, 57, 62, 68–76, 90, 91, 92, 93, 99, 102, 104, 109, 114, 115, 144, 145, 148, 155, 161
Council of the North 14
County Palatine of Chester 13
Courts
  Arches 156
  Chancery 20, 83, 85, 102, 113; [law] 17, 19, 57, 74, 77, 79, 110, 146, 154, 156; [Wales] 58, 68, 72, 73, 75, 91, 92
  Chancery of York (ecclesiastical) 156
  Common Pleas 58, 77, 83, 84, 85, 104, 133, 146, 149
  Commotal x
  Consistory 156
  County 25, 26, 27, 28, 59, 101, 105–8, 110, 111, 150, 162
  Court(s) Baron 26, 27, 28–9, 30, 59, 60, 61, 112, 113, 115, 118, 121, 124, 150, 151,
  Duchy of Lancaster 157
  Equity 21, 68, 75
  Exchequer 19, 104, 105, 106, 156; [Wales] 19, 59, 77, 78, 79, 83, 156
  Great Sessions x, 17, 19, 20, 21, 28, 29, 30, 40, 58, 60, 83–93, 99, 100, 104, 105, 109, 120, 121, 130, 140, 144, 145, 146, 149, 160, 162, 167
  Hundred x, 25, 26, 27, 28, 29, 59, 60, 61, 102, 105, 106, 108–119, 121, 146, 150, 166
  King's Bench 17, 19, 58, 83, 93, 104, 146
  Leet 26, 27, 29, 59, 60, 61, 112, 113, 115, 124, 151, 167
  Manorial x
  Petty Sessions 31
  Quarter Sessions 21, 24, 25, 26, 50, 59, 83, 93–6, 98–9, 100, 104, 105, 139, 140, 145, 150, 162, 166
  Record 123, 124, 170
  Requests 19, 79, 104, 157
  Star Chamber 16, 17, 19, 57, 68, 71, 72, 73, 75, 76, 78, 86, 104, 155

Index

T(o)urn 25, 27, 60, 61, 105, 111, 112, 113, 124, 151, 168
Wards and Liveries 19, 79, 104, 157
covenant 77
Cromwell, Thomas 22, 163
Cumberland 66
Custos Rotulorum 24
Cwmwd Deuddwr 67
Cwmystwyth 67, 126, 171
cymorthas 17, 18, 48, 68, 110, 154, 162

Dafydd Bach Brydydd 109
Dafydd Emlyn 9
Dafydd Llwyd Mathau 9
Dale 159
Dauphiné 65
Davies, Dr John (Mallwyd) 54
Davies, Richard, bishop of St David's (1561–81) 164
dedimus potestatem, writ of 25, 102, 103, 104, 166
Demetia 62, 152
demurrer(s) 84
Denbighshire 20, 66, 113, 138
Deputy Heralds 37
Deputy Lieutenant 48, 49
Descriptio Kambriae (1194) 37
Description of Penbrokshire, The (1603) ix, 1, 6, 32
Description of Wales (1602) 7
detinue 77, 123
Devereux, Robert, 2nd earl of Essex 20
Devonshire 66
Dialogue ix, x, xiv, 2, 4, 7, 10, 11, 12, 31, 32, 34, 35, 36, 39, 40, 41, 177
Dodderidge, John 175
Dorsetshire 66
Dover 66
Dudley, John, earl of Warwick 154
Durham 66
Dwnn, Lewys 8, 9
Dyffryn Clwyd 66

Ednyfed Fychan 43, 158
Edward I 111, 118, 156
Edward III 83
Edward IV 13
Edward VI 81
Edward, Prince of Wales 13
Edwart ap Raff 14
Eglwys-wen 9
Egremont 180
Egypt(ians) 80, 82, 94
Eifionydd 40
Elizabeth I 2–3, 27, 34, 46, 52, 56, 59, 67, 70, 77, 81, 82, 84, 89, 100, 103, 106, 112, 114, 122, 123, 130, 146
Elyot, Sir Thomas 1, 5, 36, 38
embraceries 83, 99
England 12, 62, 66, 67
Epiphany, Feast of 100, 155
Error, writ of 166, 167
escheat 105
Escheator(s) 20, 26, 59, 84, 85, 104, 105, 145
estrays (strays) 59, 105
estreats 105
Ewyas Harold 169
Exeter 66
Exodus, Book of 42

False Judgement, writ of 109, 167
Fetiplace (Phetiplace), George 20, 128, 129, 173
fiscus principis 77
Fitzherbert, Sir Anthony 43
Flinshire 66, 112, 138
Flint 113
forfeitures 105
France 11, 65, 85
Frankfurt x, 11, 62

Galfridian myth 3
Gascogne 65
Genealogy of the High and Mighty Monarch, James ..., The (1604) 9
Gerard, Sir William 15, 17, 154, 169
Germany 11, 19, 62, 65, 75, 76, 85, 118
Gilbert, Sir Humphrey 5
Giraldus Cambrensis 37

Glamorgan 27, 113, 115, 136
Gloucester 17
Gloucestershire 13, 103, 116
Glyndŵr rebellion 32
Graig Lwyd, Y 171
Great Inquest (Grand Jury) 21, 87, 88, 105, 167
Great Seal 124
Gresham, Sir Thomas 46
Grey, Reginald de 157
Griffith, George Wiliam 9
Gruffudd ap Rhys ap Tewdwr 132
Gruffudd Hafren 9
Gwern-y-gof 171
gwladwr 46
Gwylliaid Cochion Mawddwy 40, 171, 172
Gwynedd 163

Hampshire 66
Haroldston 2, 134
Harry, George Owen 9
Haverfordwest 2, 20, 61, 85, 132, 133, 139, 142, 178, 179, 180
Henllys 1, 4, 36, 37, 180
Henry I 132
Henry IV ix, 57, 79, 80, 84, 95, 157
Henry V 100
Henry VI 22, 94, 97, 133, 146
Henry VII (Tudor) ix, 3, 13, 23, 24, 31, 33, 34, 35, 44, 52, 58, 81, 82, 95, 96, 157, 158, 159
Henry VIII ix, 4, 6, 19, 20, 22, 23, 24, 34, 35, 42, 55, 58, 60, 61, 79, 81, 82, 83, 84, 86, 90, 94, 95, 96, 97, 105, 109, 111, 112, 114, 123, 125, 126, 135, 146, 150, 161
Herbert family (Swansea) 1
Herbert, Henry 2nd earl of Pembroke 20, 143, 154, 156, 178, 180
Herbert, William, 1st earl of Pembroke 154, 178
Hereford 136
Herefordshire 13, 115, 116
High Constable(s) 31
History of the Gwydir Family, The (*c.*1590–1616) ix, 170, 171, 172, 178

Hoby, Sir Thomas 5, 38
Holland, Robert 4
Hope (Hopesdale), lordship of 138, 176
Howells, Brian 41
Huet, Thomas 164
Humphrey, Lawrence 38
Huw Llŷn 9
Huw Machno 157
Hywel Dda (ap Cadell) 58, 90, 149

Ieuan Tew Brydydd Hen 9
Il Cortegiano (1528) 5, 38
Inns of Court 36, 38
Instructions, Council in the Marches (1586) 17, 68
Ireland 141
Is-Dulas 176
Israel(ites) 22, 80, 93, 94, 132
Italy 85
Itinerary Through England and Wales (*c.*1536–9) 6

Jacob 82
Jethro 21, 42, 93, 94, 163
Johnes/Jones, Sir Thomas (Abermarlais) 134, 142, 175, 178
Jones, Thomas (Gwent) 53
Jones, Thomas (Twm Siôn Cati) 8
Joseph 82
Juries 65, 99, 104, 122
Justices of the Peace x, 18, 20, 21, 22, 23, 24, 25, 30, 31, 41, 42, 58, 59, 84, 87, 88, 89, 94–98, 102, 107, 127, 145, 149

Kent 66
Kremer, Gerhard (Mercator) 11
Kyffin, Maurice 54

Lambarde, William 6
Lancashire 66
Lancaster 66
Laugharne 30, 61, 134, 139, 180
Lee, Rowland, bishop of Coventry and Lichfield (1534–43) 14, 15, 22, 154, 163
Leland, John 6, 45

Index

Lent 21, 90, 91, 145
Lewis, Dr David 15, 18, 22, 30, 49, 156, 165, 169, 172
Lewys Glyn Cothi 160
Lewys, Huw 54
Limousin 65
Llan-dawg 135, 139
Llanddowror 30, 132, 134, 135, 138
Llandovery 139
Llansadyrnin 139
Llanstephan 30, 61, 132, 134, 138
Lloyd, Sir John 158
Llwyd, Humphrey 3, 5, 8, 175
Llyfr y Faerdre (*Vairdre Book, The*) (*c*.1600–13) 7, 45
Llywelyn ap Gruffudd (Prince of Wales) 111, 118, 169
London 4, 7, 9, 15, 31, 59, 62, 66, 78, 82
Lord Keeper 60, 77, 86, 129, 130, 143, 151, 157
Ludlow castle 4, 9, 13, 14, 15, 18, 19, 21,

Magister Rotulorum 156
maimed soldiers 141, 142, 177, 178
Maine 65
Mansel, Sir Edward (Margam) 6
Marches 13, 32, 34, 123, 171
Maredudd ap Rhys Grug 176
Marros 139
Marshal, Isabel 138, 176
Marshal, William 176
Mary I 27, 81
Master of the Rolls 77
Mawddwy 171
Merioneth 40, 67, 111, 112, 137, 149
Merrick, Rice (Rhys ap Meurig) ix, 33, 34, 147, 171
meteing 67, 153
Meyrick, Sir Gelly 39
Middle Temple 1
Middleton, Marmaduke, bishop of St David's (1582–92) 174
Miles, Dillwyn ix
Milford Haven 81, 139, 141, 143, 177
Monmouthshire 13, 60, 83, 113, 116, 137, 149, 160, 169

Montgomeryshire 27, 40, 67, 113, 115, 127, 137, 172
More, Sir Thomas 156
Morganiae Archaiographia (1578) ix
Morgan, William, bishop of Llandaff and St Asaph (1595–1601; 1601–4) 54, 158, 164
Morus Llwyd ab Wiliam 9
Moses 4, 21, 23, 80, 83, 97
Mostyn, Sir Thomas (Mostyn) 154

Nanconwy 171
Netherlands 11
Nevern 1
Newcastle Emlyn 67
Newcastle upon Tyne 66
nisi prius, commission of 65, 153
noble 72, 155
Normandy 65
Normans 81, 132
Northumberland 66
Norwich 66

Oldsworth, William 129, 173
Ortelius 11
Ovid 152
Owain Glyndŵr 3, 33, 57, 80, 157, 160
Owen, George (Henllys) ix, x, xiv, 2, 19
Owen, William 1
Oysterlow 61, 132, 138, 151, 180, 176

Parliament 16, 26, 30, 57, 58, 62, 70, 78, 80, 84, 101, 104, 106, 113, 143, 144, 145, 146
Peacham, Henry 38
Pecham, John, archbishop of Canterbury (1279–92) 118, 169
Pembroke 61, 113, 132, 133, 139, 179
Pembroke castle 81, 138
Pembroke, earldom of 138
Pembrokeshire x, 7, 8, 9, 12, 30, 31, 35, 40, 41, 43, 51, 53, 58, 60, 61, 62, 64, 67, 82, 86, 119, 1216, 128, 130, 131, 134, 135, 137, 138, 139, 140, 141, 142, 143, 151, 158, 169, 180, 179, 180

195

Penal legislation (1401–2) ix, 3, 33, 51, 80, 157, 158
Pendine 139
Pennal policy 160
Pennant, Thomas 172
Penry, John 8, 35, 42, 131, 164, 174
Pentreath, Dolly 153
Penybenglog, 9, 10
Perambulation of Kent, A (1570) 6
Perrot, Sir John (Haroldston) 2, 39, 40
Perrot, Thomas (Haroldston) 177
Petty Constable(s) 31
Petty Jury 167
Peverall, Sir William 138, 176
Philip Fychan ap Philip ap Richard 1
Phillipps, Sir Thomas xiv
Picardy 65
placard 74
Plantagenet kings 32
plea of debt 77
Poitou 65
Poor Law 31
pound breaches 124, 170
Powel, Dr David 8, 33, 147
Praetors 77, 176
Prendergast 9
Price, Richard (Brecon) 30, 48, 151, 155
Price, Sir John (Brecon) 8, 151
Prichard, Humphrey 164
Princes of Wales 125
Principality 26, 32, 40, 111, 171
Privy Council 16, 31, 49, 102, 103, 155, 157, 161, 166, 174
Proclamation 73
prophecy 34, 52
Protestantism 35
Protonotary 20, 58, 85, 92, 149
Ptolemy 11, 12
Puckering, Sir John 20, 129, 130, 151, 173

quo warranto, writ of 28, 115, 168
quia emptores terrarum, statute of (1289) 138

Radnorshire 40, 67, 113, 127, 136
Rastall, John 20, 128, 173

Receiver(s) 20, 85, 105, 106
recognizance 87, 101, 103, 104
Register of the Council in the Marches (1569–95) 16
Religious Settlement (1559) 35
Renaissance 4, 11, 37, 153
Rhaglaw 150
Rhingyll 150
Rhodri Mawr 149
Rhys ab Owain Fychan 1
Rhys ap Thomas, Sir (Abermarlais) 175
Richard II 79, 80
Robeston West 9
Robinson, Nicholas, bishop of Bangor (1566–85) 160, 174
Rochester 66
Roman Catholic recusancy 35, 82

St Asaph 66, 138
St Clears, barony of 175
St David's 82, 174, 160
St David's Head 143
St Dogmaels 46
St Ives 62
St Michael, Feast of 100
St Thomas the Martyr, Feast of 100
Salesbury, William 164
Salisbury 66
Salusbury, John (Llewenni) 154
Saxons 132
Saxton, Christopher 30, 61, 135, 137, 152, 175
scire facias, writ of 100
Scotland 12, 66, 67
Scriptures, translation of the (1588) 35, 42, 96, 158, 164
sequestration 73
Severn 40
Sheriff(s) 18, 20, 22, 25, 26, 28, 30, 31, 59, 60, 85, 94, 95, 102–7, 110–12, 114, 115, 116, 127, 133, 145, 150, 151
Shropshire 13, 14, 103, 115, 116, 137
Sidney, Sir Henry 15, 18
Siôn Mawddwy 8, 9, 10, 37, 46
Smith, Sir Thomas 47
Smyth, William 13, 154

Index

Socrates x
Solomon 81, 158
Somerset, Edward, 4th earl of Worcester 20, 143, 178
Somerset, Sir William, 3rd earl of Worcester 178
Spain 31
'Spanish fury' 11
Stafford, Edward, 3rd duke of Buckingham 13
Starkey, Thomas 39, 47
Statute of Wales (1284) 168
Stradling, Sir Edward (St Donat's) 6
Strigoil 132, 175
Strongbow, Gilbert 61, 132, 174
Strongbow, Richard 175
subpoena, writ of 73, 155
supersedeas, writ of 109
Survey of Cornwall 6, 7
Sussex 66

Taylors Cussion, The (*c*.1598) 7
Tenant's ale 154
Tenby 61, 132, 133, 179
Tercios 11
Theatrum Orbis Terrarum (1570) 11
Thomas, Sir William (Caernarfon) 154
Three Tranes 135
tillage 91
Toulouse 65
Touraine 65
Tower of London 122
towns 29, 123
Trane Clinton 175
Trane March 175
Trane Morgan 175
Treatise of Lordshipps Marchers in Wales, A (1594) 7
Trefor, Sir Dafydd 157
trespass 77, 115, 120, 123, 145
Tristia (*De Tristibus*) 62, 152

Tudor, Edmund 81, 82, 159, 160
Tudor, Owen (Owain ap Maredudd ap Tudur) 81, 82, 158, 159
twelfth day 69

uchelwyr 37
Union, Acts of (1536/43) 2, 4, 6, 18, 23, 32, 43, 51, 59, 114, 126; [1536] 21, 27, 82, 83, 90, 105, 111, 113, 125, 138; [1543] 16, 30, 97, 103, 112, 123, 129, 134, 135
universities 36, 38, 96

Vaughan, Robert (Hengwrt) 172
Vermandois 65
Veysey, John, bishop of Exeter (1519–51) 14, 154

waifs 105, 167
Walsingham, Sir Francis 22, 49, 165, 169, 172
Walwyn's Castle 9
Warren, William (Tre-wern) 2
Welsh language 12, 66
Welshe/Walshe, John 20, 128, 173
Westminster 17, 25, 57, 65, 75, 77, 78, 79, 84, 116, 147
Westmorland 66
Whitgift, John, archbishop of Canterbury (1583–1604) 154
William I (the Conqueror) 95
William Rufus 175
Wilton 156
Winchester 66
Worcestershire 13, 115
Worthines of Wales, The (1587) 14
Wye, Richard 128, 173
Wynn, Sir John (Gwydir) ix, 3, 6, 33, 36, 40, 52, 154, 170, 171, 172

York 13